NGOs and Human Rights

STUDIES IN SECURITY AND INTERNATIONAL AFFAIRS

NGOs and Human Rights

COMPARING FAITH-BASED AND SECULAR APPROACHES

CHARITY BUTCHER
MAIA CARTER HALLWARD

THE UNIVERSITY OF GEORGIA PRESS
Athens

Paperback edition, 2025
© 2021 by the University of Georgia Press
Athens, Georgia 30602
www.ugapress.org
All rights reserved
Set in 10/12.5 Minion Pro by Kaelin Chappell Broaddus

Most University of Georgia Press titles are
available from popular e-book vendors.

Printed digitally

Library of Congress Control Number: 2020950625
ISBN: 9780820359496 (hardback: alk. paper)
ISBN: 9780820359489 (ebook)

Paperback ISBN 978-0-8203-6981-5

CONTENTS

ILLUSTRATIONS

TABLES

TEXTBOXES

ACKNOWLEDGMENTS

The authors would like to thank Hania Bekdash, Josue Chahin, Jason Ford, Vanessa Godinez, Vittorio Indovina, Kathleen Kirk, Gilbert Lopez, Marisol Mendez-Vasquez, Katie Poe, Audrey Redmond, and Hogr Tarkhani for their assistance on various parts of this project.

The authors would also like to thank Maryam Deloffre, Eva Marzi, Anwar Mhajne, and Chris Pallas for their feedback on previous drafts of chapters for this book as well as anonymous reviewers at *Journal of Human Rights* and *International Studies Perspectives* for their comments on articles published with earlier iterations of the data.

We would also like to thank our families for understanding the hours spent working on this project during holidays and summers over the past several years as well as the School of Conflict Management, Peacebuilding and Development and the School of Government and International Affairs at Kennesaw State University for their support, including funding to present our research at international conferences. This project was an equal partnership through all stages of the process; the authors are listed in alphabetical order.

ABBREVIATIONS

CEDAW	Convention on the Elimination of All Forms of Discrimination against Women
CRC	Convention on the Rights of the Child
CSW	Commission on the Status of Women
ECOSOC	United Nations Economic and Social Council
EU	European Union
FAO	Food and Agriculture Organization of the United Nations
FBOs	faith-based organizations
FGM	female genital mutilation
FIDH	International Federation for Human Rights
ICCPR	International Covenant on Civil and Political Rights
ICESCR	International Covenant on Economic, Social, and Cultural Rights
LGBTQI	lesbian, gay, bisexual, transgender, queer, and intersex
MCC	Mennonite Central Committee
MDGs	Millennium Development Goals
NGO	nongovernmental organization
OHCHR	Office of the High Commissioner for Human Rights
RNGO	religious nongovernmental organization
SDGs	Sustainable Development Goals
UDHR	Universal Declaration of Human Rights
UN	United Nations
UNESCO	United Nations Educational, Scientific and Cultural Organization
UNICEF	United Nations International Children's Emergency Fund
WILPF	Women's International League for Peace and Freedom

NGOs and Human Rights

INTRODUCTION

The protection of human rights on a global scale is an essential part of international law and order. Since the Universal Declaration of Human Rights (UDHR) was adopted by the United Nations (UN) in 1948, states have worked collectively to protect these rights. While the field of human rights has largely been studied in terms of secular international law and Enlightenment-based concern with individual rights, human rights are not solely understood in these terms. Religious actors played a "widely acknowledged role . . . in the development of the idea of human rights and in the articulation of the Universal Declaration itself" (Hogan 2015, 2), and although scholars have also documented the (evolving) contestations over human rights within and between faith-based groups from the time of the creation of the UDHR, political science scholarship has tended to emphasize secular over religious perspectives on human rights (Hogan 2015; Hoover 2013; Loeffler 2015). In fact, some authors have pointed out that the dominant narrative concerning human rights not only favors the secular but also necessarily excludes religion, because it suggests that religion actually opposes human rights (Banchoff and Wuthnow 2011; Kayaoglu 2014). According to this understanding, "traditional religious authority" is "opposed to the secular Enlightenment ideal of rational, autonomous individuals as bearers of universal rights" (Banchoff and Wuthnow 2011, 4). Kayaoglu (2014) argues that while there may be increased participation by religious groups at the UN, these voices are not treated equally with secular ones; in fact, "secular gatekeepers have effectively imposed the parameters of liberal discourse on issues, including religious issues" (64). Others, such as Baumgart-Ochse and Wolf (2019, 5), however, assert that the UN "has created an ideational opportunity-structure for a whole range of religious communities and organizations whose traditions are rich in notions of love, mercy, compassion, human dignity, and the sanctity of life."

Religious nongovernmental organizations (NGOs) at the UN have a long history, and because NGOs affiliated with the Economic and Social Council (ECOSOC) have not been categorized as "religious" or "secular," the role of religion is not always visible (Carrette and Miall 2017). Estimates suggest that between 9 and 10 percent of organizations affiliated with the UN are religious, faith-based, or spiritual, of which the largest group is Christian (Baumgart-Ochse and Wolf 2019, 8; Marshall 2013, 148).[1] As this range of labels suggests, such groups are identified differently by scholars, policy makers, and the organizations themselves, and reflect great diversity in terms of size, mission, and degree of religiosity. To further complicate the matter, the line between secular and religious organizations is not clear-cut in many parts of the world (Hershey 2016).

In addition, some faith-based NGOs have been secularized as they have moved from a mission of church diplomacy toward more general civil society activism (Lehmann 2016). Thus, some secular organizations have religious origins, while others are created out of ethical and moral concerns that are often informed by religious belief. Further, some secular organizations, like Amnesty International, have adopted "'post-Christian' accoutrements such as votive candles for the suffering" (Moyn 2015, 176). We consider religious and secular human rights organizations, not in binary terms, but on a spectrum with many gradations. As Fitzgerald (2011, 8) asserts, the creation of a religious-secular binary "exiles" those groups classified "as religions, faiths, or spiritualties . . . and simultaneously constructs the domain of the secular as in accordance with natural reason." While the dataset used in this project does categorize organizations as either religious or secular, by exploring how these groups engage with a wide range of topics, the authors demonstrate the extent to which treating religious and secular as binary, oppositional categories obscures the complexity of the relationship between religious identity and human rights activism. Indeed, we see this project as a first step in documenting and assessing the diversity of approaches to human rights activism not only between but also within the categories of religious and secular human rights organizations.

In contrast to researchers who study religious NGOs (RNGOs), this book focuses specifically on religious human rights organizations. Care for fellow humans is a core tenet in many faiths, and religious groups are increasingly venturing into the human rights arena. Given that both religious and secular groups are working on global human rights advocacy, comparison of their understanding of and approach to human rights can help us understand not only how such groups might complement each other but also how they might collaborate and cooperate in the advancement of human rights. In the past two decades, religion has been increasingly visible on the world political stage (Carrette and Miall 2017; Toft, Philpott, and Shah 2011), although this "resurgence" has generally been studied in regard to the political aims of religious groups and not in regard to religion per se (Lehmann 2016, 2). Consequently, scholars including Hefferan (2007), Lehmann (2016), and Carrette and Miall (2017) have noted that the literature tends to look at religion as simply a variable—often unquestioned and imprecisely defined—in political or development outcomes rather than as a system of beliefs or ethical values that affects sociopolitical processes. The latter approach better enables scholars and practitioners to understand how and why religion impacts human rights work.

Western scholarship tends to presume that secular approaches are somehow more modern and rational, neglecting the ways in which Western power and colonial interests have created the secular-religious binary. Fitzgerald (2011, 234) argues that "the modern invention of religion, its reification into an impossible-to-define something which incarnates universally in the 'religions' of all human groups, languages and periods of history, is a key to the dominant ideology of the secular." Marshall (2013, 4) concurs that "to speak of 'religion' as a singular concept borders on foolishness." The relationship between the secular and the religious reflects historical power struggles that are temporally, culturally, and geographically contingent. In the West, the religious/secular distinction "prescribes rules of engagement between the two realms, notably the subordination of religion to the secular state" (Martin and Catto 2012, 378).

RNGOs are incredibly diverse in their orientation and actions, and they vary in the extent to which they are affiliated explicitly with religious bodies and the extent to which they use religious symbols and belief systems in their work. This trend equally applies to religious or faith-based NGOs that work on human rights issues. NGOs vary in how they express their religiosity, with some organizations expressing a general spiritual orientation and others having members predominantly of a particular faith background (Lehmann 2016). Further, in some countries and contexts, faith-based NGOs may downplay their religious credentials in order to secure donor funding and to alleviate potential concerns of proselytizing from client populations. In secular Europe, for instance, religious organizations must "combine faith and secular goals constantly to legitimize themselves" (Marshall 2013, 176). Paradoxically, secular organizations may at times actually emphasize religious teachings or organizational moral commitments as a way of legitimizing their work in religious contexts (Flanigan 2007; Hershey 2016). In some parts of the world, including Asia and Africa, the boundaries between secular and religious are often blurred (Fitzgerald 2011; Marshall 2013). Martin and Catto (2012, 384) even suggest that the "secular" is actually "a version of the 'religious,'" grounded particularly in the Christian tradition, and may be of less use in describing other faith traditions.

While a growing body of research has examined faith-based or religious NGOs and their work in development and other service-related activities on the global stage (see, for example, Benedetti 2006; Flanigan 2007; Frame 2017;

Hefferan 2007; Johnsen 2014; Lehmann 2016; Rashiduzzaman 1997), less has been done to compare within and across religious and secular human rights organizations and their approach to human rights, as is the focus of this book. Existing research (Lehmann 2016) indicates the substantial diversity within the category of RNGOs, but the various ways in which that manifests remain understudied (Carrette and Miall 2017; Hershey 2016). Such studies are often limited to a particular organization or a particular type of service—for example, homeless services in two cities in the United Kingdom (Johnsen 2014) or two different HIV/AIDS service delivery organizations in Kenya (Hershey 2016). Baumgart-Ochse and Wolf (2019) divide RNGOs focusing on service delivery from those engaged in advocacy work. Many studies use the framework developed by Julia Berger (2003) that classifies RNGOs based on their religious orientation, religious pervasiveness, organizational dimensions, and strategic dimensions. Some of this research looks more extensively at the differing practices of faith-based organizations, such as proselytization or their use of religious practices like prayer in their activities (Davis et al. 2011).

This book explores the extent to which religiously oriented human rights groups differ from each other and from their secular kin and identifies some key areas of overlap and divergence among major world religions. In so doing, this project lays the groundwork for a better understanding of the differences across and within a diverse array of religious human rights groups in order to better capitalize on their varied strengths in addressing the world's many human rights challenges.

While some scholars may see religion and human rights as incompatible, others point to the religious traditions evident within contemporary human rights advocacy (Witte and Green 2012). Allen Hertzke (2006) has charted the rise of faith-based groups within the broader international human rights movement, arguing that this human rights movement, which includes a wide variety of religious groups, has played a strong role in shaping international politics, and particularly American foreign policy. More importantly, Hertzke argues that the influence of these groups is much greater now than it was in the past and represents an important trend in US foreign policy. Lehmann (2013, 208) concurs that "globalization processes open up new spaces for religion" since they trigger problems for which religions can provide answers. Although current global political trends include a rise in populist and authoritarian movements skeptical of internationalism and sometimes hostile to human rights (Clements 2018), human rights activism remains strong. However, approaches to human rights vary in terms of whether rights are conceptualized as divine, moral, or legal in nature. The independent states at the time of the creation of the UDHR "could not reach consensus on whether God, nature, positive law, self-evident reason, human reciprocity, social construction, class struggle, or some combination thereof should be credited with the creation of human rights" (Normand and Zaidi 2008, 7–8). Such differences could have multiple implications for how human rights are operationalized, including whether they are moral duties stemming from God-given human dignity or rights that are based on positive law and thus should be politically guaranteed by states.

Further, scholars might expect that secular organizations are more likely to view human rights as universal in nature and that religious organizations, while they may see human rights as universal, may have a modified view of whether those rights are based on particular religious or cultural traditions. Moyn (2015, 5) argues that the Catholic Church has adapted its views on human rights over time, asserting that "Christian human rights were injected into tradition by pretending they had always been there" although practices such as slavery that are now viewed as antithetical to human rights were long supported by the church. The 1990 Cairo Declaration on Human Rights in Islam affirms "fundamental rights and universal freedoms" but also qualifies these within the context of *shari'a* law (Islamic Conference of Foreign Ministers 1990). Similarly, "the compatibility of Confucianism and human rights" has been the subject of much debate (Hogan 2015; Kim 2015, 149). However, given the universalism of some religious traditions and the cultural biases of some secular ones, such categorical assumptions should not be taken for granted. The literature suggests that there is quite a range of ways religion influences NGO practices and activities (Berger 2003; Carrette and Miall 2017). Given the general findings in the literature on faith-based NGOs, we might also find that religious human rights NGOs downplay or avoid areas that may be contentious in order to attract donor funding; likewise, some secular NGOs may emphasize religious teaching and beliefs in their work as a way of legitimizing themselves in contexts that may view human rights as a foreign or Westernizing concept.

This book does not engage in thick description of religious human rights NGO practices, nor claim to provide representative or generalizable findings regarding the universe of religious human rights organizations. Instead, this book provides empirical data on the activities of religious human rights NGOs at a particular moment in time as a starting point for delving deeper into the implications of various religious orientations on human rights activism. It considers the extent to which religious human rights organizations offer a distinct framing, discussion, and operationalization of human rights. To what extent do secular and religious human rights groups differ in their approach to human rights advocacy, and what are the potential implications of these differences for the broader human rights agenda? What might religious approaches to human rights advocacy offer for countering groups like Daesh (ISIS) or the Lord's Resistance Army, which use religion in their justification of violence against civilians? Ultimately, our study contributes to a greater understanding of the diverse ways religion manifests itself in the work of human rights organizations and the ways that work overlaps with and diverges from secular human rights endeavors. In identifying similarities across assumed religious-secular divides, the book also provides avenues for finding areas of commonality in increasingly polarized societies such as the United States.

Methodology of the Book

We utilize two methods of data collection and analysis to capture how various human rights organizations frame, discuss, legitimize, and operationalize human rights issues. First, we conduct content analysis of 333 human rights organization websites. To select organizations, we drafted a list of all of the NGOs that attended the Twenty-Seventh, Twenty-Eighth, or Twenty-Ninth Session of the Human Rights Council (held in 2014, 2015, and 2016). We believe that groups that attend these sessions directly demonstrate not only their commitment to international human rights but also their will to influence human rights policy and the global human rights agenda. All organizations that attended at least one of these sessions and that had a functioning website with adequate data to code our variables were included. One problem with this sample is that it overrepresents countries from the West and Global North, which have the financial and institutional capacity to send members to the Human Rights Council sessions. To diversify the sample, we also incorporated NGOs that were members of the International Federation for Human Rights (FIDH) and located in the Global South, outside of the West, or from underrepresented countries and had websites with adequate information for us to collect data. Finally, we also included snowball sampling (through recommendations from members of organizations we interviewed and other connections with NGOs) to reach out to additional groups to increase the global reach of the sample. The final dataset includes 68 faith-based and 265 secular organizations. Specific information regarding the number of various subcategories of organizations within the dataset can be found in Appendix A.

While the sample is predominantly secular in orientation, it has a greater percentage of religious organizations (25.6 percent) than the 9 to 10 percent of religious organizations affiliated with the UN. This overselection of religious human rights organizations provides greater opportunity for identifying potential patterns and themes. Of the sixty-eight religious organizations, forty-eight are Christian, seven are Muslim, four are Jewish, and nine represent other faiths (including Buddhism, Hinduism, and Baha'i as well as some that do not identify a specific faith or are ambiguous in relation to specific faith tradition and some organizations that are interfaith). This breakdown roughly reflects the composition of religious organizations at the UN, 59 percent of which are Christian, 13 percent of which are Muslim, 7 percent of which are Jewish, 4 percent of which are Buddhist, 3 percent of which identify as Hindu, 6 percent of which identify as multireligious, and 8 percent of whose religious affiliation is classified as "other" (Beinlich and Braungart 2019, 30–32; Marshall 2013, 148). While the percentage of Christian groups is higher in the sample used for this book, the UN percentages reflect all RNGOs, while this book looks only at those groups that explicitly focus on human rights concerns. This category has tended to be dominated more by Christian and Jewish groups, whereas Muslim groups tend to focus on development issues and Buddhist groups emphasize peace (Beinlich and Braungart 2019, 34). Consequently, while our sample size for Muslim, Jewish, and other religious groups is small, it is reflective of the relative proportions of religious groups in the universe of organizations studied here, namely those affiliated with the United Nations Human Rights Council.

Second, we conducted semistructured interviews with a variety of human rights groups working to affect international human rights policy. Some of these organizations were also represented in the dataset; others attended the various Human Rights Council sessions but did not have websites available to code information for content analysis. Finally, we also included some groups that were suggested by other organizations or human rights experts with whom we spoke. In choosing organizations for interviews, we paid particular attention to broadening the scope of our study by including those that were from the Global South or outside of the West, thus increasing the global reach of our study. Overall, we interviewed members of forty-seven human rights NGOs.

We developed an initial codebook based on a review of the literature in the various areas of interest, including types of rights and justice, culture, development, and rights, women's rights, children's rights, and peace and conflict. The authors dual-coded the first forty websites and adapted this codebook as needed in the process of establishing intercoder reliability and robustness of the codebook. As coding progressed, several emergent themes were identified and added to the codebook, such as democracy promotion and support for the environment and sustainability; these were not in our initial list of focus areas but were added when we noticed that many of the organizations identified these as key areas of work.

We classified groups as religious if they identified as a religious or faith-based organization or were affiliated with a religious denomination. In addition, we coded whether the organization clearly referenced religious beliefs or used religious symbols in its mission, vision, or about us section of its website. We collected basic information regarding location of headquarters and used it to determine whether the organization was part of the Global South or Global North and whether it was Western or non-Western. For the purposes of our coding, we considered organizations to be part of the Global South if they were listed as in a "developing" country using the M49 standard that the UN employs and part of the Global North if they were listed as in a "developed" country.[2] Because one of the critiques leveraged against human rights movements is that they are a "Western" construct, we coded organizations based on whether they were considered Western or not. For the purposes of our research, we defined Western organizations as those with headquarters in Europe, North, Central, or South America, the Caribbean, Australia, or post-Soviet countries with membership in the EU. An exception to this classification is that we coded as non-Western any organizations that identified as indigenous regardless of where they were located geographically.

Although we recognize the limitations of these definitions in that they overlook diversity within countries and regions, we used them to get an initial cut into the data to identify emergent themes and general tendencies. Further, by breaking apart some of these additional categories of membership, we determined whether differences between organizations were in fact due to religion or other factors, such as the socioeconomic conditions of the country or cultural beliefs.

We conducted interviews in person or by phone or Skype and recorded and transcribed them whenever possible. A semistructured interview guide was developed and approved by the Institutional Review Board (IRB) to address the main research questions of the study regarding how the organizations conceptualize, prioritize, and address human rights issues.[3] We analyzed interview transcripts according to the same topical themes as the website content analysis.

Overview and Organization of the Book

In contrast to much of the previous research that compares secular and religious human rights organizations, which has often focused on small-N comparative case studies or in-depth anthropological or sociological inquiries into a single organization, this book considers a larger number of organizations using a mixed-method approach (as discussed above). Further, this study delves more deeply into the broad field of human rights by analyzing how these organizations approach and are affected by a variety of human rights issues, including culture, development, women's rights, children's rights, and peace and conflict.

Chapter 1 provides a theoretical overview of the differences between secular and RNGOs and outlines how these groups approach human rights more broadly. In particular, the chapter considers whether secular and/or religious human rights organizations focus more on political and civil or economic and social rights, whether they address legal or social justice, and the extent to which they focus on matters of human dignity and equity. The chapter also compares funding patterns for these groups.

Chapter 2 examines the role of culture in approaches to human rights, specifically investigating the extent to which religious and secular human rights organizations differ in their attention to issues of culture as well as whether they tend to focus more on matters of individual or collective rights, a key dimension of culture that is often highlighted in the literature. Because religion is often seen as a component of culture, this chapter also explores other dimensions of identity that may affect orientation to cultural dimensions, such as whether organizations are based in the Global North (so-called developed countries) or Global South (so-called developing countries) and whether or not they are based in the so-called West, that is, Europe, North, Central, and South America, and Australia. By teasing apart the influence of religion as opposed to cultural, socioeconomic, and sociopolitical categories, the chapter differentiates the influence of religion and culture on approaches to human rights.

Chapter 3 examines varying approaches to second-generation, or socioeconomic, rights as well as the somewhat related third-generation right to development between religious and secular organizations. Given that many religious traditions commend caring for the poor and advocate for a range of social welfare concerns, this chapter investigates whether religious and secular human rights organizations vary in the extent to which they work on economic and social rights. The chapter also examines whether organizations based in the Global North and Global South differ in their approach to these rights, and particularly to the right to development, given the history of competing claims regarding colonialism and development and differential socioeconomic status. Overall, very few organizations in the sample mention the right to development, regardless of where they are based.

Chapter 4 focuses more narrowly on questions related to gender and rights. The role of women can be politicized in and across religions, with women's rights and responsibilities often differentiated from those of men in conservative religious populations. Many religious figures view Western feminism as a threat to traditional culture, and religious institutions serve as one of the remaining glass ceilings facing women globally (Marshall 2013, 186–87). In addition to exploring whether religious and secular human rights organizations have a specific focus on women's rights, the chapter explores whether organizations engage in specific advocacy related to women's education and leadership development. Rights related to women's bodies, notably gender-based violence, reproductive rights, and abortion rights, are also explored in this chapter, particularly given various religious beliefs regarding birth control and the start of life. Religion also shapes views on lesbian, gay, bisexual, transgender, queer, and intersex (LGBTQI) rights, and this chapter compares the extent to which religious and secular human rights organizations address these issues.

Chapter 5 looks at the rights of children as codified in international law and compares how religious and secular human rights organizations approach children's rights. Religious communities have a long history of working in areas of health and the education of orphans (Marshall 2013, 155). Thus, we have particular interest in whether organizations focus on issues of the physical well-being, basic needs, and survival of children, whether they concentrate on the development of children and helping children flourish, thrive, and meet their full potential, and/or whether they consider children as active agents in their own growth and development and as advocates for their own rights.

Human rights violations often occur in situations of conflict, and areas of conflict may be the least equipped to document and handle human rights violations. Chapter 6 looks at how secular and religious human rights organizations respond to and engage in areas of peace and conflict, if at all, and how their work differs in those cases. This chapter also considers the debate on the "right to peace" and how religious and secular groups may differ in their support for this right.

The book concludes with a focus on the main themes as well as questions remaining to be addressed in further studies of human rights organizations more broadly and the role of religion in human rights work more specifically. While religious organizations seem slightly more likely than secular organizations to focus on socioeconomic rights, human dignity, and humanitarian issues and to emphasize peace and conflict resolution, both religious and secular organizations address political, civil, and individual rights and generally neglect third-generation rights. Overall, we note that there are many more areas of convergence than divergence between religious and secular organizations and that in certain areas like collective rights or gender rights, culture or specific religious orientation carry significant weight. However, given the dramatic differences between the organizations in this study in terms of size, scope, and budget, more refined case study analysis is required to investigate these patterns.

CHAPTER 1

Religious and Secular Approaches to Human Rights

History of Human Rights International Law

The UDHR was adopted by the UN General Assembly on December 10, 1948, and includes political and civil rights as well as social, economic, and cultural rights. However, international actors have often differed in their conceptual approaches to human rights, including which rights are considered universal, and these approaches, generally termed "generations," have changed over time. First-generation human rights are political and civil rights and include life, liberty, and security as well as freedoms of religion, opinion, expression, assembly, and association. These first-generation rights are often considered "negative rights," as they are meant to restrict government behavior and express rights upon which governments should not infringe. The International Covenant on Civil and Political Rights (ICCPR), which more specifically outlined civil and political rights, entered into force in March 1976 with 172 state parties to the treaty (UN 1966a).

Second-generation human rights include social and economic rights, including the rights to education, to work, and to housing. These rights are often called "positive rights" because they are rights that the government should take action to provide. The International Covenant on Economic, Social, and Cultural Rights (ICESCR) similarly entered into force in March 1976 and has since been ratified by 169 states. While the United States signed the convention in 1977, it was never formally ratified, so the United States is not party to it (UN 1966b). The Cold War context and the association of some second-generation rights with communism have shaped some of the discussion around these rights, particularly in the United States.

Third-generation human rights are often referred to as "solidarity rights" and are the most controversial of the various generations. These rights often include those that are claimed by groups (in contrast to the more individual-oriented rights of the first two generations) and include collective rights for ethnic groups or indigenous peoples, the right to development, the right to peace, and the right to a healthy environment. Solidarity rights are newer within the international system and do not have as wide support as other political, civil, and socioeconomic rights.

A variety of conventions have attempted to deal with some of these third-generation rights. For example, the 1972 UN Conference on the Human Environment, also known as the Stockholm Conference, was the first major UN conference on international environmental issues. This conference resulted in the Declaration of the United Nations Conference on the Human Environment, which promotes the preservation of the human environment (UN 1972). Similarly, the Rio Declaration on Environment and Development of 1992 recognizes the importance of preserving the environment, stating, "Human beings are at the centre of concerns for sustainable development. They are entitled to a healthy and productive life in harmony with nature" (UN 1992). The Rio Declaration both combines concerns for the environment with issues of development and promotes "the right to development" (UN 1992). As of 2019, the UN Human Rights Council has not passed a declaration on solidarity rights, though in 2005 the Commission on Human Rights (the predecessor to the Human Rights Council) created an independent expert on human rights and solidarity with the mandate to develop a draft declaration on such a right. This process remains under way (Office of the High Commissioner for Human Rights [OHCHR] n.d.).

In addition to these broader human rights conventions, there are a variety of more specialized treaties and conventions on human rights issues, such as the Convention on the Elimination of All Forms of Discrimination against Women (CEDAW) and the Convention on the Rights of the Child (CRC). This chapter, however, focuses on human rights as broadly conceived, with subsequent chapters considering these more specialized treaties and conventions as appropriate.

Secular versus Religious Organizations and Human Rights

Before considering the similarities and differences between secular and religious human rights organizations, it is important to define the boundaries of these classifications. Clarke and Jennings (2008, 6) discuss a faith-based group as "any organization that derives inspiration and guidance for its activities from the teachings and principles of the faith or from a particular interpretation or school of thought within the faith." Similarly, Berger (2003, 16) defines "religious NGOs" as "formal organizations whose identity and mission are self-consciously derived from the teaching of one or more religious or spiritual traditions and which operate on a nonprofit, independent, voluntary basis to promote and realize collectively articulated ideas about the public good at the national or international level." We agree with these conceptions of religious and faith-based groups and use these terms interchangeably.

Secular organizations, in contrast, are those whose identity and mission are not spiritual or religious in nature, although in practice this can be difficult to ascertain. Much of the literature comparing faith-based and secular organizations does not actually provide explicit definitions; instead authors either identify secular groups as those that are not religious or use self-identification for classifying secular groups (Berger 2003; Ebaugh et al. 2003; Ferris 2005; Twombly 2002). Furthermore, the literature on secularism does not really provide a single definition, emphasizing that the concept is locally negotiated and thus has different meanings in different contexts (Freeman 2004; Hallward 2008). For example, when we interviewed a member of one self-identified secular organization, they noted that they often feel some individuals and groups within their country view the term "secular" as synonymous with "atheist." Consequently, in line with Berger (2003) and Ebaugh et al. (2003), we classify groups as secular based on cues during interviews and from their own self-identifications on their websites. As discussed in the introduction, although this dichotomy sidelines the nuanced variations in degree of religiosity or secularity of organizations, it provides a useful starting point for comparing secular and religious human rights organizations.

Why might religious and secular NGOs be expected to differ in their approach to human rights? As Koschmann (2013, 129) notes, "Religious faith influences how people make and justify decisions, how they resolve conflict, how they make sense of their circumstances, and how they interact with multiple stakeholders." Consequently, it is not unreasonable that RNGOs would use different processes within their organizations than secular NGOs might to define human rights. Religious groups may have some general commonalities that set them apart from their secular counterparts. However, individual religions may have elements that set their human rights work apart from that of other groups, including other religious groups. For example, Salih (2002, 2) suggests that "Islamic NGOs distinguish themselves from other NGOs by the fact that voluntarism is a religious duty in Islam, and those NGOs which profess an Islamic identity claim also to be advancing a Muslim way of life and expanding the Islamic *umma* (community) world-wide." Dicklitch and Rice (2004, 660) note the Mennonite Central Committee's (MCC) "holistic approach to basic human rights."

Other scholars have considered the distinctive contributions of religious groups to development. For example, Melissa Caldwell (2012) observes that, in comparison to their secular counterparts, religiously affiliated groups appeared to be more successful "at doing the kind of work that mattered . . . in terms of providing client-centered services that were humane, compassionate, and emphasized the dignity of clients" (Caldwell 2012, 262). In Caldwell's study, secular groups perceived that religiously oriented groups were not as constrained and restricted by bureaucracy as they themselves often were. Clarke (2006) suggests that faith-based organizations have several characteristics that distinguish them from their secular equivalents, including drawing on spiritual and moral values in their development work.

In her foundational work on RNGOs, Berger (2003) documents the increasing number of groups that refer to themselves as religious, spiritual, or faith-based groups. Berger suggests that although NGOs overall have long been moral entities that have challenged what is "wrong" in the world in favor of what is "right," RNGOs and secular NGOs identify different origins for the values that they support (Berger 2003, 19). In contrast to secular-oriented groups, RNGOs articulate a religious rather than a more "purely 'reasoned' origin of these values." Of particular relevance to our research here, Berger states, "In contrast with the rights-based approach of many secular NGOs, the starting point for RNGOs is the duty-oriented language of religion characterized by obligations toward the divine and toward others, by a belief in transformation capacities, and a concern for justice and reconciliation" (19). Similarly, Braungart (2019) notes that many RNGOs are highly focused on reconciliatory and restorative justice approaches, which are more about social than legal justice. A focus on human dignity also has been characteristic of religious actors. Moyn (2015, 4) suggests that in the context of post–World War II Europe it was "quite difficult to find non-Christians who enthused about human rights, and more especially their basis in human dignity." Chapter 2 provides further discussion of the importance of duty-oriented approaches for religious organizations.

However, as Berger notes, there is great diversity among religious groups, including religious orientation and pervasiveness, or the extent to which the religious identity defines the structural and strategic dimensions of the organization (Berger 2003, 23). Further, religious human rights groups span the political spectrum from right to left, with great variation in their acceptance of the liberal human rights paradigm (Moyn 2015). In relation to organizational elements, Berger finds that donor patterns and financing may be an area in which secular and religious groups differ. Most RNGOs, in order to maintain their organizational independence, are largely privately funded through member donations (Berger 2003, 28). However, she also notes that some RNGOs, such as Catholic Charities, do receive substantial finances from government sources, but overall many of these organizations avoid government funding. Butcher and Hallward (2018) find that religious organizations that are involved in humanitarian work, in addition to their human rights advocacy, are more likely to take money from governments than those groups that are not so involved. Further, they argue that some secular organizations may see themselves as government watchdogs, and to maintain this autonomy and impartiality, they may be reluctant to receive government funding. Similarly, Clarke (2006) finds that Western donors tend to support religious organizations primarily when they focus on charitable and development issues—of which humanitarian aid would be part. These findings suggest that the relationship between funding and secular/religious organizations may be more complex than noted by Berger (2003).

Considerable variation exists in the degree to which mission statements of RNGOs emphasize the religious or spiritual origin or foundation of the organization's actions (Berger 2003, 29). Further, whereas some RNGO processes—including network building, advocacy, monitoring, and providing information—are used by all types of NGOs, others—such as seeking spiritual guidance, praying, and using dialogue to consider disparate views—are more unique to RNGOs. For example, the Friends World Committee for Consultation (Quakers) is well known for its mediation at the UN and for its conflict resolution and reconciliation efforts. Although there are potential differences in how RNGOs and secular organizations approach their work, no research has specifically connected these differences to human rights advocacy or considered how these differences might impact the ability of these groups to find mutual ground. Additionally, Berger finds that the strategies RNGOs use to promote human rights also vary. For example, while a key characteristic of the mission of many RNGOs "is recognition of the spiritual nature of the individual and of a divine source of guidance," considerable variation exists in the degree to which mission statements emphasize the religious or spiritual origin or foundation of the organization's actions (Berger 2003, 29).

While the research presented above discusses the uniqueness of RNGOs more generally or in other issue areas, recent studies have specifically considered RNGOs within the human rights field. Religious groups often view human rights as divinely proffered and as such may link human rights to other concepts, such as peace and development, in a holistic way (Dicklitch and Rice 2004; Hallward 2013; Johnston 2014; Klager 2014). In their analysis of 237 human rights groups, Butcher and Hallward (2017) find that faith-based groups are more likely to mention peace and to connect human rights and peace on their websites. Other authors argue that a "development perspective" is particularly useful for understanding the link between human rights and religion (Petersen 2015). Religious groups also tend to place a greater emphasis on positive rights, those that relate to social and economic rights, versus secular groups (Berger 2003; Johnston 2014; Butcher and Hallward 2018). In contrast, secular human rights groups often focus on political and civil rights, which emphasize "neutrality" and "impartiality" (Johnston 2014, 907). Such political and civil rights are often encompassed within a broader legal tradition—providing legal protections for the political and civil rights of individuals without necessarily situating these rights in a social justice or development framework.

The literature is divided regarding potential and actual cooperation between religious and secular human rights organizations. Koschmann (2013, 108) suggests that although research has considered structural and organizational aspects of religious human rights organizations, it has failed to fully consider collaboration between secular and religious organizations within human rights specifically. He argues that as religious organizations and other NGOs begin to work together, along with government agencies and other stakeholders, such collaboration requires "the negotiation and transformation of identities." Not all the partners in collaboration will share the religious views of faith-based groups, and some may even work for organizations that specifically restrict religious influence within their work.

Negrón-Gonzales (2012) suggests that the human rights movement provides space for secular and religious factions within the country to reconcile some of their differences. More specifically, she argues that a human rights master frame emphasizing the common fate that a diverse group of individuals share as citizens within the state helps bridge the gap between secular and religious groups. Diplomatic and government actors "simply tend not to see [religious groups] as central and competent" even though religious actors may run the most sustainable and locally rooted programs due to the faith link (Marshall 2013, 178). Civil society partnerships can perhaps help offset the neglect of religious organizations by elites and raise the profile of religious actors in the human rights field. However, some religious actors may push back against such cooperation, particularly those who worry about LGBTQI and reproductive rights (Beinlich 2019; Marshall 2013, 188; Moyn 2015).

Interreligious Differences

The literature review suggests that differences likely exist between religious human rights organizations from different faith backgrounds. For example, while Christian, Jewish, and Muslim groups emphasize justice, Buddhists, Hindus, and other non-Abrahamic faith traditions emphasize harmony (Glaab, Fuchs, and Friederich 2019). Some authors have considered the potential friction between different types of RNGOs or between Western organizations (including Christian NGOs) and Islamic groups. For example, Benthall (1997, 170) discusses the tensions between the Red Cross and the Red Crescent Movement over a variety of issues, including the organization's emblems and the potential Christian connotation of the cross, differences on issues such as the rights of nonbelievers, and friction between the way that the International Committee of the Red Cross attempts to be more inclusive by providing a "humanist representation of Islam," while Muslims attempt, at the same time, to maintain "the distinctiveness and originality of their religion." Benedetti (2006) considers potential collaboration between Islamic and Christian humanitarian/relief

NGOs, finding that strongly religious Christian and Islamic NGOs were more likely to have negative perceptions of one another than those that had a lower level of religiosity. Similarly, in their discussion and comparison of Muslim and Western relief aid organizations, Barakat and Strand (1999, 30) suggest that Muslim organizations "have at times been greeted with suspicion by long-established western organizations who are concerned about their possible religious and political intentions," while many Muslim agencies also "appear to have an ingrained prejudice that one of the key aims of western NGOs is to spread Christianity and promote Western governments' political interests." Indeed, Muslim organizations may downplay their faith connections due to "harsh sanctions and financial difficulties" toward Islam in some areas (Marshall 2013, 176). In contrast, Petersen (2010) suggests there are many examples of cooperation and partnerships between NGOs from different religious organizations and even between religious and secular groups, but there tends to be less cooperation between RNGOs from the same religious group. Furthermore, Petersen found that the primary RNGO divide seems to be between "progressive" and "conservative" organizations, particularly regarding issues such as women's and homosexuals' rights. This divide can manifest even within the same denomination, including churches part of the Anglican Communion in Southern Africa, East Africa, Nigeria, and Australia, which are split over questions of gay and women priests (Marshall 2013, 68).

Hypotheses

Based on previous research, we expect secular and faith-based human rights organizations to use different language in defining, framing, and operationalizing human rights advocacy. In this chapter, we examine the types of rights organizations emphasize, how they frame them, and their approaches to justice. We also consider issues related to organizational funding. Specifically, we examine the following hypotheses:

1. Secular organizations will be more likely than religious organizations to frame their work using a rights discussion.
2. Secular organizations will be more likely than religious organizations to consider civil and political rights.
3. Secular organizations will be more likely than religious organizations to promote democracy.
4. Secular organizations will be more likely than religious organizations to focus on legal justice.
5. Religious organizations will be more likely than secular organizations to consider social and economic rights.

6. Religious organizations will be more likely than secular organizations to focus on human dignity.
7. Religious organizations will be more likely than secular organizations to focus on social justice.
8. Religious organizations that are focused on humanitarian aid, in addition to human rights, will be more likely to receive government funding than those that are not.
9. Both religious and secular organizations will rely on funding from grants from external NGOs, churches, and individuals.
10. Religious organizations will be more likely than secular organizations to be funded through membership support.

Findings

This chapter considers how the religious and secular organizations in the sample of 333 human rights organizations and forty-seven interviews of human rights organizations vary in terms of which types of rights organizations consider (political and civil rights compared to social and economic rights) and their conceptions of justice (legal versus social justice). Further, this chapter compares the funding sources of secular versus faith-based organizations in the sample.

While the organizations in the sample associate themselves with the broader international human rights agenda, not all of them explicitly frame their work on their websites in terms of rights, though most do. Of the 333 organizations in the sample, 278 (84 percent) mention rights in their mission statement, vision statement, about us statement, advocacy page, or other page directly related to their work at the UN. As noted in Table 1.1, secular organizations were more likely than religious groups to mention rights, 88 to 65 percent, a difference significant at the $p < .001$ level. There is little variation between different faith organizations in terms of whether they discuss rights, although Muslim and Jewish organizations are slightly more likely to discuss rights. Around 71 percent of Muslim and 75 percent of Jewish organizations in the sample discuss rights, compared to 65 percent of Christian and 55 percent of other religious organizations. Still, groups from all faith backgrounds are less likely than secular organizations to discuss rights explicitly on their websites.

Which Rights?

Civil and political rights are indicated by an organization's concern for physical and civil security (such as the prevention of torture, slavery, inhumane treat-

TABLE 1.1

Comparison of Types of Rights (in percentages)

	Religious organizations	Secular organizations
Rights	65	88
Civil and political rights	52	80
Democracy	9	33
Social and economic rights	93	81
Human dignity	57	25

ment, and arbitrary arrest and equality before the law) as well as support for norms pertaining to civil and political liberties or empowerments, such as freedom of thought, conscience, and religion; freedom of assembly and voluntary association; and political participation in one's society. Social and economic rights are those that are more concerned with the social and economic wellbeing of individuals and include promoting the provision of goods for meeting the social needs of society and individuals (such as nutrition, shelter, health care, and education) and promoting the norms of provisions to help meet the economic needs of society and individuals (such as work and fair wages, an adequate living standard, and a social security net). Discussions of the rights to education, work, housing, and subsistence as well as minority rights and equality/inclusion are all part of social and economic rights.

The vast majority of organizations in the sample, 247 (74 percent), consider political and civil rights in their mission statement, vision statement, about us section, advocacy page, specific section on political/civil rights, recent annual reports (less than five years old), or document/page directly related to their work at the UN. As expected, secular organizations are more likely than religious organizations to consider political and civil rights and to promote democracy, 80 to 52 percent (see Table 1.1), and only 9 percent of religious organizations actively promote democracy, compared to 33 percent of secular organizations.[1]

As shown in Table 1.2, Christian organizations in particular are less likely than those from other faith traditions to consider political and civil rights. While the small sample size means that the differences between Christian and other types of religious organizations are not necessarily statistically significant, the distinction between Christian and Jewish organizations is significant at the $p < .05$ level. Only Christian and Muslim organizations in the sample are found to promote democracy, albeit at low levels, and none of the Jewish and "other" religious organizations explicitly mention democracy promotion in their human rights work.

TABLE 1.2

Religious Differences in Considerations of Types of Rights (in percentages)

	Civil and political rights	Democracy promotion	Human dignity
Christian organizations	42	10	67
Muslim organizations	71	14	29
Jewish organizations	100	0	0
Other religious organizations	67	0	45

As shown in Table 1.1, religious organizations were slightly more likely than secular groups to consider social and economic rights, and this difference is significant at the $p < .05$ level. There does not appear to be much difference between faith backgrounds and support for social and economic rights—each tradition shows strong support for these rights. Further, religious organizations are statistically much more likely to consider social and economic rights than political and civil rights. Secular organizations, on the other hand, appear equally likely to support civil and political rights as socioeconomic rights. Chapter 3 discusses social and economic rights along with the right to development in more detail.

Use of "human dignity" rather than "human rights" is often connected to social and economic rather than political and civil approaches to human rights. Further, conceptions of dignity are often grounded in faith traditions, including conservative ones (Caldwell 2012, 262). Moyn (2015, 2, 5) claims that by emphasizing the dignity of the human person as stemming from God, the Roman Catholic Church "made what had been secular and liberal into a set of values that were now religious and conservative." As expected, religious organizations were more likely than secular organizations to mention "human dignity" (see Table 1.1). When disaggregating the data by religion, as shown in Table 1.2, Christian organizations are, by far, the most likely to mention human dignity, followed by other religious organizations and Muslim groups. None of the Jewish organizations in the sample mention human dignity; the difference in percentages between Christian groups (which are the most likely to mention human dignity) and Jewish organizations (least likely) is significant at the $p < .01$ level, with the remaining differences failing to attain statistical significance.

The qualitative interview data reveal similar findings, namely, that secular organizations are more prone to emphasize political and civil rights and that while both types of organizations heavily focus on social and economic rights, religious groups are more likely to focus on these rights. For example, the Federation of Environmental and Ecological Diversity for Agricultural Revampment and Human Rights (FEEDAR & HR) promotes "the basic fundamental rights like rights to working, rights to public opinion, rights to participate in public and political issues," while Djazairouna mentioned "defense of their civic and political rights." Several secular organizations focus explicitly on imprisonment and torture, including the Center for Prisoners' Rights Japan, which works to "improve the human rights conditions of those that are held in penal institutions in Japan" and "to abolish the death penalty," while the Lebanese Center for Human Rights and Public Foundation "Kylym Shamy" work to prevent arbitrary detention and torture. In contrast, Franciscans International noted the "church has a key role in . . . promoting a better use of business in sharing resources equitably," and the Baha'i International Community emphasized the importance of social and economic issues in addition to nondiscrimination. Catholic groups such as Dominicans for Justice and Peace also used a human dignity focus, sharing that their work includes dealing with poverty and development because of the need to "ascribe to the full dignity and equal dignity of every individual . . . at every level of life."

Work on the different generations of rights was not exclusive to either religious or secular human rights organizations, however, and our results indicate that the vast majority of groups in our sample focus on social and economic rights. The Women's International League for Peace and Freedom (WILPF), for instance, speaks of the importance of investing in social and economic welfare instead of the military. Djazairouna, which mentions working on civic and political rights, also specifically mentions fighting for socioeconomic rights, particularly for women. The Organisation Guinéenne de Défense des Droits de l'Homme et du Citoyen (OGDH) says, "We defend ALL human rights; we don't separate areas . . . we don't separate civic, political, cultural, [economic], etc." Similarly, the Association Africaine d'Éducation pour le Développement said, "Human rights are universal, indivisible and interdependent; that is to say there are civil and political rights, economic rights, social and cultural issues; it's unacceptable to privilege civil and political rights while at the same time abandoning social, economic, and cultural rights."

Conception of Justice

A significant amount of human rights advocacy addresses issues of justice, either for victims of human rights violations or for the perpetrators of human rights abuses. Legal justice places an emphasis on laws and legal institutions and their role in correcting human rights abuses. Issues of "accountability" are often a key part of legal justice. On the other hand, social justice speaks to issues of equal access to wealth, opportunities, and privileges within society, such as promoting equality and ending racism and other oppressive structures. In the sample, a focus on social justice is much more common than one on legal justice. Only 41 percent of organizations consider legal justice, compared to 77 percent that focus on social justice. Given the additional resources and costs associated with providing legal assistance and the difficulties that many organizations may have in gaining access to courts, this is perhaps not surprising.

However, as expected, secular organizations were more likely than religious groups to consider legal justice, and this difference is significant at the $p < .001$ level (see Table 1.3). Christian organizations are least likely to discuss legal justice (8 percent), compared to 14 percent of Muslim, 50 percent of Jewish, and 33 percent of other religious organizations. There is a strong tradition of Jewish law, the halakha, which may account for the larger percentage of Jewish organizations that focus on legal justice.

TEXTBOX 1.1

Conceptions of Justice

Caritas Internationalis

Caritas Internationalis is a confederation of member organizations working at a grassroots level around the world. The organization is inspired by the Catholic faith and considers itself "the helping hand of the church—reaching out to the poor, vulnerable and excluded, regardless of race or religion, to build a world based on justice and fraternal love." They are guided by the "deep moral and spiritual principles of dignity, justice, solidarity and stewardship." The organization provides emergency assistance during humanitarian crises and promotes "human development" so people are "free to flourish and live in peace and dignity." Caritas further seeks "a world where women and men in the poorest and most disadvantaged communities are able to influence the systems, decisions and resources that affect them" so that they "can then live under governments, institutions and global structures that just and accountable."

Caritas. n.d. "Our Mission." https://www.caritas.org/who-we-are/, https://www.caritas.org/who-we
-are/mission/.

International Bridges to Justice

International Bridges to Justice promotes the basic legal rights of all people, particularly in the event of arrest and judicial accusation, focusing specifically on the right to legal representation, freedom from torture, and the right to a fair trial. One of their primary objectives is to "advocate and support the prioritization of just and effective criminal justice systems on the agenda of organizations involved with international human rights and legal development." The organization also provides technical support and training to legal aid organizations, particularly within the developing world, including country-specific eLearning courses and defenders' manuals for public defenders. Further, the organization hosts a competition for JusticeMakers Fellows; the 2017 JusticeMakers Fellows competition focused on the prevention of torture in Francophonie Africa, and the ten chosen fellows were legal experts representing a variety of African countries.

International Bridges to Justice (IBJ). n.d. "JusticeMakers." https://www.ibj.org/programs
/justicemakers/about/.
IBJ. n.d. "Lawyer2Lawyer." https://www.ibj.org/programs/lawyer2lawyer/.
IBJ. n.d. "Mission." https://www.ibj.org/meet-ibj-2/mission/.

TABLE 1.3

Comparison of Types of Justice (in percentages)

	Religious organizations	Secular organizations
Legal justice	15	48
Social justice	87	75

In contrast, religious human rights organizations were more likely than secular organizations to promote social justice, and this difference is significant at the $p < .05$ level (see Table 1.3). Muslim organizations in the sample were the most likely to consider social justice (with all seven of the Muslim organizations in our sample focusing on social justice), but this comparative difference is not statistically significant. Around 88 percent of Christian, 75 percent of Jewish, and 78 percent of other religious organizations consider social justice, indicating that the vast majority of all religious groups were focused on social justice.

The qualitative data also support the social justice orientation of religious organizations, with interview subjects identifying efforts to tackle the root causes of poverty and injustice. Franciscans International pointed to the strong antipoverty message of Pope Francis, and Dominicans for Justice and Peace also emphasized their history combatting poverty and promoting the right to development and the rights of indigenous people. Baha'i International also underscored the importance of "the eradication of extremes of wealth and poverty, and social justice for everyone," and Soka Gakkai shared that one can "attain enlightenment only after having first saved others from suffering" and also noted the need to combat "passive violence." Similarly, Islamic Relief Worldwide (2014, 6) emphasized that "human rights are a means to achieving justice and preserving human dignity."

Legal rights language was more commonly used in the interviews with members of secular organizations. For example, the FIDH and the Human Rights Observatory in Rwanda mention their fight against impunity and working toward "accountability for the most serious human rights violations." The Center for Prisoners' Rights Japan files lawsuits to counter human rights abuses. Similarly, the Public Foundation "Kylym Shamy," Djazairouna, the Lebanese Center for Human Rights, the Association Rwandaise pour la Défense des Droits de la Personne et Libertés Publiques, and OGDH all mention providing legal support for victims of human rights abuses. Finally, the Union for Civil Liberty discusses the importance of reforming the justice system to help victims.

Comparisons of Funding

Human rights organizations pursue a variety of funding types, including from state or local governments, from international organizations such as the European Union (EU) and UN, from members, and from grants allocated by other NGOs, foundations, churches, or businesses. Where money originates can impact how organizations approach human rights advocacy. Funders usually have their own agendas and thus may choose programs or organizations that align with their view or may attempt to reorient the work of groups that they fund. Many organizations in the sample do not provide information regarding their funding sources, so there is more limited data when comparing the funding for religious and secular organizations and the potential implications this has for their human rights advocacy. The results (see Table 1.4) indicate that religious organizations were less likely than secular organizations to receive government funding of all types (state/local, EU, UN), though these differences are generally not statistically significant. Both secular and religious organizations were most likely to receive funding from individual state and local governments, followed by UN funding, with EU funding being the least likely. These findings are consistent with those of Berger (2003) and suggest that the secular nature of many governments may make them more reluctant to fund religious organizations.

In terms of state and local government funding, of the organizations with data, 52 percent of religious organizations received this type of funding, compared to 67 percent of their secular counterparts. While religious were less likely than secular organizations to receive this funding, the difference is not statistically significant (due to small sample sizes). Further, it should be noted that more than half of the religious organizations with data received government funding, suggesting this is not a rare occurrence. Similarly, 22 percent of religious organizations with data received EU funding, compared to 39 percent of secular organizations, and 32 percent of religious organizations with data received UN funding, compared to 48 percent of secular organizations, with neither of these differences being statistically significant. Overall, religious groups seem to be less likely to receive funding from state and local governments as well as from the EU and UN, but the differences between secular and religious organizations, particularly given the small sample sizes, are not statistically significant.

As predicted, religious organizations in the sample were more likely to receive funding through memberships, with 74 percent of faith-based organizations with data receiving membership funds, compared to 54 percent of secular organizations, a significant difference at the $p < .05$ level (see Table 1.4). Religious and secular organizations appear equally likely to receive funding through grants from NGOs, churches, businesses, and foundations. Funding

TABLE 1.4

Comparison of Funding (in percentages)

	Religious organizations	Secular organizations
Government funding (states or local)	52	67
EU funding	22	39
UN funding	32	48
Membership funding	74	54
Grants from NGOs, foundations, churches, businesses	93	94

159 organizations had data for government funding; 149 organizations had data for EU and UN funding; 229 organizations had data for membership funding; and 168 organizations had data for grants.

through grants was the most common type (aside from donations from individuals, which is not included in the dataset since nearly all organizations accept such donations).

While the data demonstrate patterns in funding for secular and religious organizations, they also show significant variation in types of funding, and while religious organizations may be less likely than secular organizations to receive government funding (of all kinds), there are still many religious organizations that receive government funding. These trends in funding, as well as the diversity of funding, are also seen throughout the interviews.

Many of the organizations, both religious and secular, emphasized the importance of funding from their members as a way of providing more control over their activities. Religious groups including Soka Gakkai and Baha'i International noted that they receive all of their funds from members of their faith communities; other groups, such as the secular International Association for Jewish Lawyers and Jurists and Mazlumder, a Muslim group based in Turkey, receive most of their funding from members and individual donors. Religiously affiliated groups receive money from their faith communities as part of fulfilling obligations or acting on value commitments. Islamic Relief Worldwide reports receiving a substantial amount of money through Muslims donating their zakat (one of Islam's five pillars that requires donating money to the poor), and T'ruah, a rabbinic association, reports most of their grants coming from Jewish organizations, in part because "we have a harder time as allies convincing the non-Jewish funders to invest in us."

Large religious organizations, particularly those engaged in humanitarian and development activities, such as the World Council of Churches, Lutheran World Federation, Catholic Relief Services, and Islamic Relief Worldwide, receive money not only from member churches and committed individuals but also from bilateral government donors and multilateral donors within the world system. For example, Islamic Relief has received funding from the UN (including from the UN High Commissioner for Refugees and the World Food Programme) as well as from Britain, Sweden, and Canada. This is one of the ways that the large religious organizations differ substantively from smaller grassroots, member-driven groups.

Secular organizations vary widely in their funding sources, with some organizations, such as BADIL, even receiving church-based funding. Other secular groups, such as the International Service for Human Rights, receive most of their funding from states, particularly Western governments. WILPF, the International Peace Bureau (IPB), and FIDH received funds from foundations and from some Northern European governments and agencies as well as private donations. European governments, including the EU, the Netherlands, Norway, Switzerland, Germany, and France, fund a range of organizations in Africa and Asia, including the Commonwealth Human Rights Initiative, Le Réseau des Éducateurs aux Droits de l'Homme, à la Démocratie et Genre, Human Rights Commission of Pakistan, Djazairouna, OGDH, B'Tselem, and Informal Sector Service Center. One major divide that emerged through speaking with organizations, particularly in the Global South, is that while some organizations like FEEDAR & HR receive all their funding from individual and member donations, others have a difficult time raising money from their membership since, as the IPB notes, "our members are poor." Further, many Global South groups have a difficult time securing funds in part due to the highly professionalized processes for applying for and receiving funds from governments and donor agencies. One organization from Algeria noted that they had received funding through foundations but generally found it difficult to get funds for their association, noting that they "have searched for donations, but can't find any." Overall, the interviews emphasized wide variation in funding sources for human rights organizations, with funding varying more by size and scope of the organization than whether it was religious or secular per se. However, religious organizations tended to receive more of their funding from members, while secular groups tended to receive more from governments.

Funding and Humanitarian Aid

We hypothesized that human rights organizations that provide humanitarian aid will be more likely to receive government funding than those that do not provide such aid, and this would include funding from local and state governments as well as from the UN and EU. This is particularly important when considering religious groups, which are hypothesized to generally be less likely to receive government support; humanitarianism may serve as an intervening factor that can improve the chances of receiving government aid. Although this book focuses on human rights organizations, not humanitarian activity per se, many religious organizations, in particular, also engage in humanitarian work as part of their mandate of serving those in need, and thus the intersection between the two types of activities is explored here.

The data support our hypothesis (see Table 1.5). Religious organizations that also provided humanitarian aid were significantly more likely to receive state and local government (71 vs. 43 percent), EU (50 vs. 14 percent), and UN (60 vs. 21 percent) funding than those religious organizations that did not provide humanitarian aid. On the other hand, similar trends are found for secular organizations; those that provided humanitarian aid were more likely to receive various types of government funding. However, religious organizations appear to benefit more than secular organizations from their humanitarianism (see Table 1.5), with the differences between groups larger for religious organizations than for secular ones.

In terms of EU funding, 149 human rights organizations in the sample have data regarding whether they receive EU funding or not, and 16 also provide humanitarian aid. In terms of the interaction between EU funding and humanitarian aid, of these 16 organizations, 9 (56 percent) receive EU funding, compared to 46 of the 133 (35 percent) organizations with data that do not provide humanitarian aid; this difference is significant at the $p < .10$ level. There are a total of 18 religious organizations in this subsample, 4 of which also provide humanitarian aid. Of the 4 religious organizations that provide humanitarian aid, 50 percent (or 2) also receive EU funding. Of the 14 religious organizations that do not provide humanitarian aid, only 2 (14 percent) receive EU funding.

TABLE 1.5

Comparison of Funding for Organizations That Provide Humanitarian Aid versus Those That Do Not (in percentages)

	Government funding (states or local)	EU funding	UN funding
Religious organizations providing humanitarian aid	71	50	60
Religious organizations not providing humanitarian aid	43	14	21
Secular organizations providing humanitarian aid	86	58	58
Secular organizations not providing humanitarian aid	65	37	47

159 organizations had data for government funding; 149 organizations had data for EU and UN funding; 229 organizations had data for membership funding, and 168 organizations had data for grants

Thus, religious organizations providing humanitarian aid are more likely to receive EU funding than those that do not.

Finally, when considering UN funding, 149 human rights organizations in the sample have available data, 17 of which provide humanitarian aid. Of these 17 organizations, 10 also receive UN funding (59 percent); of the 132 organizations that do not provide humanitarian aid in the sample, 58 receive UN funding (44 percent), though this difference is not statistically significant. There are a total of 19 religious organizations in this subsample, 5 of which provide humanitarian aid. Of these 5 organizations, 3 (or 60 percent) also receive UN funding, compared to 3 out of 14 (22 percent) religious organizations that do not provide humanitarian aid. Of the 130 secular organizations in this subset, 12 also provide humanitarian aid. Of these 12, 7 (59 percent) receive UN funding, compared to 55 out of 118 (47 percent) secular organizations that do not provide humanitarian aid. Similar to state and local government funding and EU funding, while providing humanitarian aid seems to increase the likelihood of receiving UN support for both secular and religious organizations, this change was smaller for secular than religious organizations. Overall, the results of this section suggest that humanitarianism increases the likelihood that human rights organizations will receive government funding, whether it be from state and local government or from intergovernmental organizations like the EU or UN. However, the results also demonstrate that religious organizations, which are less likely to receive government funding more generally, benefit the most from this humanitarianism. These findings are significant because they provide a more nuanced understanding of the factors that impact the funding of religious and secular organizations and indicate ways that religious groups may be able to mitigate the potential secular bias of governments in funding decisions.

Conclusion

Overall, the results from this chapter indicate that there are clear differences in the ways that religious and secular organizations approach human rights advocacy, conceptualize and frame human rights, and obtain funding. Even though all the organizations in the sample associate themselves with international human rights, not all explicitly frame their work in terms of rights; religious organizations are less likely than their secular counterparts to use rights language when discussing their work, with many using the term "dignity" instead. When considering which types of rights organizations focus on, the findings suggest that, consistent with previous research, secular organizations are more likely than religious groups to consider political and civil rights, while religious organizations are more likely to focus on social and economic rights. However, contrary to previous research, secular organizations appear equally likely to consider civil and political rights as to focus on social and economic rights (Berger 2003; Johnston 2014; Butcher and Hallward 2018). This finding suggests that social and economic rights are increasingly prominent in the international human rights framework. In fact, in the sample analyzed here, more organizations focused on social and economic than on civil and political rights, and religious organizations are significantly more likely to consider social and economic than political and civil rights. Christian organizations in the sample are particularly unlikely to advocate for civil and political rights, which could be due to their strong focus on helping the poor and less fortunate, but could also be related to a reluctance to get involved with issues that might seem more politically oriented. For example, many Christian organizations are opposed to abortion as well as LGBTQI rights (discussed more in chapter 4), which might make them more likely to shift their focus from political and civil rights more generally to social and economic rights.

A far greater percentage of the organizations in the sample focused on social justice than on legal justice. This could be due to the amount of resources, in both time and expertise, required to work through the courts. As predicted, religious organizations were more likely to discuss social justice, whereas secular organizations were more likely to discuss legal justice. Given the social justice focus of many religious traditions, it is not surprising to see religious organizations emphasizing that area.

Finally, the results suggest that religious organizations were less likely than secular organizations to receive all types of government funding (state and local governments, UN, and EU). Further, the most common type of government funding for both types of organizations was from state and local governments, followed by UN funding, with EU funding being the least likely. Even though religious organizations were less likely to receive government funding, many religious groups did in fact receive it, and more than half of the religious organizations with funding data received funding from state and/or local governments. These data suggest that government funding for religious organizations is not uncommon and that all organizations actually received a wide variety of funding. Further, the results indicate that organizations that provide humanitarian aid are more likely to receive government funding and that this effect may be particularly strong for religious organizations. This is important because it indicates that the potential secular bias of governments can be overcome depending on the focus of an organization and the types of services it provides. For religious human rights organizations, adding a humanitarian focus might lead to more government aid. In fact, religious organizations largely focused on human rights may be making conscious choices to increase humanitarian aid in the hopes of securing greater government funding. While human rights law is distinct from humanitarian work, much of humanitarian law deals with issues similar to those of concern to human rights organizations, particularly those focused on peace and conflict issues.

While this chapter has considered broader issues related to human rights (such as different types of rights and justice), subsequent chapters delve more deeply into the various areas of human rights advocacy, such as culture, development, children's rights, women's rights, and peace and conflict, and discuss the differences between secular and faith-based approaches to these rights.

CHAPTER 2

The Role of Culture

Discussions of religion inevitably bring about considerations of culture and the ways in which culture influences understandings of and approaches to human rights. While culture and religion sometimes are treated as interchangeable, this chapter seeks to separate their respective influences on the theory and practice of human rights. Making this distinction is particularly important for this project since at times cultural practices, such as female circumcision, are confused with religious tenets and have been challenged by civil society actors using religious teachings. This chapter explores the extent to which religious and secular human rights organizations engage with culture, given that culture and religion have been used to justify recusals from particular sections of human rights instruments and the liberal, universal approach to human rights has been deemed a "secular" religion. Culture shapes many dimensions of human rights operationalization, including whether rights are understood in collective or individual terms, and the extent to which human rights are deemed universal or particular to specific groups. This chapter explores the various ways in which culture shapes conceptions of and approaches to human rights in religious and secular human rights organizations and traces the variations between different cultural and faith backgrounds. This chapter also engages in initial explorations of themes that are developed further in other chapters, notably differences between organizations based in the Global North, Global South, West, and non-West as well as the relatively unique positionality of women's rights when it comes to debates of religion and culture.

International Law and Culture

The UDHR is based on the presumption that human rights transcend culture. The preamble of the document "proclaims this Universal Declaration of Human Rights as a common standard of achievement for all peoples and all nations," clearly indicating that rights are not culturally specific. While Article 18 asserts the right to freedom of religion—on an individual basis—and Article 27 provides the right to freely participate in the cultural life of one's community, there is no specified "right to culture" per se. Cultural rights are covered in the ICESCR, which is also discussed in chapters 1 and 3. The ICESCR was adopted and opened for signature in December 1966 and entered into force almost a full decade later, January 1976. The ICESCR is framed in terms of both individual and collective rights, with the preamble focused on the "inherent dignity of the human person" and individual rights and duties; the first article switches focus to the rights of "peoples" (UN 1966b).[1] Therefore, cultural rights can be discussed in the context of either individual or collective rights, and Article 3 of the ICESCR clearly states that state parties "undertake to ensure the equal rights of men and women to the enjoyment of all economic, social and cultural rights set forth in the present Covenant" (UN 1966b). However, at the same time Article 2, Number 3, highlights some of the tensions inherent in economic, social, and cultural rights as well as differences between how countries in the Global North and Global South may address them. These tensions include ideological differences between states and groups more inclined toward the individual pursuit of wealth and capitalist economic approaches and those preferring a more socialist or communal approach to sharing resources and ensuring the welfare of all as well as differing socioeconomic positionality of states in the Global North versus South. For example, Article 2, Number 3, states that "developing countries, with due regard to human rights and their national economy, may determine to what extent they would guarantee the economic rights recognized in the present Covenant to non-nationals." Article 1, Number 1, states, "All peoples have the right of self-determination. By virtue of that right they freely determine their political status and freely pursue their economic, social and cultural development." By noting states' freedoms to define their own culture and recognizing differences in economic capacity in the international system, the covenant suggests a distinction between countries in the Global South and Global North as well as between different cultures when it comes to implementing the ICESCR. Consequently, we disaggregate the data on religion and secular human rights organizations according to this socioeconomic classifying scheme as well as based on cultural orientation to account for the possibility of influences other than culture on any observed differences between religious and secular human rights organizations.

Overall, the ICESCR says little about cultural rights, with most of the covenant focusing on economic and social rights. While "cultural development" is mentioned in Article 6 and Article 15 recognizes the right "to take part in cultural life," specific "cultural rights" are not elucidated in the text. Thus, much is left assumed or implied, devolved to states and cultures themselves to determine, as seen in Article 13, Number 3, which says that parents have the liberty "to ensure the religious and moral education of their children in conformity with their own convictions" (discussed more fully in chapter 5). However, the UN asserts that the pursuit of one's own rights should not impinge on the rights of others; Article 4 of UNESCO's 2001 Universal Declaration on Cultural Diversity, for example, states that "no one may invoke cultural diversity to infringe upon human rights guaranteed by international law, nor limit their scope" (UNESCO 2001). Thus, according to the UN culture cannot be used as an excuse for violating the human rights of others (as defined in international covenants), illustrating the universal nature of the UN human rights framework, even as it may be used to protect the rights of cultural self-determination. This tension between individual rights to a culture and the collective rights of peoples to define and enforce their own cultures recurs in this field, the evolution of which is also reflected in different generations of international human rights approaches. While first-generation rights are nominally "culture blind" and individually focused, third-generation rights substantively engage with culture and its role in shaping the rights afforded to collectivities.

The Global Agenda for Dialogue among Civilizations, a resolution adopted by the UN General Assembly in November 2001, is another international agreement related to culture. The resolution highlights a range of tensions discussed throughout this book, including statements like "all civilizations celebrate the unity and diversity of humankind" and "human rights" and "fundamental freedoms" should be pursued "without distinction to race, sex, language or religion" (UN 2001). While talking extensively about individual rights, the declaration also affirms the rights of peoples, that is, collective identity groups, to "freely pursue their economic, social and cultural development." Although as a General Assembly resolution the declaration is nonbinding, the Global Agenda for Dialogue among Civilizations does identify key themes and goals such as the promotion of "common understandings of human rights" and "enhancement of respect for cultural diversity and cultural heritage" in Article 2. The document also explicitly references the role of religion in Article 3, calling for the "recognition of diversified sources of knowledge and cultural diversity as fundamental features of human society and as indispensable and cherished assets for the advancement and material and spiritual welfare of humanity at large." Thus, while culture and religion are both seen as "fundamental" and "indispensable," their influence is deemed distinct, even as they are interrelated.

Overall, international law is limited in its coverage of cultural rights, and culture is often a contested and sensitive subject, as who is to define culture? This question is further compounded by the intersection of culture with nationality, state sovereignty, and at times religion. When added into debates over the pros and cons of globalization, seen as Westernization by many, culture becomes a contested and sensitive topic (Barber 1995). Joffe (2019, 111) suggests

that the "human rights industry" and the West are unable "to deal with patriarchal, theocratic, authoritarian cultures" and that "the growth of relativist
ideologies in the West, which refuse to judge non-Western cultures according
to Western standards, have undermined the universal application of human
rights concepts." Thus, questions of religion, culture, and rights are intimately
intertwined in question of universality versus particularism.

Literature Review: Culture and Human Rights

There is a long tradition of debates between those asserting the universality
of human rights and those favoring cultural relativism (Donnelly 1984; Tesón
1985; Fagan and Fridlund 2016). Many states that are currently members of
the UN were colonial possessions at the time the UDHR was penned, although they have since signed on to the document and, as Penna and Campbell (1998) argue, despite the tendency of Western human rights discourse to
dismiss non-Western cultures, many precolonial societies did respect the values underlying human rights norms. The debate over whether human rights
are another form of "Western" neocolonialism, however, continues in various
forums. While some dismiss culture-based arguments against the relevance of
human rights in former colonial countries as reflective of ruling class desires
to maintain their status—in other words, that entrenched elites use culture to
maintain control over their populations by refusing certain rights—others assert that Western notions of individualism may in fact conflict with understandings of rights held in other parts of the world (Penna and Campbell 1998;
Mamdani 2000). The universality of human rights, based on an assumption of
human dignity and increasingly equated with "democracy" and "good governance," was presumed and imposed on the newly independent states in Africa
and Asia. Yet, some argue, "not all cultures perceive the promotion of human
dignity as comprising recognition of the same set of rights" (Sawad 2017, 102).

Other scholars suggest that human rights are part of the "culture wars"
that emerged during the period of intense globalization in the late 1990s and
that rejecting human rights as Western reflects the desire of some to assert
their own identity (Howard 1998, 94). Human rights are also caught in the globalization debate as it relates to corporate globalization and an individualist
pursuit of wealth (often by the United States) for the few at the expense of those
living in poverty around the world. Culture can also be used in these contexts
as a pretext for "curb[ing] the content and reach of universal human rights"
(Arat 2006, 437). As one scholar argues, "Many of the world's cultures, especially those associated with the great religions and philosophies such as Confucianism, Buddhism, Judaism, Christianity, and Islam are ancient, widespread,
and deeply rooted in the lives, beliefs, and values of billions of people" (Free-

man 2004, 376). However, despite the level of acceptability of human rights standards among communities of people, reservations to human rights treaties on cultural grounds may provide a means for states to "navigate their cultural norms within a universalized system" (Sawad 2017, 103). As these debates indicate, culture as a concept is contested, and debates over culture and human rights are intimately tied with other issues such as identity, economics, and colonial history. Further, since culture is not static but dynamic and can include exclusionary and harmful aspects as well as positive expressions of identity, the question is "*who* decides to what extent cultural diversity should be promoted and which cultural aspects should be protected?" (Donders 2016, 23).

Individualism versus Collectivism

The UDHR is based on the rights of the individual and offers "promises of liberation from constraining national boundaries and alternatives to caste, gender and racial hierarchies" (Markowitz 2004, 331). Some cultures emphasize collective identity more than others. Geert Hofstede, for example, classifies cultures around the world on a scale measuring whether they tend more toward individualism, in which individuals feel independent and autonomous, or collectivism, where people feel like they are interdependent with others, part of a broader social structure that is more deterministic. According to Hofstede, the United States scores 91 out of 100 for individualism, whereas India scores 48 and China only 20, suggesting different orientations to individual rights.[2] Hofstede's classification is based on national (state) cultures, but reified culture can create forms of oppression within society, and claims for collective rights are sometimes used precisely by marginalized groups in an effort to gain recognition and representation from hegemonic state cultures.

Cultural rights are seen as both individual and collective in nature, as individuals have the right to be part of their cultural communities and cultural communities have the right to speak their own language, for example (Donders 2016). However, some argue that human rights discourse is based in a "cult of the individual," which leads to hesitation from states, which irrespective of their location on Hofstede's scale of individualism, worry about losing power over their populace. This individual focus is evident, for example, in the individual focus on workers rather than unions in the context of labor rights and the more limited number of legal instruments focused on peoples or groups (Elliott 2007, 358; Reidel 2010). The uneasy relationship between individualism and culture is further evidenced in the idea that "as long as culture does not violate the basic rights of individuals, the co-existence between human rights and cultural practices is unproblematic" (Alldén 2007, 9). This begs the question, however, of whether this individual focus violates the basic rights of groups and/or certain cultural practices.

Universality versus Particularity

One of the ongoing debates in the realm of culture and human rights is the extent to which human rights are truly universal, that is, whether they apply to all cultures in all places. Cultural relativism (particularism) asserts that "members belonging to one culture should not 'judge' the members of another culture" (Sawad 2017, 104). It further asserts that there is no universal moral standard against which human rights can be judged. As one critic suggests, human rights is "the elaboration of a specific culture that has made claims of universal validity without those claims originally being agreed to universally or even within that very culture" (Siani 2014, 24). In contrast to the universalism enshrined in the UDHR, which holds that all humans have the same set of rights simply for being human, cultural relativism presumes that moral commitments differ substantively across cultures. Much of the pushback against the UDHR from non-Western cultures, however, is partially due to the equation of human rights with Western-imposed values and thus as a reminder of colonial rule, as discussed above (Saghaye-Biria 2018; Sawad 2017, 110). While the debate over the universality of human rights is often culturally, not necessarily religiously, based, the "shari'a reservations" to human rights treaties, in which certain Muslim-majority states agree to all provisions of a given treaty except for those deemed incompatible with shari'a law, are one significant illustration of the way religion and culture interplay in the tension between universal human rights norms and particular cultural-religious norms. The inconsistency of the shari'a reservations across Muslim-majority states further demonstrates that religion and culture are not synonymous; rather Muslim countries differ politically, culturally, and philosophically (Sawad 2017).

Donders (2016, 25, emphasis original) argues that universality and cultural particularism are not necessarily mutually exclusive since the universality of human rights, including that all human beings are free and equal, does "not necessarily imply the *uniform implementation* of these rights." In other words, one can have equality of rights and also respect cultural diversity. Further, despite universal assumptions embedded in human rights discourse, "concern for human rights and freedoms has not found expression across the world" (Stevenson 2013, 187). However, the universalist assumptions of some liberal proponents of human rights, such as Rorty's view of a human rights culture, are predicated in their own ethnocentric notions of how societies and governments should function, that is, a universality based solely on Western ideals (Staples 2011). In other words, "it is not the difficulty of justifying universality but the desire for universality that is the problem" (Hoover 2013, 941). Such debates illustrate the political, not merely cultural, nature of the tension between universality and particularity in that value for the Other, as well as histories of political, economic, and social domination, shape state and societal views of human rights. The extent to which human rights are equated with a particular version of Western-imposed values impacts whether and how they are universally accepted.

Culture and Democracy

For many Western states, democracy, development—particularly in terms of economic markets—and human rights are interlinked. Human rights scholar Jack Donnelly (1999, 609) argues, "Most obviously, international human rights norms require democratic government." Donnelly also asserts that democracy is focused on "the people" and thus is collective in nature; however, human rights can be antidemocratic given that they may not align with the will of the people. This is why judicial review—another pillar of democracy—is needed to ensure that human rights are not sacrificed to majoritarianism or nationalist waves (Sloss 2017). In contrast to Donnelly's view that democracies are "collectives," others suggest that capitalist democracies tend to focus on individual rights, particularly political and civil rights, as opposed to the focus of other political systems on duties (Moghaddam 2000). Debates over the suitability of democracy for all peoples as well as the extent to which democracy is a requirement for human rights enforcement remain contested (Langlois 2003, 993–94). The lack of agreement on a definition of democracy, namely the distinction between procedural democracies based on elections and substantive democracies based on a commitment to human rights, poses a further challenge in ascertaining the relationship between democracy and human rights, since by definition human rights are embedded in certain types of democracy (Villaseñor 2015). Based on the equation of liberal democratic culture with the secular universalist approach to human rights in some of the literature, we expect to see democracy promotion more in secular than in religious human rights organizations.

Culture, Religious Traditions, and Human Rights

The idea of human rights is rooted in the idea of duty and responsibility to others, a feature in all of the world's major religions, and religious leaders were involved in the crafting of the UDHR (Elliott 2007). The quest for laws upholding religious freedom helped drive the fight for rights in Western Europe, but religions also provide their own binding doctrines; for many faithful, God's law trumps the law of humankind (Lee and Lee 2011, 891). At the same time, religion is increasingly subjective and contested in parts of the contemporary world, with individual interpretations of religion challenging the idea of authoritative and hierarchical traditions (Seljak 2016, 544). Some suggest that human rights are a new civil or "secular" religion, a basis of moral authority and belief disconnected from divine sanction, which may be deemed threatening by some religious officials (Joffe 2019; Lee and Lee 2011). The perceived tension between what religion calls one to do and what state and/or national laws grounded in human rights doctrine may require or prevent is related to culture as well. As Lee and Lee (2011, 898) observe, "The ethical imperatives behind religious doctrines . . . and the accompanying narratives should not be ignored; for otherwise society will be deprived of an important source of a cultural self-understanding, shared by believers or non-believers alike."

Christianity

Within Christianity, the pursuit of human rights is connected to the idea of human dignity and God's creation, although these values are grounded in conservative as well as liberal traditions within the church (Moyn 2015). Christianity has not uniformly applied human rights values over time and place, for example subjugating women, enslaving Africans and native peoples, and oppressing colonial subjects. Elliott (2007, 353) argues that human rights are a "means of protecting and empowering the 'sacred' in modern society." Even before the emergence of human rights discourse, the Catholic social doctrine focused on the obligation of the church to help the poor (van Kersbergen and Manow 2009).

Christian approaches to rights are historically linked to concerns for socioeconomic welfare of the weak and marginalized, although cultural divides within Christian traditions shaped how these concerns manifested themselves. Research suggests that the history of interaction between religious and state authorities accounts for differential welfare policies in Northern and Southern Europe (Morgan 2009, 58). Alexis de Tocqueville attributed much of American culture, including individualism and independence, to Protestant religion (Cohen and Hill 2007). Within the United States, debates over welfare policy and health care policies have been impacted by Catholic social teachings that support medical care as being among the most basic human rights but that also oppose abortion, as well as by Calvinist doctrine that the poor should be required to work (Quadango and Rohlinger 2009). Such tensions illustrate how multiple religious cultures can exist within a religious and/or national community and that there are both more liberal and more conservative strands within most faiths. Further, while Protestant Christianity tends toward individualism, Catholicism and some branches of non-Catholicism, like the Amish, tend toward collectivism (Cohen and Hill 2007). Thus, rather than considering religious and secular human rights organizations as binary opposites, such examples illustrate the diversity within the category of religious organizations.

Bonney (2004, 26) asserts that religions are "incultured" through historical processes, and in the case of Christianity, this has led to "distinctive African, Indian, and Asian forms of Christianity that have come up against the preceding traditional religions." Further, there are divides not only between Catholics and Protestants in the Western tradition of Christianity but also between the Western traditions and the Orthodox or Eastern strand of Christianity. The difference between these two variants involves culture as well as theology. Within the Russian Orthodox Church, some argue, human rights should be subordinate to higher Christian values. Further, in contrast to the individualism of the Western church, the Russian Orthodox Church emphasizes collective and socioeconomic rights, placing unity above social strife and looking for the common good over the individual (Agadjanian 2010). Because of the diversity of cultures in which Christianity is found and due to the disparate traditions of Eastern and Western Christianity, we expect to find more individualism on the whole in Christian groups, particularly those influenced by Western Christianity, but some collective rights as well due to the inculturation effect.

Islam

As a religion, Islam began in the Arabian Peninsula and thus has many elements of Arab culture associated with it. However, the Islamic empire spread the religion across a wide array of cultures, and local practices that are often ascribed to Islam are cultural in nature. For example, the *hijab*, or the head covering worn by many Muslim women, is cultural, not Qur'anic, in nature. Likewise, polygamy, female circumcision, and other practices that may be seen as contrary to human rights doctrine are not actually rooted in Islam per se (Bonney 2004). Saudi Arabia did not sign the UDHR in 1948—unlike other Muslim-majority states including Pakistan and Egypt—because it claimed it did not account for non-Western culture and religion (Russell 2012). In contrast to the UN official discourse that asserts the universal validity of international human rights law, the Cairo Declaration on Human Rights in Islam places the authority on such matters firmly within shari'a, Islamic law (Fagan and Fridlund 2016, 26). Consequently, the Cairo Declaration prioritizes a particular culturally informed reading of Islam over the universality of rights. Even as the Cairo Declaration and some culturally based interpretations of Islam privilege the collective over the individual, fundamentally Islam is an individually based religion, with the individual directly accountable to Allah through praying five times a day—no intermediary required—and structuring one's life around the five pillars of Islam (Monshipouri 2013). However, this tension between concern for the Muslim *umma*—the community of believers that transcends national boundaries—and the individual believer suggests that there will be a mix of emphasis on individual and collective rights in the Muslim groups studied.

Judaism

One of the basic tenets of Judaism is that all human beings are created in the image of God, and many Jews feel an obligation for *tikkun olam*, "repair" of the world, which is reflected in the mission statements of many Jewish organizations (Cotler 1999). While this is a fundamental principle cited by many Jewish human rights organizations, traditionally Judaism is a collective religion, aimed at preserving the needs specific to the community (Cohen and Hill 2007). While a focal point of rights in the Jewish tradition is "the communal right to the land God promised the nation (Goodman 1998, 55), at the same time the Torah "extends its laws to the stranger" and "casts a wide net of protection over strangers, widows, orphans and the poor," indicating a concern for rights beyond that of the collective (52). Further, the creation of the UDHR was partly a response to the horrors of the Holocaust, and thus Jews have supported international human rights law as a means to protect individuals and groups from such horrors recurring. Thus, we expect a degree of universalism among Jewish organizations.

However, the situation of Judaism is further complicated by the fact that Jews identify as an ethnonational community, one with a state of their own (Israel) as well as a religious community (Joffe 2019, 112), making the differentiation between religion and culture challenging, particularly given the large number of secular Jews. Further, Goodman (1998) argues that ancient norms do not neatly differentiate entitlements from freedoms and that biblical language focuses more on the language of duties than the language of rights. Given the history of the Holocaust and the subsequent creation of the state of Israel as a state for the Jewish people, the identity of Jews as a collective seeking to protect themselves from actual and potential external threats has been further ingrained in Jewish cultural identity. Thus, we expect an emphasis on collective identity in the Jewish groups studied even more than we expect an appreciation for universal elements of human rights law.

Other Faith Traditions

In many faith traditions, culture and religious practice are intertwined. In China, for example, Confucian ideals of women's obedience and duty and harmony in the home are attributed by some to patriarchal culture, and together these tendencies can create an environment that is not conducive to women's rights as understood by many in the human rights arena (Xie, Eyre, and Barker 2018). Further, faith traditions including Hinduism and other Asian religious traditions tend toward collectivism, in which "spiritual identity and motivation are conceptualized as emphasizing social integration, ritual, and tradition" (Cohen and Hill 2007, 715). Aboriginal and native people have also identified cer-

tain cultural practices and customs that are enshrined in international treaties and conventions, such as CEDAW, to which they have reservations (Sawad
2017, 121). Often, however, these traditions do not speak explicitly of "rights,"
and the "Asian values" argument, which suggests Asian culture values community, order, and harmony in contrast to Western values of individual freedom,
put forth by political elites in Southeast Asian countries, was not based on religion per se and, further, does not reflect many Asians, who differ profoundly
in terms of culture (Song 2016; Tew 2012).

Culture and Imperialism

Human rights, some argue, is a profoundly liberating discourse, which can
"provide avenues for resisting local structures of power and asserting identity claims via supranational organizations and the state" (Markowitz 2004, 331).
Yet the UDHR was "born to a colonialist world order, with almost two-thirds
of world countries still under European colonial rule and thus without a voice"
(Saghaye-Biria 2018, 62). However, treating everyone alike under the rule of
law can neglect how cultural differences may impact the enjoyment of human
rights (Almqvist 2005). Further, at times human rights can be seen as a tool of
neoimperialism in which the weak are rescued by the Western intervention-
ists; this critical perspective suggests that human rights discourses serve the
power of national authorities and of Western states (Hoover 2013). Some argue that "the definition of human rights leads to the creation of experts who
are designated to speak to the colonized and other marginalized peoples about
the rights that they possess" (Maldonado-Torres 2017, 129). Regilme (2018) suggests that such power struggles make the terminology of human rights fraught,
signifying a move toward the language of human dignity to capture both the
agency of grassroots movements as well as the desire for national sovereignty in the face of North-South tensions. Stevenson (2013) also advocates for the
concept of human dignity, challenging arguments that human rights is merely
a form of neoliberalism. Instead, he asserts that human rights and human dignity provide a channel for expanding circles of freedom to include the marginalized, the working class, and women.

Hypotheses

International law is primarily written in terms of individual rights, and so we
expect a focus on individual rights in most of the organizations studied. However, based on the discussions in this chapter, we do expect variation between
secular and religious organizations in the extent to which they emphasize collective identity, duties, and culture. In addition, we expect differences between

Western and non-Western organizations and between those organizations in the Global North versus those in the Global South, particularly since these parts of the world have had different colonial experiences and have different current concerns related to self-determination (and thus collective identity) and varying views on the universality of rights. Specifically, we declare the following hypotheses:

1. Religious organizations will be more likely than secular organizations to emphasize culture.
2. Religious organizations will be more likely than secular groups to focus on collective identity rights.
3. Jewish organizations will be the most likely of the religious organizations to focus on collective identity rights; Christian organizations will be the least likely.
4. Religious organizations will be more likely than secular groups to focus on duties.
5. Organizations in the West will be more likely than those outside the West to emphasize individual rights.
6. Organizations in the Global South will be more likely than those in the Global North to emphasize collective rights.
7. Organizations in the Global South and outside of the West will be more likely than those in the Global North and West to mention culture.
8. Organizations in the Global North and West will be more likely than those in the Global South and non-West to emphasize the universality of rights.

Findings

Given the intersection of religion and culture, we expected that more religious than secular organizations would emphasize culture in their work. Indeed, this was the case, with 56 percent of religious as compared to 45 percent of secular organizations mentioning culture in a main section of their website, although this difference is not quite statistically significant. Organizations representing faiths other than Christianity, Islam, and Judaism are the most likely to mention culture on their websites, with 67 percent of the other organizations in the sample discussing culture. These organizations include both Buddhist organizations in the sample, World Barua Organization and Soka Gakkai, Baháʼí International Community, Arigatou International, Aliran Kesedaran Negara National Conscious Movement (in Malaysia), and the Institute for Planetary Synthesis. As this list indicates, most of these organizations are located out-

TABLE 2.1

Approaches to Culture (in percentages)

	Mentions culture	Mentions duties	Rights of individuals	Collective rights
Religious organizations	56	18	93	32
Secular organizations	45	9	96	36
Global North	46	11	96	28
Global South	54	8	94	56
Western	48	12	97	30
Non-Western	49	7	92	50

side of the West. Half of the Jewish organizations in the sample discuss culture, along with 42 percent of Christian organizations and only 29 percent of Muslim ones.

Although we expected that organizations based in the Global South or non-West would be more likely to emphasize culture than those based in the Global North or the West, given discourses asserting that universal human rights are a form of neocolonial or cultural imperialism, we did not find this to be the case. While a slightly higher percentage of organizations based in the Global South mentioned culture (54 percent) than those based in the Global North (46 percent), this difference is not statistically significant. Further, there was minimal difference between organizations based in the West and non-West. These differences are captured in Table 2.1.

One of the differences in regard to human rights that emerged in some literature on religion and culture is the focus on rights versus duties. While some religious and cultural traditions focus on the obligation of duty bearers, such as states, or those who benefit from existing social and political institutions, toward others, including the unfortunate or marginalized, others focus more on the rights of individuals. Religious groups were particularly focused on duties, with 18 percent of organizations mentioning duties and/or responsibilities in the context of human rights work, as compared to 9 percent of the secular organizations. This difference is statistically significant at the $p < .05$ level. Muslim organizations in the sample were the most likely to mention duties, with 43 percent of these organizations discussing duties. Around 17 percent Christian organizations, 11 percent of the other religious organizations, and none of the four Jewish organizations mentioned duties. The higher percentage of Muslim organizations mentioning duties may be related to the Muslim obligation to give alms to the poor, zakat, one of the five pillars of Islam.

Several of the religious groups we interviewed mentioned this responsibility, with Soka Gakkai, for example, noting that "we all have the opportunity and responsibility to move our lives in a better direction." Islamic Relief shared that they are the fourth largest charity in Britain despite Muslims representing only about 4 percent of the British population, noting that this "underpins the importance of charity within the Muslim community." Both Mazlumder and Dominicans for Justice and Peace described their work in terms of "religious motivation," although neither used the term "duty"; they both emphasized their religious beliefs as the impetus for human rights actions. Similarly, T'ruah discussed their work in terms of acting "on the moral imperatives found in our tradition to support and protect the human rights of all."

Individual versus Collective Rights

As expected, the vast majority of groups—317 out of 333—in the sample focus on the rights of individuals. The difference between religious and secular groups is very slight, with 93 percent of religious groups and 96 percent of secular ones focusing on individual rights. Given that one approach to supporting minority rights is through individual rights guarantees—such as freedom of religion—it is not surprising that religious groups would focus on such rights. There are also only minor differences between religions when it comes to supporting individual rights. All seven of the Muslim organizations in the sample discuss individual rights; three out of four Jewish organizations, forty-five out of forty-eight Christian organizations, and eight out of nine other religious organizations all mention individual rights. Thus, in the sample Jewish organizations are the least likely to discuss individual rights, which is consistent with

TEXTBOX 2.1

Collective Identity Rights

World Council of Churches

The World Council of Churches (WCC) brings together member churches and denominations in more than 110 countries and territories to reflect, speak, act, worship, and work together on issues including engaging in Christian service by serving human needs, breaking down barriers between people, seeking justice and peace, and upholding the integrity of creation.

The WCC has a long-standing commitment to work in solidarity with Indigenous Peoples and has a section of their work program dedicated to that purpose. WCC states, "The worldviews, spiritualities, cultures and experiences of Indigenous Peoples are distinct. At the heart of their struggles for survival as distinct self-determining peoples is the maintenance of Indigenous Peoples' spiritual, cultural, social, economic, and political integrity." To this end the WCC strengthens and supports Indigenous Peoples' networks, helps develop capacity, and engages in advocacy for Indigenous Peoples' Rights and strengthening Indigenous theologies and spiritualities.

World Council of Churches. 2020. "About Us." https://www.oikoumene.org/en/about-us.
World Council of Churches. 2020. "Solidarity with Indigenous Peoples." https://www.oikoumene.org/en/what-we-do/indigenous-peoples.

TEXTBOX 2.2

Collective Identity Rights
Comparing Muslim Organizations

World Muslim Congress

The World Muslim Congress, the Motamar Al-Alam Al-Islami, promotes solidarity and cooperation among the global Islamic community (*ummah*). It has "championed Muslim causes such as
Palestine, Kashmir, the Filipino Muslims' struggle, freedom for Muslim people from European
colonial rule, and the economic emancipation of the Muslim Ummah."

World Muslim Congress. n.d. "History." http://www.motamaralalamalislami.org/history.html.

Imam Al-Khoei Foundation

The Al-Khoei Foundation carries out charitable and educational functions. In 1997 it became the
only Shi'a Muslim organization to hold General Consultative Status in the United Nations, where
it works to promote human rights and minority rights. The foundation runs schools, carries
out development projects such as digging wells, and helps victims of war and natural disasters.
The foundation "endeavored to bring honor and respect to disadvantaged Shi'a in the Muslim
world by training them in the professions, providing nurseries for women, and founding indus-
trial schools and universities." The importance of collective identity markers is evident in the
description of moral values in one of the foundation's school websites: "Female teachers have to
be appropriately and modestly attired so that the hijab-clad female students learn appropriate
dress-code and modestly in behavior. The male-teacher is expected to grow a beard so that he is
seen as a person of probity and Islamic credential."

Al-Iman School. n.d. "Faculty and Staff." http://www.al-imanschool.org/faculty-and-staff/.

Jewish collective identity norms, and Muslim organizations are the most likely,
which is consistent with the individual nature of Muslim spirituality, but overall very few religious organizations did not mention individual rights. There
was also little difference between groups based in the Global North and Global
South or between those based in the West and non-West (see Table 2.1).

The aggregated data suggest there is no statistically significant difference
between religious and secular groups when it comes to a focus on collective
rights. In fact, 32 percent of religious groups focus on collective rights, as compared to 36 percent of secular groups. This finding may reflect that culture and/
or ethnicity more than religion per se is a driving factor in focusing on collective rights, but this would require further investigation. However, when one
disaggregates the data by religion, differences appear. In particular, as expected, the data suggest that Jewish organizations are very likely and Christian organizations are the least likely to consider collective identities, and these differences are significant at the $p < .01$ level. All four of the Jewish organizations
in the sample focus on collective rights, compared to only 25 percent of the
Christian organizations in the sample. This is consistent with the sociology of
both religions, given that Judaism is considered both a religion and an ethnic

group and that Jewish collective identity is strong for a number of factors, including centuries of persecution. Christianity, in contrast, particularly within its Western traditions, is very individually focused, as exemplified by Max Weber's ([1905] 2002) study on the Protestant work ethic.

Islam is also a religion based on individual belief and practice, in which individual believers can communicate directly with God (Allah), although many countries where Islam is practiced have collectivist cultural traditions. Around 29 percent of Muslim organizations and 44 percent of other religious organizations have a focus on collective rights. The fact that Islam's focus on collective identity groups is also low is worth exploring further, and it may reflect an important distinction between religion and culture in terms of the individual-collective spectrum. It could also reflect a different variant of the colonizer-colonized dynamic given that the Islamic empire superimposed the Muslim faith on a range of local cultural traditions as it expanded beyond the Arabian Peninsula into Africa and Asia. It is difficult to draw any conclusions regarding the other religious organizations given their small number (nine) and diverse traditions, including Aliran Kesedaran, Arigatou International, and Baha'i International Community. However, the percentage focusing on collective identity rights is larger than that of the full sample as well as both Muslim and Christian groups, although it is much smaller than the sample of Jewish organizations. This may be due to the persecution some of these communities face as a result of being distinct from the majority religion. For example, the Baha'i International Community noted their advocacy on behalf of the Baha'i as a group given their persecution in Iran, where they are "denied employment,

TEXTBOX 2.3

___

Collective Identity Rights

___

World Jewish Congress

The World Jewish Congress (WJC) website banner states "All Jews are responsible for one another," a sentiment that reflects the collective identity rights orientation of the Jewish organizations in the sample. The WJC represents Jewish communities and organizations in over a hundred countries around the world, is politically nonpartisan, and "represents the plurality of the Jewish people." Self-described as the "diplomatic arm of the Jewish people," the WJC advocates on behalf of Jews for restitution or compensation for property stolen by Nazis and supports the state of Israel.

The mission of the WJC includes "to secure the rights, status and interests of Jews and Jewish communities and to defend them wherever they are denied, violated or threatened; to encourage and assist the creative development of Jewish social, religious, and cultural life throughout the world."

World Jewish Congress. n.d. "About WJC." https://www.worldjewishcongress.org/en/about.
World Jewish Congress. n.d. "Mission." https://www.worldjewishcongress.org/en/about/mission.

___

TEXTBOX 2.4

Collective Identity Rights

World Barua Organization

The World Barua Organization is a nonprofit sociocultural and welfare organization with head-quarters in Switzerland that seeks to create a community of the Barua people—who claim to be the original inhabitants of Burma and Greater India—and who adhere to the teachings of Buddha, Dhamma, and Sangha. The organization carries out research, collects and disseminates information about human rights and nondiscrimination, and provides for various community members to increase their education and to share their concerns. Their website states that the Barua "seek a common cultural identity within different states," and the organizational mission includes working "towards a world where all people enjoy freedom of conscience, expression and religion, free exercise of cultural rights, as well as freedom from all kinds of discrimination."

World Barua Organization. n.d. "Constitution." http://www.worldbarua.org/about%20us.html.

their homes are confiscated, their shops are burnt, even cemeteries are bull-dozed."

When comparing Christian groups (the lowest percentage) with Jewish groups (the highest percentage), the difference is statistically significant at the $p < .01$ level. Comparing Jewish groups to the full sample, of which 35 percent consider collective rights, the difference is also statistically significant at the $p < .01$ level. A similar comparison between Christian groups and the full sample does not meet the threshold of significance. The percentage of other religious traditions focusing on collective identity rights is larger than that of the full sample as well as both Muslim and Christian groups, although it is much smaller than the Jewish sample.

Although a focus on collective identity rights was not significantly different between religious and secular groups writ large, as seen in Table 2.1 there is a statistically significant difference between groups based in the Global North (28 percent) and those in the Global South (56 percent) at the $p < .001$ level. Some of this difference may be explained by different economic systems, with the Global North tending toward capitalist and industrialized societies that are more focused on individual achievement and competition, in contrast to the Global South where economies may include more communalistic traditions. Further, the societies of the Global South may have more diversity in terms of collective identity groups and often less democratic societies, which may also result in a greater focus on the rights of collective identity groups than in the Global North, where there tends to be a focus on the more individually oriented political and civil rights than the more group-oriented economic, social, and cultural rights. The difference between organizations based in the West (30 percent) as compared to the non-West (50 percent) is also statistically signifi-

TEXTBOX 2.5

Collective Identity Rights

The International Movement against All Forms of Discrimination and Racism

The International Movement against All Forms of Discrimination and Racism (IMADR) is a global network of concerned individuals and minority groups that was originally founded by the Buraku people in Japan. The organization's main focus is to combat racism and racial discrimination, and it seeks to uphold the rights of indigenous peoples and minorities through empowerment, solidarity, and advocacy. IMADR builds bridges between communities, shares information through its network, and engages in advocacy campaigns, including working with the rights of Argentina's migrant and indigenous communities. IMADR has supported the Roma, Ainu, and Ryukyu peoples. The Latin America base is active in a number of areas including "study on the indigenous language and culture of Toba/Qom peoples," "legal support to Mapuche peoples' struggle against environmental damages from hydraulic fracturing for oil and shale gas," and activities that "contributed to self-empowerment of indigenous peoples and the realization of their rights."

International Movement against All Forms of Discrimination and Racism (IMADR). n.d. "About IMADR." https://imadr.org/about/.
IMADR. n.d. "Upholding the Rights of Indigenous and Minority Peoples." https://imadr.org/activity/minority-indigenous/.

cant at the $p < .001$ level. This aligns with expectations given that Western societies tend to be more individually focused than those of the non-West, which tend to be more collectivist in orientation.

Interview data align with the quantitative data in the prevalence of support for individual rights across the sample. However, a number of the groups interviewed in the Global South did not differentiate between types of rights when describing their work. As explained by one such group, they work for "family, individual, and collective rights for which we fight every day." The Organisation Guinéenne de Défense des Droits de l'Homme et du Citoyen stated, "We defend ALL human rights, [we] do not divide into civic, political, cultural." Several organizations based on the Indian subcontinent, such as the Feminist Dalit Organization and the Informal Sector Service Center, discussed their work advocating for Dalits and fighting against the caste system, illustrating the role of human rights discourse in combating local cultural norms. One group suggested they were distinctive among human rights organizations because they "promote the local view point both in terms of specific ethnic, cultural, indigenous identity and other issues." For their part, the Western-based organization OIDEL noted that "one of the most important challenges right now concerning human rights is that . . . in most parts of the world [human rights] is perceived as a Western values thing." The Lutheran World Federation observed increasing division in debates at the UN between those who advocate for universal human rights and national sovereignty. Several interview subjects and a wide range of websites also mentioned the increasing prevalence of attacks on human rights defenders as well as groups working to promote human rights, including the closure of offices of some well-known international NGOs by certain governments, again indicating the tension between whether human rights are seen as consistent with local or foreign norms.

A number of organizations are explicitly dedicated to collective rights. Adalah's website, for example, states that its "mission is to promote human rights in Israel in general and the rights of the Palestinian minority, citizens of Israel, in particular." Organizations focusing on indigenous rights also tend to emphasize collective identity rights, focusing on peoples' rights, such as Advocates for Human Rights and the Asia Indigenous Peoples Pact, whose website states it "is committed to the cause of promoting and defending indigenous peoples' rights and human rights."

Some groups underscore the fact that advocating for individual or collective rights is not necessarily an either/or situation, promoting both within the minority rights framework of political and civil rights as well as within the realm of group rights found more in the social and cultural rights framework. For example, the East and Horn of Africa Human Rights Defenders Project website says, "Wherever and whenever there is persecution and oppression, minorities and other vulnerable groups are threatened and human rights are denied or human dignity is threatened, defenders tend to emerge and strive to protect the weak and hold the authorities to account," highlighting both the minority (political/civil, individual based) and group rights (collective) approaches. Similarly, the website of the International Partnership for Human Rights states it works "with our partners to improve respect for the rights of groups and individuals who are among those most vulnerable to human rights violations."

A few organizations made evident the gaps between Global North and Global South in terms of orientation to human rights issues, including development (see chapter 3). Nord-Sud XXI, for example, states on its website that it rejects "economic and financial doctrines that impose dependency and underdevelopment on all peoples, in particular the people of the South. Such doctrines manifest the continuity of centuries old genocide of Indian-Americans, the Slave Trade and colonialism." The Comisión Jurídica Para el Autodesarrollo de los Pueblos Originarios Andinos described mining as an "invasion in indigenous people's territories" and asserted that indigenous "groups are different because they have a spiritual and material relationship with the earth." The tension between Northern and Southern approaches to the human rights of collective groups was also identified by organizations based in the Global North, such as the Dominicans for Peace and Justice, who, when speaking about the work of Brothers in Peru, shared, "Some say you should just leave indigenous people on their own, don't contaminate them with our development. . . . Others say obviously we need to respect where they are coming from but that doesn't stop you from . . . still engaging with them and taking responsibility for them."

The Role of Democracy and Human Rights

Although democracy promotion was not initially part of our codebook when we began studying organizational websites, it emerged as a theme when we noticed repeatedly that democracy promotion was among the categories of action undertaken by human rights organizations. As the research progressed, it seemed that democracy promotion was linked not only to which types of rights were advanced by organizations—political and civil rights or social, economic, and cultural rights, as discussed in chapter 1—but also to cultural questions regarding a focus on individualism and the universality of rights. Fewer than one-fourth of all organizations mentioned universality (see Table 2.2). Further, there is no statistically significant difference between religious and secular organizations in their approach to universality, although one religious, non-Western organization in the Global South, Mazlumder, actively opposes the idea of universal human rights (the only one in our sample to do so explicitly) in their materials. Contrary to expectations, organizations in the Global South appear slightly more likely than those in the North to support the universality of human rights, although this is statistically significant only at the $p < .10$ level. There is no real difference between the percentages of Western and non-Western organizations supporting the universality of rights. There are several possible explanations for the difference between the Global North and Global South. One may be an artifact of our sampling strategy, which focused on organizations affiliated with the UN Human Rights Council. This may suggest an overall bias in our sample, as groups attending these sessions presumably give some credence to international organizations and the suitability of human rights discourse for advancing organizational goals. Thus, it may be that organizations from the Global South, where state institutions may not be sufficiently capable—for whatever reason—of upholding human rights, focus more on universality as a way of gaining leverage vis-à-vis the state. This strategy of the weaker party appealing to international norms has been seen elsewhere, for example, in discursive struggles between Palestinians and Israelis (Hallward 2011). Further, groups explicitly aligning themselves with global human rights discourse are more likely to use this same language, which is often deemed Western and oriented toward the Global North.

As expected, secular organizations are more likely than religious groups to promote democracy, 33 percent to 9 percent, statistically significant at the $p < .001$ level. Given that many religions are hierarchical in nature and religious doctrine is often taken as a given rather than open for majoritarian deci-

TABLE 2.2

Democracy and Universality (in percentages)

	Positively mentions universality of rights	Promotes democracy
Religious organizations	15	9
Secular organizations	18	33
Global North	16	20
Global South	24	49
Western	18	23
Non-Western	18	42

sion making, this intuitively makes sense. Contrary to our expectations, organizations in the Global South as well as those outside the West are more likely to promote democracy than those in the Global North and West, and these differences are statistically significant at the $p < .001$ level (see Table 2.2). If we break these differences down into religious and secular organizations, we find that there is no statistically significant difference between religious organizations based in the Global North and Global South in terms of promoting democracy, although those in the Global South are actually slightly more likely to support democracy. Similarly, slightly more religious organizations in the West than those outside the West promote democracy, but again this difference is not statistically significant.

Instead, it seems that the variance between organizations in the Global South and Global North, as well as between those in the West versus outside of the West, is largely driven by differences within secular organizations, as religious perspectives across these divides are relatively constant. When examining secular organizations promoting democracy, however, the differences between the Global North (23 percent) and Global South (53 percent) are statistically significant at the $p < .001$ level. Secular organizations outside the West are also more likely to promote democracy (48 percent) than secular organizations in the West (27 percent), statistically significant at the $p < .01$ level. There are several possible reasons for this difference. One is that many societies in the Global North and West are already democratic and thus do not feel the need to promote democracy and/or believe that promoting democracy abroad in nondemocracies may violate the right to self-determination of those peoples. Related, those organizations based in the Global South and/or outside the West may see enhancing democracy in their societies as a means to better enforce human rights. Indeed, the literature suggests a correlation between substantive democracy and human rights promotion, and most nondemocracies are in the Global South. Secular organizations outside the West are also more likely to promote democracy (48 percent) than secular organizations in the West (27 percent), which is statistically significant at the $p < .01$ level.

In looking to see whether there is an alignment between individual rights and democracy promotion, we find that overall 29 percent of the sampled organizations focus on individual rights and democracy, while 13 percent of the organizations that do not focus on individual rights also promote democracy. Due to the small number of organizations that do not support individual rights, this difference is not statistically significant, and the data indicate that there is not an automatic alignment between individual rights and democracy, although there seems to be a greater likelihood that those organizations that support individual rights also support democracy. There was a slightly larger correlation of groups that focus on collective rights that also consider democracy, with 35 percent of such groups, and 25 percent of groups that do not consider collective rights that also consider democracy. Thus, those promoting collective rights are more likely to also promote democracy, though this is statistically significant only at the $p < .10$ level. Given Donnelly's argument that democracy is a collective phenomenon, the linkage between collective rights and democracy is not surprising.

Women and Culture

Although chapter 4 looks at the question of women's rights more generally, several interviewees specifically mentioned women's rights when discussing the intersection of culture and human rights. Repeatedly, organizations, particularly those in the Global South, discussed challenges faced by women due to cultural traditions that impede their rights, such as a ritual that keeps women in the house for six months after their husband dies or other traditional practices such as genital mutilation. As one interviewee from the Federation of Environmental and Ecological Diversity for Agricultural Revampment and Human Rights noted, "We do not destroy any part of the culture, but improve the lives of the girls and the boys." WILPF, another secular organization, discussed the problems regarding rape culture in many countries around the world, and asked, "Why aren't [the men who do not rape] saying this is absolutely unacceptable?," suggesting that much had to do with cultural norms regarding masculinity. Several interviewees from religious organizations spoke about the intersection between religion and culture regarding women. For example, Islamic Relief Worldwide mentioned that because some Islamic law is based on culture, there are ways religious officials should help differentiate between what is cultural and what is religious obligation. Dominicans for Justice and Peace shared that "unfortunately, often the church collaborates with other oppressive cultures that are seeing women in an inferior light."

Conclusion

This chapter suggests that in certain areas culture—approximated in this study based on location in the Global North, Global South, West, or non-West— seems to have its own distinct influence on approaches to human rights advocacy distinct from religion, with a few exceptions. Across the sample, the vast majority of organizations focus on individual rights, which is not surprising given the individual basis of the UDHR and the international human rights regime. There is little difference between organizations from the Global North and Global South in terms of focus on individual rights; non-Western organizations are slightly less likely than Western ones to emphasize individual rights, but in both groups over 90 percent of organizations support individual rights.

Contrary to our expectations, there is little difference between religious and secular organizations as a whole in terms of a focus on collective rights. However, when disaggregated by religion, 100 percent of Jewish groups and 44 percent of other faith traditions focus on collective identity rights. This finding may be explained by the fact that organizations from the Global South and non-West are between 20 and 30 percent more likely than organizations from the Global North and West to focus on collective identity rights. Given that Judaism is considered both a cultural and a religious category and that most of the other faith traditions are non-Western, culture influences approaches to rights more than religion per se.

The findings also suggest a significant difference between religious and secular groups in terms of democracy promotion, with secular organizations promoting democracy at a significantly higher level than religious organizations. Interestingly, organizations in the Global South and non-Western groups promote democracy at a significantly higher rate than those in the Global North or West. Little difference exists in terms of democracy promotion among religious organizations in the Global North and Global South or West and non-West, suggesting again that the difference has more to do with culture, particularly among secular organizations. Despite the relatively high support for democracy by some organizations, there is relatively little support for the universality of rights among all of the organizations in the sample, with fewer than 20 percent of the organizations in nearly all categories supporting universality; the only exception was those from the Global South, where 24 percent mention the universality of rights. These findings suggest that even those groups who advocate for human rights do not explicitly advocate for their universality. Additional, more nuanced research needs to be conducted to examine more specifically the relationships between universality and particularity.

Overall, the findings in this chapter suggest that religion and culture interact distinctly when it comes to human rights and that differences between how organizations based in the Global North and Global South and the West and non-West approach human rights are present, although not necessarily in predicted patterns. Power and national interests, more than cultural or religious norms, may account for international discourses related to cultural relativism and exceptions from international human rights. Further, the findings suggest that organizations in the Global South and non-West may use human rights as a tool to advocate for changes in sociopolitical structures, particularly in terms of promoting democracy. If this is the case, then discourses suggesting that democracy (and/or political/civil rights based on the individual) is culturally foreign or Western undermine the agency of local human rights activists. It is incumbent on those exploring these narratives around rights to investigate the power dynamics inherent not only on the global scene but also within respective national and religious institutions.

CHAPTER 3

Rights-Based Approaches to Socioeconomic Development

As noted by Katherine Marshall (2013, 155), "Religious work on health, education, and care of society's most vulnerable members . . . generally draws on deep historic and philosophical roots." Further, many organizations that now work on human rights began with a more humanitarian mission but evolved to tackle challenges related to development as well (Marshall 2013, 172). As noted by Lehmann (2019, 402), socioeconomic development and charitable activity is one of five thematic areas for faith-based organizations involved in international politics. Consequently, it seems relevant to explore how religious human rights organizations approach socioeconomic development, including the overlap between such work and humanitarian relief, since often organizations began with one mission and expanded to include the other. However, the focus of this chapter is whether religious human rights organizations are more prone to engage in socioeconomic and humanitarian efforts than are secular human rights organizations given the philosophical and moral commitment of many faith-based organizations in this area as well as the fact that "religious actors may run the most lasting, sustainable of the development efforts" (Marshall 2013, 177).

The secular, liberal, Western approach to human rights has tended to emphasize political and civil rights rather than social, economic, and cultural rights or the right to development, although the number of state parties to the ICCPR is only slightly higher, at 169, than the 165 countries that are state parties to the ICESCR. There is strong reason to believe that religious and secular organizations may have divergent views on the importance of these various generations of rights. Many faiths have a historical moral commitment to serving the less fortunate, and given the precarious circumstances of minority religious communities in many parts of the world, religious human rights organizations may be likely to focus on social and ethnic minorities.

Religion is not the only reason why we might expect variance among human rights groups in regard to socioeconomic development. Other factors, including the relative wealth of the country, may also affect how groups decide which rights to emphasize. Further, given historical geopolitical divides regarding the relative priority of these rights stemming from the Cold War and antiglobalization backlash in some parts of the world, we may expect to see differences between countries based in the Global North and Global South. After reviewing the evolution of socioeconomic rights and the right to development in international law, this chapter examines the extent to which religious and secular human rights organizations prioritize social and economic rights, considering also the intersectionality of religion with the North-South divide.

History of Socioeconomic Rights and Development in International Law

Socioeconomic rights, also known as second-generation rights, are laid out in the ICESCR, which was adopted by the UN General Assembly in 1966 and entered into force on January 3, 1976.[1] The ICESCR outlines rights for just working conditions, including the right to fair wages and the right of trade unions; the right to social security; the right to a basic standard of living, including freedom from hunger; the right to education and physical and mental health; and the right to take part in cultural life as well as scientific research. These rights have historically been associated with countries of the developing world (previously known as the Second and Third worlds) as well as welfare states, whereas civil and political rights, known as first-generation rights, were typically associated with the United States and other Western powers (Snyder 2011, 5). However, many states in the EU also have incorporated some degree of protection of socioeconomic rights in their constitutions, although these rights "are often protected poorly and inefficiently" (Černič 2016, 229). Second-generation rights have been criticized for being costly and lacking fixed content, which makes them complex and difficult to enforce, in contrast to first-generation rights, which such critics view as a set of ground rules for democratic political processes (Pemberton 2017).

In addition to their connection to so-called developing countries, second-generation rights have been linked to particular religious and cultural traditions, such as Confucianism, which holds that society should provide people with a right to education in order to enable them to pursue the *dao*, or the "good" (Carr 2016, 12). Article 22 of the African Charter specifically asserts that "all peoples shall have the right to their economic, social and cultural development with due regard to their freedom and identity" and that "states shall have the duty, individually or collectively, to ensure the exercise of the right to development" (African Commission on Human Peoples' Rights 1981). However, given that upholding socioeconomic rights requires financial resources, such rights "have often been subjected to budgetary restrictions" (Černič 2016, 246), even in European states. Countries including South Africa, India, and Brazil have been engaged in efforts to interpret how judicial systems should promote and enforce socioeconomic rights clauses (do Valle 2016). In the absence of state capacity to enforce and/or promote such rights, however, NGOs often provide such services.

Sustainable Development Goals (SDGs)

Although not part of international law per se, international thinking and action around socioeconomic development is shaped by the UN's efforts at first identifying the Millennium Development Goals (MDGs) and subsequently the Sustainable Development Goals (SDGs), articulated as part of Agenda 2030. The SDGs had their origin in the Rio Earth Summit that called for mainstreaming sustainable development in the UN system by identifying goals that were "global in nature and universally applicable to all countries while taking into account different national realities, capacities and levels of development" (Johnson 2017, 91). However, what resulted in June 2015 was a series of seventeen goals that were not only duplicative but "virtually unimplementable and unmonitoriable" (Johnson 2017, 93). The seventeen SDGs include no poverty, zero hunger, good health and well-being, quality education, gender equality, clean water and sanitation, affordable and clean energy, reduced inequalities, climate action, peace, justice, and strong institutions, and partnerships for the goals.[2] While some of these goals overlap with the ICESCR, there is no rights language included in the SDGs, and they are not explicitly grounded in the human development paradigm that includes human needs, security, and rights (Johnson 2017).

Historically the UN has treated human rights as a tool or object of development, suggesting that it is more than economic growth and instead incorporates all dimensions of human progress (Brems, Van Der Beken, and Yimer 2015). However, the SDGs focus primarily on the economic and social aspects of development (Johnson 2017, 94). Pogge and Sengupta (2016) even argue that the SDGs make it easy for governments to slow down their human rights efforts because the goals do not explicitly reference political and civil rights, including the rights of ethnic minorities, and are not framed universally, thereby posing a challenge to those who face discrimination. However, the linkage of human rights and development did not occur until the 1990s (Uvin 2007), and so the disassociation of the two may reflect a return to the status quo of the international system.

The setting of goals and targets such as the SDGs often involves friction between governments and civil society as well as between the Global North and the Global South, as poorer countries often agree to such goals only if wealthier countries provide more financial assistance and less trade protectionism so they can attain them (Browne 2017). Debates around the role of rights in development can be seen in two areas of international practice—discussion surrounding the right to development and the so-called rights-based approach to development work.

The Right to Development:
Differences between the Global North and the Global South

The question of economic development has been at the heart of debates between the Global North (industrialized "core" states) and Global South (non-industrialized "peripheral" states) for decades but has attracted scholarly attention particularly since the 1990s, when the end of the Cold War, combined with the failure of the International Monetary Fund's neoliberal structural adjustment programs, created space for bringing together the ideas of development and human rights (Offenheiser and Holcombe 2003; Uvin 2007, 597).[3] Historically, the Non-Aligned Movement wished to enshrine development as a human right; however, the United States and other Western powers strongly opposed it, supporting instead the right of citizens to democratic participation in development policy (Normand and Zaidi 2008, 290). From the perspective of the Global South, "the right to development emerged from the legacy of colonialism and Third World demands for economic self-determination and equality" (Normand and Zaidi 2008, 291), whereas from the Global North's perspective, the Third World's request for resource transfer to offset global economic inequity sought to divert attention from the corruption and mismanagement of national leaders (Normand and Zaidi 2008, 290). At the same time, actors in the Global North and Global South sometimes promoted differing conceptions regarding what constitutes development. For some critics in the Global South, development is a means for the Global North to dominate the world system, for external "experts" to artificially determine communal needs and destroy ways of life (Cavalcanti 2007). During the colonial era, development interventions were part of a scheme to "modernize" colonial subjects and to raise standards of living in line with Western norms. However, anticolonial forces viewed this process as a means of underdeveloping the colonies, who were "bled" to enhance the wealth of the colonial powers (Nilsen 2016, 275; Ngang 2018). Further, the right to development is entwined with the right to self-determination, as the struggle for development in Africa has been framed as "the right of countries to determine their own development unconstrained by external forces" (Cheru 2016, 1268). In addition, many decry the economic destruction that accompanies industrialization and seek a means of development that preserves their land, water, and autonomy (Nilsen 2016, 270).

The right to development, originally introduced by Senegalese jurist M'Baye in 1972 as part of the debates around the New International Economic Order (Uvin 2007), was included in the 1981 African Charter on Human and People's Rights and the 1986 United Nations General Assembly Declaration on the Right to Development. According to the declaration, development is "an inalienable human right by virtue of which every human person and all peoples are entitled to participate in, contribute to, and enjoy economic, social, cultural, and political development, in which all human rights and fundamental freedoms can be fully realized." Differing views on development, poverty, and the appropriate means to address these issues continue to shape debate regarding the right to development (Cheru 2016; Du Plessis 1999; Ngang 2018). In 1993 the right to development was incorporated into the Vienna Declaration and Programme of Action. However, several critical issues remain under debate: whether the right is one of individuals or states and whether the duty bearer is the state or the international community. The theory of unequal exchange suggests that unfair colonial trading practices contributed to the poverty of the Global South, whereas the United States asserts that prosperity results from a combination of capitalism plus democracy (Dargin 2013) and will support only rights of individuals vis-à-vis their own governments, not those of other states (De Feyter 2015, 32).

A few states, including Ethiopia and Malawi, have enshrined the right to development in their constitutions. In Ethiopia, the right has both procedural and substantive components, the former giving citizens the right to be consulted regarding policies and projects affecting their community, the latter involving the right to improved living standards and sustainable development (Brems, Van Der Beken, and Yimer 2015). Independent expert to the Human Rights Commission Arjun Sengupta (2004, 180) asserts that "development is a comprehensive process, going beyond economics to cover social, cultural and political fields and aiming at 'constant improvement,'" contrasting this with GNP growth or industrialization.

The discourse on the right to development has continued to evolve. Although human rights scholar Jack Donnelly has dismissed the right as a nonexistent "unicorn," in the over twenty-five years since the UN declaration, it has become "firmly embedded in the institutional framework of the UN" (Kuosmanen 2015, 316). The issue of poverty was front and center in the (largely unrealized) MDGs, and the discourse on sustainable development has been integrated further in the SDGs, which now serve as guidelines for the work of UN-affiliated organizations. However, the goals of the SDGs and the purposes of development aid, which are inherently political, are not always aligned, and the United States provides funds even to countries deemed human rights violators if other strategic interests are at stake (Braaten 2017). Uvin (2007, 599) suggests that many organizations "colonise the human rights discourse" by making statements that suggest "that human rights is what these development agencies were doing all along. Case closed; moral high ground safely established." Writing a decade after Uvin, Nelson and Dorsey (2018) note that there has been an increase in rhetoric surrounding rights-based development, but it is unclear how significantly this has impacted programming choices and grant making. Human rights NGOs sometimes step in where states cannot or will not take action. Offenheiser and Holcombe (2003, 277), writing from the perspective of Oxfam America, assert that human rights "are given by the people to themselves" and as such do not depend on state authority. Consequently, Northern NGOs have a duty to support marginalized groups in their efforts to attain their rights, while finding a balance between rights campaigning and development practice (Offenheiser and Holcombe 2003). Perhaps in part due to the importance of donor engagement and distrust of potential legal obligations under the right to development, some development NGOs have begun to use the term "rights-based" (Davis 2009, 174). Often, use of the rights-based approach is found in secular human rights organizations, although some Christian aid agencies have also used this language (KindornayRon, and Carpenter 2012). Nelson and Dorsey (2018, 101) also note that international organizations like the World Bank have renamed programs to appear more rights-based, such as the shift from "governance" to "social accountability." As a consequence, when evaluating the extent to which development organizations ascribe to the human rights (or the rights-based) agenda, one should focus less on statements and more on the extent to which development processes respect and fulfill human rights (Uvin 2007; Sengupta 2000).

Literature on Religion, Socioeconomic Rights, and Development

Although, as noted in chapter 1, there is increasing attention paid to similarities and differences between religious and secular organizations in a variety of nonprofit fields, few scholars have examined how socioeconomic rights are approached. Further, while there is a growing literature looking at RNGOs in the development field, researchers have not considered human rights or the right to development per se. Are faith-based human rights organizations more likely than their secular counterparts to engage with socioeconomic rights issues? Are there differences between faith-based organizations (FBOs) and secular organizations based in the Global North versus those in the Global South? Do religious and secular human rights organizations differ in their approaches to development?

Religious Perspectives on Socioeconomic Needs

According to Pew data, just over half of the world's population professes adherence either to Christianity (31 percent) or to Islam (24 percent), and the birth rate of these populations is growing at a faster rate than that of the religiously unaffiliated (Pew Research Center 2017). Around the world, those living in poverty are often religious, and religious leaders often command trust. Clarke (2016, 181, 184) argues that teachings within faith communities, including "protecting the poor, reducing economic inequality and having economic growth serve the wider society," are distinct from standard international development policies. For Catholics, "economic outcomes must serve not those with economic influence and power, but the marginal and powerless. Moreover, economic outcomes should not be the end goal, but rather serve to bolster improvements in all human realms, including the spiritual." Further, Catholic social teaching asserts that humans have "an inherent dignity which cannot be compromised at any cost" and that dignity consequently "takes priority in economic life" (Tablan 2015, 294). In addition to showing compassion to disadvantaged groups, Islam also emphasizes equity; this obligation to be charitable is enshrined in the zakat, a tax on wealth used to provide for the needs of the poor (Clarke 2016). Social justice, including values of equality and equitable distribution of goods and burdens, is also a core element of Jewish identity, particularly among liberal Jews (Lough and Thomas 2014). The common roots of these three Abrahamic faiths include prophets who actively spoke in support of the poor and the powerless (Loy 2014).

Although Buddhism does not share the same emphasis on social justice as the monotheistic traditions, it does speak strongly against greed as one of three "poisons" and emphasizes the importance of human relationships as well as ending *dukkha*, or suffering (Loy 2014). Many indigenous spiritual traditions view everything as part of creation and therefore sacred (Razak 2017).

At the same time, however, religious traditions have also been used to socially and economically oppress others, such as the Christian enslavement of Africans and Hindu mistreatment of Dalits (Razak 2017). Thus, not all FBOs will necessarily interpret scripture the same way regarding socioeconomic rights and may not view rights as universally applicable. Further, development organizations are not always certain regarding how to integrate faith into their work given that it can have net positives and negatives in terms of inclusion and human rights impact. The UK Department for International Development launched a set of "faith partnership principles" in 2012, but not all organizations have such guidelines (Deneulin and Zampini-Davies 2017). Thus, more research is needed to examine how the interaction between religion and socioeconomic rights informs development processes and influences the ideas and practices of religious traditions (Deneulin and Zampini-Davies 2017).

Role of Religion in Development Practice

One of the distinguishing factors between faith-based and secular human rights organizations is the motivation for their work. While individuals working for FBOs and secular organizations may share certain values, FBOs can be motivated by a sense of "duty" (Tomalin 2013) and an integration of religious practices in the daily activities of the organization (Ebaugh et al. 2003; Hugen and Venema 2009). Some studies suggest FBOs focus more on human services, counseling, and self-help through faith and prayer (Ebaugh et al. 2003; Graddy and Ye 2006; Ferguson et al. 2007) and can include spiritual goals such as "restoring broken lives" (Frame 2017; Davis et al. 2011). FBOs vary in terms of the scope and focus of their work; in the realms of socioeconomic rights and development, organizations vary in the extent to which they are focused on development in terms of the material and spiritual dimensions of life as well as the extent to which they seek to convert those they serve (Bradley 2009; Leurs 2012; Johnsen 2014). Further, some differences exist between religious groups; for example, one Muslim NGO suggested that Christians do good deeds out of goodness, whereas Muslims do them because God ordered them to (Mittermaier 2014, 523–24). There is also variance within religious traditions, and religious views shape how actors—state and non-state alike—conceptualize development work and how to go about "poor relief." As discussed by Kahl (2009), even ostensibly secular policies toward the poor are shaped by religious traditions, including whether society has a duty to provide for all or whether individuals have a duty to support themselves. Secular organizations also vary in their approach to their clients' faith and the extent to which they engage with it directly (Frame 2017).

FBOs and secular organizations do not always have disparate approaches to human rights, however. For example, Bompani and Smith (2013, 25) examine a Catholic organization that promoted the cultivation of a biotechnological product, emphasizing development first and Christian teachings second. A rights-based approach is seen as a product of Western culture by some communities (Harris-Curtis 2003), and getting the buy-in of local FBOs can provide a sense of legitimacy and respect for development projects (Bradley 2009). This is particularly the case when "the state finds it increasingly difficult to criticize practices carried out in the name of 'religion' or 'tradition' that contrast with the goals of its secular development programs" (Tomalin 2013, 62). FBOs may be able to interpret their development missions in a way that conforms with local belief systems rather than the language of secular NGOs, which may be informed by the international donor agenda (Davis et al. 2011). FBOs may also approach development as a means for emphasizing the common good and improving society spiritually and morally and not just materially (Institute for Studies in Global Prosperity 2013). Further, some FBOs focus on poverty alleviation rather than development in the sense used by many international donors and policy makers, at times using ethical frameworks rather than rights-based language alone to promote their goals (Mittermaier 2014).

Contending Approaches to Development

Beyond sometimes differing religious and secular conceptions of socioeconomic rights and their motivations for engaging in development work as a means of achieving these rights, challenges exist in defining development. While the wide-ranging and overlapping nature of the SDGs compounds the challenge of defining development, this issue precedes the creation of the SDGs and is evident in the contention surrounding the right to development. In brief, economic development, often equated with economic growth, is one approach to development, whereas a second conception focuses on the human aspect of development and opportunities created for communities to achieve economic, social, and cultural rights (Villaroman 2011). In contrast to the more material conception of economic development, human development examines capacities, including individual freedom, well-being, and opportunities. The UN Human Development Index measures more than just gross domestic product (GDP), the basic measure of economic development, also including health and education measures to gain a more complex view.[4]

The literature comparing religious and secular development organizations discusses differences in how FBOs examine not only the material but also the faith-based aspects of development (Bradley 2009). As described by Salek (2016, 367), "In Islam the basic goal of development is to create an environment that enables people to enjoy spiritual, moral and socio-economic well-being in this world and success in the Hereafter." Overall, the literature suggests that FBOs are more holistic in their approach to development and focus more on the means rather than the ends (Davis et al. 2011). At the same time, faith-based NGOs involved in global health may have very specific views regarding women's rights to sexual and reproductive health based on their theological views (Karam and Marshall 2016). As Du Plessis (1999, 381–82) observes, "development" is a "value concept," and focusing on economic development alone may actually reinforce existing disparities and even cause social unrest. Not all organizations are explicit regarding their development values. Oxfam, however, created a set of five program aims to clarify the rights-based model for staff:

the right to a sustainable livelihood, the right to basic social services, the right to life and security, the right to be heard, and the right to an identity (Offenheiser and Holcombe 2003). The multifaceted nature of these different rights as they relate to the value-laden concept of development poses challenges to defining and measuring the development activities of human rights groups. To illustrate this challenge, we examine organizational efforts aimed at water and sanitation.

Water and Sanitation

Clean water and sanitation is SDG Goal 6 and intersects with Goal 5, on gender equity, and Goal 3, which focuses on good health and well-being. The literature demonstrates an important link between water, human rights, and issues of gender and children's rights, further evidence of the cross-cutting nature of the SDGs and the varying components of the international human rights agenda. Water is associated with a wide array of freedoms and the right to life, as exemplified by the oft-cited proverb "water is life" (Hellum, Kameri-Mbote, and Van Koppen 2015). However, external development organizations do not necessarily account for local norms affecting how to operationalize this right, such as assumptions regarding women's roles in gathering water (Hellum, Kameri-Mbote, and Van Koppen 2015, 30). Water and sanitation programs also intersect with the right to education, since in many places inadequate facilities at schools mean that families will not send their daughters to school due to challenges related to menstruation (Hellum, Ikdahl, and Kameri-Mbote 2015; Karam and Marshall 2016).

Water and sanitation efforts are also linked to children's rights, as the lack of water and sanitation facilities has a particularly harsh impact on children, who can become sick and die of otherwise treatable illnesses as a result of these conditions. According to one study, over half a billion children (27 percent) had no toilet facilities and over 400 million (19 percent) either had unsafe drinking water or had to travel too far to fetch sufficient water to meet their daily requirements (Nandy and Gordon 2009). Additionally, water and sanitation disasters can "negatively affect societies and economies in many regions, spur migration and spark conflict" (Seung-Soo 2018), due in part to the interaction between water and sanitation systems, which are stressed by rapid urbanization and can be impacted by mud slides, earthquakes, and other natural disasters caused by climate change. Thus, water and sanitation efforts are linked not only to SDGs related to gender equality and good health but also to climate action (Goal 13) and building sustainable cities (Goal 11). Consequently, although the link between water and sanitation and human rights may not be immediately apparent, inadequate access to water and sanitation has far-reaching rights-related impacts.

Hypotheses

Based on the review of the literature related to the social teachings of various faiths, particularly Abrahamic faiths, we expect differences in how FBOs and secular organizations approach human rights related to development. We also expect, however, that many organizations within our dataset will focus on socioeconomic rights, as they have been explicitly discussed in international human rights discourse and agreements, including the MDGs and SDGs. Similarly, we expect most organizations in the sample to promote human development since they are focused on human rights and issues related to the well-being of humans. Still, we expect some variation between religious and secular organizations as well as between organizations based in the Global North and the Global South. Specifically, we examine the following hypotheses:

1. Religious organizations will be more likely than secular groups to focus on socioeconomic rights, development, and the right to development.
2. Religious organizations will be more likely than secular groups to frame their work in terms of poverty and human development.
3. Secular organizations will be more likely than religious groups to frame their work on development using liberal economic discourse of economic growth (like income generation and job creation).
4. Religious organizations will be more likely than secular groups to provide humanitarian aid.
5. Secular organizations will be more likely to refer to development and other human rights issues using rights-based language.
6. Organizations in the Global South and outside of the West will be more likely to focus on socioeconomic rights, development, and the right to development than those based in the Global North and West.
7. Organizations in the Global South will be more likely than those in the North to frame development rights in terms of human development.
8. Organizations in the Global North and West will be more likely than those in the Global South and outside of the West to frame their work on development by emphasizing the liberal economic discourse of economic growth (including income generation and job creation).
9. Organizations in the Global North and West will be more likely than those in the Global South and outside of the West to refer to development and other human rights issues using rights-based language.

10. Organizations in the Global South will be more likely than those in the Global North to include water and sanitation issues as development issues.
11. Organizations with sections on women and/or children will be more likely than those without these sections to include water and sanitation as development issues.

Findings

This section examines the various hypotheses laid out above. To do so we examine quantitative data generated from the analysis of 333 organizational websites in conjunction with qualitative data gathered from forty-seven interviews and illustrative information pulled from organizational websites.

Socioeconomic Rights

Based on the fact that social justice and care for the poor are key tenets in many world religions, we expected that religious organizations would be more likely than secular organizations to include socioeconomic rights in their work (also discussed in chapter 1). This expectation was partially correct; 93 percent of religious organizations in the sample do in fact focus on socioeconomic rights, as compared with 81 percent of their secular counterparts. While this difference is significant at the $p < .05$ level, the percentages indicate the overwhelming majority of human rights organizations focus on socioeconomic rights to some degree, even if religious groups do so to an even greater extent. Further, as discussed in chapter 1, there is little difference between religious organizations of different faith backgrounds and their likelihood of supporting socioeconomic rights, particularly since such a large percentage of organizations in the sample support these rights.

We also expected that organizations based in the Global South would be more likely than those in the North to focus on socioeconomic rights, due to the varying degrees of socioeconomic development and the tendency of countries like the United States to focus on political and civil rights. For similar reasons, we thought that organizations based in Western societies would be less likely to focus on socioeconomic rights, which were historically disregarded by the United States given the association of these second-generation rights with their archrival, the Soviet Union, during the Cold War era. However, the data show only very minor differences between organizations based in the Global North and South and between Western organizations and others. These data, captured in Table 3.1, suggest not only that human rights organizations over-

TABLE 3.1

Organizations Focusing on Socioeconomic Rights and Development (in percentages)

	Supports socioeconomic rights	Focuses on development	Supports right to development
Religious organizations	93	46	6
Secular organizations	81	37	5
Global North	84	42	5
Global South	85	32	5
Western	84	42	5
Non-Western	83	32	4

whelmingly focus on socioeconomic rights but also that this happens across socioeconomic, geographical, and religious lines.

Overall, interviewees did not often specifically mention socioeconomic rights. Djazairouna was one organization that specifically used the language of "socioeconomic rights" to discuss their work with women, "through the implementation of several projects and activities . . . [including] embroidery and cakes, secretarial and computer [courses]." A few organizations mentioned their efforts with workers. For example, the Informal Sector Service Center discussed their campaign to help fix minimum wages for agricultural laborers as part of a broader effort to end bonded labor in Nepal. T'ruah, a religious organization, spoke of how using the language of rights provided space for considering workers as human beings and prevented the inevitable stalling that would have occurred with a focus on fair wages. This message, inherent in many faiths, of the human being as created in the divine image helps remind one of the "whole life" of workers. A few of the organizations did not speak explicitly about their work in terms of socioeconomic rights but did discuss social and economic issues they were working on. For example, the International Peace Bureau spoke of how military spending diverted funds from social and environmental needs, and the Franciscans highlighted human rights issues as related to abusive business practices, specifically in the need to share resources more equitably.

Organizational websites were often more explicit in their use of rights language. According to the website of Advocates for Human Rights, for example, they created a manual "to strengthen the capacity to use human rights to combat entrenched poverty, discrimination and injustice," and the website of APRODEH (Asociación Pro Derechos Humanos) asserts that it "promotes the protection of economic social, cultural and environmental rights." In particular, APRODEH emphasizes how collective rights are affected by extractive industries and discriminatory government policies. Elsewhere in the world, the Asia Forum for Human Rights and Development uses similar language on their website, talking about building a "peaceful, just, equitable and ecologically sustainable community . . . where all human rights of all individuals, groups and peoples—in particular, the poor, marginalized and discriminated—are fully respected and realized in accordance with internationally accepted human rights norms." Likewise, the website of Bir Duino Kyrgyzstan promotes "civil, political, cultural, and economic rights and other social useful objectives"; similar language is also used on the websites of Human Rights Now and the Movement for Protection of the African Child (MOPOTAC), affirming the lack of geographic specificity for these rights.

Development

Similar to our expectation that religious organizations would be more likely to promote socioeconomic rights, we also expected that they would be more likely to mention development as part of their work or have a section devoted to development. While this was indeed the case, with 46 percent of religious organizations mentioning development as compared to 37 percent of secular groups, this difference was not statistically significant. There was some notable difference between organizations of different faith backgrounds. Of the Christian organizations in the data, 50 percent discussed or had a section devoted to development. Similarly, 57 percent of the Muslim organizations focused on development, while all of the Jewish organizations mentioned or had a section specifically on development. Finally, other religious organizations in the sample were the least likely to consider development, only 33 percent. Thus, Jewish organizations were the most likely to consider development, followed by Muslim and then Christian organizations, with other religious organizations being the least likely. The difference between Jewish and other organizations is significant at the $p < .05$ level, with none of the other differences being statistically significant. While the number of Jewish organizations in the sample is small, this is an interesting finding for future research and perhaps is linked to the fact that many Jewish human rights organizations are committed to the development of the Jewish community at home and around the world. It may also be related to the idea of *tikkun olam*, commonly understood as improving the world, prevalent in some forms of Judaism.

It was expected that more organizations in the Global South than in the North would mention development or have a development section. However, this was not the case. Though the difference is statistically significant only at the $p < .10$ level, a greater percentage of organizations based in the Global

North, 42 percent, highlight development, as compared to those based in the Global South at 32 percent. This finding may be due to the fact that organizations based in the Global North are more likely to have the funds and mission to promote development and/or are more likely to receive donor funding given their ability to meet the metrics for donor financing requirements (Neufeldt 2016). As with socioeconomic rights, the findings for Western versus non-Western organizations paralleled those for Global North versus Global South, with 42 percent of the organizations based in the West as compared with 32 percent of those outside the West mentioning development, though this difference was statistically significant only at the $p < .10$ level.

Right to Development

Based on the review of the literature, we did not expect many organizations to emphasize the right to development, although we did expect more religious organizations and more of those from the Global South and outside of the West to mention the right to development. Overall, as reported in Table 3.1, very few organizations mentioned the right to development, and there was very little difference between organizations along any of the three axes of difference— secular versus religious, Global North versus Global South, and Western versus non-Western. These results indicate that the vast majority of organizations distanced themselves from officially supporting development as a right that should be upheld. This finding could be the result of several different factors that arose in our research, including the many different ways that development is understood by various organizations (economic vs. human) as well as the increasing focus on environmental sustainability and protection of the natural world that was evident across organizations. One interesting finding is that all four of the religious organizations that mentioned a right to development are Catholic. This is consistent with Catholic social teaching and the Vatican's teachings regarding economic development over the decades, which emphasize concern for the poor and cooperation to end the underdevelopment of some while others grow wealthy.[5]

Consistent with these findings, the single organization whose members we interviewed who explicitly mentioned the right to development was Catholic. The Dominicans stated that the right to development, as part of a broader approach including education, health rights, and ending poverty, had been a major focus of their work. Another Catholic organization, the International Catholic Child Bureau, states on their website that they have a "constant focus on the right to development, a right which is fundamental to the life, well-being and dignity of human beings." Asia Forum for Human Rights and Development, a secular organization, mentions on their website that they work "to promote and protect human rights, including the right to development, through collaboration and cooperation among human rights organization and defenders." Thus, while this group states their support of the right, they do not differentiate it from their overall support of human rights more generally. More frequently websites speak of efforts to promote development or sustainable development without using rights language.

Approaches to Development

Within the international community, and especially in light of the multi-faceted SDGs, development is defined according to a range of topics and indicators. This section focuses more specifically on the subareas of human development, poverty, and water/sanitation efforts.

Given the nature of human rights as human centered, we expected that many organizations would focus on human development rather than taking an economic growth approach to development. At the same time, given the social teachings of many religions, we expected that religious organizations would be more likely than secular organizations to have a focus on human development. We also expected that organizations based in the Global South would be more focused on human development than those based in the Global North. As outlined in Table 3.2, there are indeed slightly more religious organizations and those in the Global South focused on human development. However, these differences are not statistically significant. There are some clear differences between religious faith traditions. Christian organizations are the most likely to discuss human development (81 percent), followed by other organizations (78 percent). Around 43 percent of Muslim organizations and 50 percent Jewish organizations discuss human development. The difference between Christian and Muslim organizations is statistically significant at the $p < .05$ level. None of the other differences are significant. This distinction may simply be a factor of sample size or could be due to the focus within Islam on charity, as opposed to development per se, whereas many Christian denominations have associated relief and development agencies, that is, Catholic Relief Services and MCC. Western and non-Western organizations are similarly likely to emphasize human development. Again, this is not surprising given that these groups are focused on human rights and thus are likely to be interested in the human side of development.

The human development angle of organizations' efforts emerged clearly from the qualitative data. The Federation of Environmental and Ecological Diversity for Agricultural Revampment and Human Rights (FEEDAR & HR), for example, stated, "We go for things which will improve the social, political, socioeconomic, you know, bring life to people, smiles on people's faces. So we think that what we do is certainly related to development." A member of B'Tselem, an Israeli human rights organization, reflected that "even the smallest projects we do and the way that we incorporate and teaching Palestinian

TABLE 3.2

Comparison of Development Approaches (in percentages)

	Human development	Poverty	Income generation / job creation	Humanitarian aid
Religious organizations	75	41	18	25
Secular organizations	65	15	13	9
Global North	66	24	14	14
Global South	71	12	12	8
Western	67	23	14	12
Non-Western	69	13	12	12

volunteers about their rights and giving them a voice and the platform to tell their stories is something that is certainly development work." A number of organizations spoke of human development in terms of training, capacity building, or raising awareness regarding issues related to good governance or legal justice. The representative from the Human Rights Commission of Pakistan differentiated the type of development work her organization does by stating, "We don't go out and build schools or set up health centers, not that kind of development work, but development in terms of creating awareness, empower[ing] people so they continue or are able to fight for their rights. Not [development] in brick and mortar sense of the word." Femmes Développement et Droits Humains en Guinée (F2DHG) observed, "Development is materialized by the evolution of attitudes and the commitment of young people and women we train to participate actively in the life of the nation." Another example of this human development approach is from the Observatoire des Droits de l'Homme au Rwanda, a Rwandan organization that asserted, "Our work will contribute to development by raising people's awareness of good governance the fight against impunity, corruption and injustice."

Religious organizations used slightly different language than did the secular human rights organizations, focusing more on the holistic development of the person. Islamic Relief, for example, shared, "We defined development in a multidimensional way according to the priorities of prophetic law which are protection of faith, of life, of wealth, of intellect, and of progeny." Soka Gakkai spoke of themselves "as a movement for human development and evolution," and the Lutheran World Federation noted that development empowerment efforts reinforce other components of their work as a whole. Thus, initial findings seem to suggest that for religious organizations development is a broader, almost spiritual concept, distinct from the definition found with aid agencies and in UN policy documents, although this issue requires further study.

Few organizations across the board emphasized the income generation or job creation side of development work. This is not surprising given that job creation per se is not part of economic and social rights. Although the ICESCR does mention that individuals have the rights to work and to fair wages, economic rights are much more broadly construed than the creation of income alone. The idea of development as income creation is much more closely tied to the neoliberal model of development advocated by some donor agencies primarily in the West and Global North. However, the data (see Table 3.2) do not show any real differences between organizations based in the West and non-West or Global North and Global South in this context. While there are a few more religious organizations than secular organizations with a focus on income generation or job creation, these numbers are still small and not statistically significant. A few organizations mentioned job creation or income generation in their interviews. Two of these organizations focused particularly on the link between economic empowerment and political voice for women, with FEEDAR & HR discussing a cocoa bean cooperative for women intended to give them a voice in decision making and F2DHG referencing their efforts to economically empower women as a way of influencing the electoral process.

In terms of poverty, we expected that religious organizations would focus more on this area given religious commitments to caring for the unfortunate in several major faiths, including the obligation to give alms to the poor in Islam. Indeed, religious groups are significantly more likely than secular groups to have a focus on poverty, 41 as compared to 15 percent, statistically significant at the $p < .001$ level. We also expected that organizations based in the Global North and the West would focus more on poverty than groups in the Global South and non-West given the orientation toward poverty as a monetized economic measure as opposed to a livelihoods-based conception. The findings support this expectation; 24 percent of organizations in the Global North and 23 percent of organization in the West focused on poverty, compared to 12 percent of those in the Global South and 13 percent of those in the non-West, both significant at the $p < .05$ level.

A related finding, consistent with our hypothesis, is that 25 percent of religious organizations include humanitarian aid as part of their mandate, as compared to 9 percent of secular organizations, and this finding is statistically significant at the $p < .001$ level. Further, Muslim organizations are the most likely to provide humanitarian aid (43 percent). Around 29 percent of other religious organizations, 25 percent of Jewish organizations, and 23 percent of Christian organizations provide humanitarian aid. Although these differences are not statistically significant, it is not surprising to see a stronger focus on humanitarian aid from Muslim organizations due to the alms-giving tradition within Islam. This finding suggests a link between the mandate of religious groups

TEXTBOX 3.1

Approaches to Development and Poverty

HOPE International

HOPE International is a Christian organization that began with one man's humanitarian work in the post-Soviet Ukraine and evolved into a microfinance organization operating in sixteen countries around the world focusing on poverty reduction through microenterprise rather than the provision of charity. The organization states, "We share the hope of Christ as we provide biblically based training, savings services, and loans that restore dignity and break the cycle of poverty." HOPE International's efforts are based in the belief that "families in poverty have the God-given talents and skills to provide for their families. What they don't have is a lump sum of money to invest in their potential."

HOPE International. 2020. "Our Mission." https://www.hopeinternational.org/about-us/our-mission.
HOPE International. 2020. "Why Christ-Centered Financial Services?" https://www.hopeinternational.org
/what-we-do.

ATD Fourth World

ATD Fourth World seeks to build a world without poverty, bringing people together to work based on their own experiences with poverty. The organization prioritizes education, respect, and long-term sustainable change. They say, "The most disadvantaged people can free themselves from the dependence and indignity of poverty when their courage and their capacity for action are recognized and when everyone takes responsibility for overcoming the prejudice and discrimination that continue to exclude people in poverty, on every continent." Further, they note that "today's economic systems subject people in extreme poverty to punishing exploitation and often condemn them to uselessness. Around the world there are many initiatives for the public good, fair-trade, and promoting self-sufficiency and community resilience. We work to ensure that people in extreme poverty be able to participate in these projects."

ATD Fourth World. n.d. "One Central Focus, Four Priorities: ATD Fourth World's Strategic Ambitions 2019–2023."
https://www.atd-fourthworld.org/what-we-do/our-priorities/.
ATD Fourth World. n.d. "Our Mission." https://www.atd-fourthworld.org/who-we-are/mission/.

to care for the poor and those in need and humanitarianism, which does not seem to apply to secular organizations that are more narrowly focused on human rights alone. Further, given that international law differentiates between human rights law and humanitarian law and religious organizations ascribe to higher (divine law), this distinction is likely more important to secular organizations than to religious ones. However, the relationship between human rights and humanitarianism in religious organizations as compared to secular ones is a topic worthy of additional study. Aside from religious/secular differences, there are no other statistically significant differences between the other categories (North/South and West/non-West) examined, although there are more organizations based in the Global North than the Global South that provide humanitarian aid.

The qualitative data mirror the quantitative data in terms of the focus on poverty found in the religious organizations. Of those organizations interviewed that explicitly discussed poverty as a main focus of their work, three were Catholic and one was Muslim. Catholic Relief Services mentioned that "with this Catholic social teaching principle of the 'preferred option for the poor,' we typically try to reach out to the most marginal, most vulnerable within a population," and the Dominicans also noted that "issues of poverty and inequality I think are major things that we have to deal with." The Franciscans shared that they have a "thematic, global policy strategy on extreme poverty . . . promoting a rights-based approach to extreme poverty." Islamic Relief emphasized that in terms of poverty "the rights-based discourse is fundamental to our faith teaching."

The secular interviewees had an array of views on humanitarianism and the extent to which their work was considered humanitarian; this reflects a disjuncture between those defining humanitarian in terms of voluntary, free, or in the service of humanity and those defining humanitarian in accordance with international statutes. For example, the Lebanese Center for Human Rights said, "We provide legal assistance to the poor and vulnerable, regardless of ethnicity and religion . . . so yes, it is humanitarian work." FEEDAR & HR said, "All of our work [is] humanitarian. We do everything for free." Others, however, differentiated between human rights and humanitarian efforts, suggesting the two endeavors are "very different," and several others, such as the Human Rights Commission of Pakistan and B'Tselem, noted they are not providing shelter or food for those in need. Several religious groups, however, noted their humanitarian efforts, with Islamic Relief self-identifying primarily as a humanitarian agency that has increasingly focused on rights. At the time of the interview, Lutheran World Relief was the fourth largest partner for the UN High Commissioner for Refugees and was the largest faith-based partner, emphasizing the important role of humanitarianism in the organization's mandate.

The distinction between human rights and humanitarian foci between religious and secular organizations is similar to another distinction that emerged in the interviews. In contrast to some of the interviewees quoted in this chapter, several others stated that they do not consider their work to be development, and that human rights and development are not the same thing. For example, the representative from the Center for Prisoners' Rights Japan shared, "I have never thought that our activities are for development." These observations are particularly noteworthy given the lack of a human rights framing in the SDGs. Given differing views on the relationship between these concepts among human rights organizations and the lack of integration in the international policy arena, the ongoing relationship between the concepts of rights and development should be monitored.

Rights-Based Approach

We expected that secular organizations, particularly those based in the Global North and West, would be more likely to emphasize the "rights-based" approach to development, given that organizations like Oxfam initiated it. However, very few organizations specifically mention a rights-based approach, perhaps because they are committed to human rights more broadly and therefore do not find it necessary to frame their work using "rights-based" language. Further, as the sample consists primarily of organizations affiliated with the Human Rights Council that may also do development work, rather than development organizations that might also do some human rights work, these low percentages are not surprising. We did find, however, that religious organizations (13 percent) are more likely than secular organizations (5 percent) to mention the rights-based approach. However, this difference is not statistically significant. Further, seven of the nine religious organizations that mentioned a rights-based approach are Christian, one is Jewish, and one is an other religious organization (Arigatou International). As expected, organizations based in the Global North (8 percent) and West (7 percent) mention the rights-based approach more than those based in the Global South (4 percent) and non-West (5 percent), but these are small differences and not statistically significant.

Reflecting the quantitative findings, only a few interviewees mentioned the rights-based approach; interestingly enough, most of these are religious organizations. For example, the Franciscans noted how their strategy comes "from a human rights based approach." A representative from Islamic Relief opined that "obviously we deliver rights through all our programs, but it's not as rights-based as you might find in some agencies such as Christian Aid or Oxfam." No secular organizations discussed a rights-based approach explicitly in their conversations, although the Commonwealth Human Rights Initiative observed that "without rights you don't have development. If you don't have implementation of rights and access to rights there cannot be development because it would be empty." The Organisation Guinéenne de Défense des Droits de l'Homme et du citoyen noted that "without peace there would be no development, and without human rights there would be no peace, and no development, so the human rights aspect is indispensable for these two things." Perhaps one reason why the rights-based approach was not discussed much on websites or in the interviews has to do with the lack of reference to human rights in the 2030 Agenda for Sustainable Development. As observed by the representative from the World Council of Churches, "Nonetheless [the 2030 Agenda] is portrayed, and I think legitimately, as being human rights related in a sense of its holistic approach to human wellbeing and flourishing." However, the reframing of development work through the articulation of the SDGs may have resulted in a shift away from "rights-based" language to terminology more in keeping with the new UN-led initiative.

Water/Sanitation

In the literature on development, water and sanitation efforts are often linked to gender and children's rights for several reasons, including the health impacts on children lacking adequate water and sanitation, the negative impact a lack of sanitation facilities has on girls' education, and the inordinate amount of time fetching water requires of women and girls in so-called developing areas. For these reasons, we expected to see more efforts at water and sanitation—at times discussed in terms of WASH, water, sanitation, and hygiene—in organizations with women's and children's sections and also in those based in the Global South. However, as evident in Table 3.3, there are few statistically significant differences across any of the categories of distinction for water and sanitation efforts, although religious organizations mention such efforts more than their secular counterparts. Of the eleven religious organizations that did, nine are Christian and two are Muslim, with no Jewish or other religious organizations discussing this issue. Almost exactly the same percentages of organizations based in the Global North and Global South focus on water and sanitation; likewise for organizations in the West and non-West. This set of relatively similar percentages could reflect the inclusion of water as Goal 6 of the SDGs, which gives a common focus to development-oriented organizations.

Although there does not seem to be a difference between religious and secular organizations when it comes to a focus on water/sanitation, the data do show a connection between development and water/sanitation. If we consider only those organizations with a development focus, we find that a higher percentage of these organizations (24 percent) consider water/sanitation issues than those without such a focus (4 percent), and this difference is significant at the $p < .001$ level. Further, there are observable differences between women's organizations and groups with women's sections as compared to others in terms of water and sanitation efforts. When looking at women's organizations 16 percent consider water/sanitation, compared to 12 percent of non–women's organizations; similarly, 14 percent of organizations with a women's section discuss water/sanitation, compared to 11 percent of organizations without a women's section. A similar pattern is evident in the children's organizations and those with a children's section. With children's groups, one sees the same trend, with 21 percent of children's organizations and 15 percent of organizations with a children's section considering water/sanitation, compared to 11 percent of non–children's organizations and organizations without a children's section.

TABLE 3.3

Water and Sanitation Efforts by Organizational Type (in percentages)

Religious organization	16
Secular organization	11
Global North	12
Global South	11
Western	12
Non-Western	10
Organizations with a development focus	24
Organizations without a development focus	4
Women's organization	16
Non–women's organization	12
Women's section	14
No women's section	11
Children's organization	21
Non–children's organization	12
Children's section	15
No children's section	11

Although the small numbers of children's (nineteen) and women's organizations (thirty-one) affect the ability to determine statistical significance, this trend is worthy of further study and is similar to the patterns seen in the focus on gender issues within women's organizations and organizations with gender-specific sections found in chapter 4.

Overall, water and sanitation efforts were not mentioned in the interviews, with only two organizations, one religious (Islamic Relief) and one secular (Feminist Dalit Organization), mentioning the topic at all, and then only briefly, although water was previously one of the five sectors of Islamic Relief's work. However, water and sanitation efforts are mentioned on the websites of Edmund Rice International and Franciscans International, both FBOs. While some organizations, like the International Work Group for Indigenous Affairs, emphasize on their websites that lack of water disproportionately affects certain groups, such as pastoralists in Tanzania, certain American Indian tribes in the United States, and Arab Bedouin in Israel, others, like Medical Care Development International, take less of a values-based equity approach to water/sanitation. As is logical based on the SDGs related to water and sanitation efforts, a number of the organizations that emphasize water and sanitation efforts are environmental, women's, or children's organizations, including the Mexican Environmental Law Center, the Women and Child Support Organization, and the Sudanese Environment Conservation Society. Given that "water is life," it is not too surprising to find both religious and secular organizations emphasizing water, sanitation, and hygiene efforts, including World Vision, LDS Charities, Catholic Relief Services, and World Federation of Khoja Shi'a Ithna-Asheri Muslim Communities on the religious side and WILPF, Family Health International, World Resources Institute, and Action Against Hunger on the secular side.

Conclusion

One of the major findings of this chapter is that although the differences between religious and secular organizations were not always statistically significant, there was often a greater percentage of religious organizations focusing on issues of socioeconomic rights and development, and this difference is significant when looking at poverty and humanitarian work. While more investigation is needed to explore the reasons for this difference, particularly given that ending poverty is one of the SDGs, it suggests that the more holistic and spiritual view of human rights and the obligation to serve humanity found in some of the religiously based organizations impacts these two metrics in particular. However, this commitment to address poverty and engage in humanitarian efforts does not lead religious organizations to view development as a right. In fact, the data overwhelmingly suggest that the right to development is not widely supported, as less than 6 percent of organizations across all the various categories of difference mention the right to development on their websites.

A second major finding is that contrary to expectations, there is little difference between organizations based in the Global North and the Global South when it comes to issues of socioeconomic rights and development. Further, despite the history of Cold War divides between the United States and the Soviet Union regarding their respective prioritization of political and civil rights versus social and economic rights, we did not find evidence of a divide between organizations based in the West and non-West regarding these issues either. Several possible explanations exist for these results, the first of which has to do with an evolving understanding of development in the international community, particularly with the 2030 Agenda and the SDGs that provide a very broad view of development. Further, because the sample in question focuses on human rights organizations, some of which also do development work, rather than development organizations per se, our findings are not representative of the broader universe of organizations working on these issues. Additionally, our definition of West and non-West does not neatly line up with Cold War lines but rather is more cultural and geographic in nature (see chapter 2) and thus may not be a good proxy for a reflection of Cold War legacies in terms of rights.

A third major finding of this chapter relates to the difficulty of defining development, which may be partially related to the hesitation to promote a "right" to development. The 2030 Agenda includes seventeen SDGs, which are wide ranging, including an end to poverty, an end to hunger, gender equality, clean water and sanitation, decent work and economic growth, industry, innovation and infrastructure, and peace, justice, and strong institutions. The wide-ranging and all-encompassing nature of these goals makes it difficult to determine what exactly "development" is, as opposed to other social change efforts. Further, some of the goals can be construed as paradoxical, with climate action, life below water, and life on land (Goals 13–15) contrasting—and some might say even contradicting—decent work and economic growth (Goal 8) and industry, innovation, and infrastructure (Goal 9). Coding the websites for the various development indicators was challenging given the sometimes opposing ways in which development was construed by those with "development" sections: although some organizations spoke of sustainable development and livelihoods in their development sections while also working against extractive industries and neoliberal models of economic growth, others had development sections focused on infrastructure projects and growth more in line with practices condemned elsewhere. These data point to the need for additional research on the intersection of development and human rights, particularly in regard to the multifaceted nature of the 2030 Agenda and the lack of human rights language integrated into the SDGs.

CHAPTER 4

Exploring the Intersection of Gender and Human Rights in Religious and Secular Organizations

This chapter focuses on the particular ways in which gender and women's rights are conceptualized and operationalized in religious and secular human rights organizations, exploring whether and how diverse groups around the world address women's rights as a particular subset of their human rights agenda. While gender concerns are not exclusively about women, women's rights often serve as a focal point for debates over culture and religion. Consequently, we expect that the conception of women's rights will reflect this broader global struggle. Further, as demonstrated at the Fourth World Conference on Women held in Beijing in 1995, debates over women's rights can also reflect different perspectives from women's movements in the Global North, which have often privileged issues of wage equality and reproductive rights, and women's movements in the Global South, which have often privileged issues more fundamental to survival and socioeconomic development. After discussing the major bodies of international law that address the rights of women, this chapter explores how women's rights are discussed in the literature, before examining to what extent women's rights are emphasized in the religious and secular organizations studied in our sample, examining patterns related to not only the type of rights emphasized but also whether there are broader patterns between Northern and Southern organizations. The chapter also engages with broader questions regarding gender, particularly by exploring to what extent organizations support LGBTQI rights.

History of International Law as It Relates to Gender

The UDHR, proclaimed by the UN General Assembly on December 10, 1948, attempts to provide a common standard for human rights. The declaration uses gender-inclusive language, such as "all human beings," "men and women," and "everyone" (UN 1948). In relation to women's rights, the document explicitly recognizes both men and women when discussing various rights, including equal rights to marriage and the dissolution of marriage. However, while the document does provide a long list of rights that apply to both men and women, there is no real discussion of issues that may be more relevant to women or any attempt to specifically address gender-based discrimination. Further, at the time the document was written, many women around the world either had recently acquired (e.g., France in 1944) or still had no voting rights (e.g., most countries in the Global South, still under colonial rule).

The ICCPR, which opened for signature, ratification, and accession by the UN General Assembly in December 1966, promoted human rights and equality between men and women. Article 3 specifically states that the parties to the covenant should "undertake to ensure the equal right of men and women to the enjoyment of all civil and political rights set forth in the present Covenant" (UN 1966a). As with the UDHR, there is little additional discussion of women's rights or discrimination against them, with the exception of a prohibition on carrying out a sentence of death on a pregnant woman. A series of international conferences, starting with the World Conference on the International Women's Year hosted in Mexico City in 1975, followed by a 1980 World Conference in Copenhagen and a 1982 World Conference in Nairobi, raised the profile of women's rights.

In 1979, the UN General Assembly adopted CEDAW, defining discrimination as "any distinction, exclusion or restriction made on the basis of sex which has the effect or purpose of impairing or nullifying the recognition, enjoyment or exercise by women, irrespective of their marital status, on a basis of equality of men and women, of human rights and fundamental freedoms in the political, economic, social, cultural, civil or any other field" (UN 1979, Article 1). The treaty entered into force on September 3, 1981. CEDAW not only excludes culture as a justification for discrimination but also specifically targets culture and tradition as a force shaping (unequal) gender relations while also affirming women's reproductive rights. Article 5, for example, affirms that state parties will endeavor to "modify the social and cultural patterns of conduct of men and women, with a view to achieving the elimination of prejudices and customary and all other practices which are based on the idea of the inferiority or the superiority of either of the sexes or on stereotyped roles for men and women," and Article 10 specifies state parties should ensure "access to specific educational information to help to ensure the health and well-being of families, including information and advice on family planning." Article 12 further stipulates women's equal rights to health care services, "including those related to family planning." Although much of the treaty focuses on political and civil rights, Article 14 focuses particularly on the rights of women in rural areas, again emphasizing family planning but also including access to economic opportunities, adequate sanitation, and water.

The text of CEDAW does not explicitly mention religion, although the web page discussing reservations to CEDAW states that "neither traditional, religious or cultural practice nor incompatible domestic laws and policies can justify violations of the Convention" (UN Women n.d.-a). However, many states have noted reservations to the treaty, some of which have to do with religious teachings and beliefs, such as shari'a law or Catholic views regarding children born out of wedlock, which indicate the significance of religion in shaping how women's rights are viewed.[1] Most UN member states have ratified or acceded to the convention, which means they are legally bound to it and are required to submit periodic national reports on compliance. It is worth noting, however, that while the United States signed the treaty in 1980, it never ratified the convention, and thus the United States is not party to the treaty.

Paragraph 18 of the Vienna Declaration and Programme of Action, adopted at the 1993 World Conference on Human Rights, states, "The human rights of women and of the girl-child are an inalienable, integral, and indivisible part of universal human rights" (UN High Commissioner for Human Rights 2014). The 1994 International Conference on Population and Development also emphasizes women's human rights, particularly in regard to gender equality, preventing violence against women, reproductive health, and birth control (OHCHR 2014, 13). In 1995, the United Nation's Fourth World Conference on Women, held in Beijing, produced the Beijing Declaration and Platform for Action. The Mission Statement of the Platform for Action specifically states, "Equality between women and men is a matter of human rights and a condition for social justice and is also a necessary and fundamental prerequisite for equality, development and peace" (UN 1995). This conference helped solidify the idea that women's rights are fundamental human rights. At the same time, tensions at the conference between women from the Global North, who focused more on issues such as reproductive rights and pay equality, and those from the Global South, who focused more on economic justice and livelihood issues, illustrated the varying ways issues of women's rights are identified and operationalized in different socioeconomic and political contexts (Barton 2004).

Subsequent to the Beijing Conference, ECOSOC expanded the role of the Commission on the Status of Women (CSW), originally created in 1946, to include monitoring the implementation of the Beijing Declaration and Platform for Action as well as mainstreaming a gender perspective in UN activities. In 2010, the UN General Assembly created UN Women, the United Nations Entity for Gender Equality and the Empowerment of Women, bringing together previously separated programs and funds for women into a single entity. UN Women helps with the formulation, implementation, and monitoring of various policies, global standards, and norms related to gender equality and women's empowerment and supports the work of the CSW (UN Women n.d.-a).

Through the creation of UN Women and its efforts to mainstream a gender perspective, the UN highlights two competing approaches to women's rights: one that attempts to bring gender explicitly into all discussions of human's rights and another that focuses more specifically on issues relevant to women through gender-specific programming. The first approach helps to ensure that women are always integrated as part of the equation, although it can also gloss over ways in which women's needs are distinct from those of men. The second approach identifies women's distinct needs yet may contribute to a view that women's rights are not equivalent to human rights more generally. The creation of dedicated focus areas on women in the MDGs through Goal 3, promote gender equality and empower women, and the subsequent SDGs through Goal 5, gender equality, illustrates this second approach to advocating for women's rights.[2]

Sexual Orientation and Gender Identity

Although CEDAW and other international legal documents specify "sex," in recent decades there has been a shift toward discussing "gender," further emphasizing the socially constructed nature of what it means to be male and female and broadening the scope to include individuals who do not identify with either such category and/or who identify as lesbian, gay, bisexual, transsexual, queer, intersex, or other, referred to by the acronym LGBTQI. Concerns about the rights of LGBTQI individuals have been raised by the human rights bodies of the UN since the early 1990s, although sexual identity was not mentioned explicitly in the UDHR. In 2011 the Human Rights Council adopted Resolution 17/19, which "*express[es] grave concern* at acts of violence and discrimination, in all regions of the world, committed against individuals because of their sexual orientation and gender identity" (UN 2011). According to the UN, consensual same-sex relationships are targeted by discriminatory laws in seventy-seven countries, and in five countries LGBTQI individuals can face the death penalty (UN High Commissioner for Human Rights 2014). To address these concerns, OHCHR launched a public information campaign titled "UN Free and Equal" in July 2013, promoting equal rights for LGBTQI people. On June 30, 2016, the UN Human Rights Council adopted a resolution calling for protection against violence and discrimination for LGBTQI individuals. However, this vote was not unanimous (Henneberg 2016, 16).

Like questions concerning the role of women in society, discussions surrounding gender and sexual identity are often highly sensitive in some religious communities; further, views on LGBTQI rights vary significantly within and between sectarian groupings. Some religious traditions, like Buddhism, are highly decentralized and thus have varied teachings and practices in regard to LGBTQI rights, marriage, and ordination as monks or nuns. While the more centralized Roman Catholic Church does not recognize same-sex marriages or allow homosexuals to be ordained, the Catholic laity increasingly supports same-sex marriage, an illustration of how religious views can differ between official doctrine, institutional leadership, and individual believers. Protestant denominations also differ in their views regarding LGBTQI rights. The 2016 Book of Discipline of the United Methodist Church, for example, states that "the practice of homosexuality is incompatible with Christian teaching" (Human Rights Campaign n.d.-b). In contrast, denominations including the Evangelical Lutheran Church in America and the Presbyterian Church (USA) have allowed ordination of LGBTQI individuals since 2010, although such practices are at the discretion of individual congregations.

A lack of recognition for LGBTQI rights is not unique to religious bodies, however. Many countries around the world have laws prohibiting what is often called sodomy, and a number of countries, including Mauritania, Sudan, Iran, and Saudi Arabia, have legislation leading to the death penalty for LGBTQI people (Felter and Renwick 2019). Even in the twenty-three countries around the world where same-sex marriage is legal, political candidates run on platforms for reducing their state's existing rights protections for the LGBTQI community (Felter and Renwick 2019). Thus, despite a changing international legal environment toward LGBTQI rights, political, economic, social, and religious discrimination persists, in both secular and religious contexts.

Gender Mainstreaming versus Dedicated Programs

Since 1997 the UN and major development agencies have sought to "mainstream" gender in their work, an approach that organizations sometimes call a transversal or a cross-cutting theme. There are many arguments organizations provide for having gender integrated into all aspects of their work. Paragraph 189 of the report that came out of the 1995 Fourth World Conference on Women held in Beijing states, for example, "In addressing the inequality between men and women in the sharing of power and decision-making at all levels, Governments and other actors should promote an active and visible policy of mainstreaming a gender perspective in all policies and programmes so that before decisions are taken, an analysis is made of the effects on women and men, respectively" (UN Women n.d.-b). The UN has continued to emphasize the importance of gender mainstreaming in all of its organizations as a means of pursuing the goals of gender equality and women's empowerment, reiterating this position in June 2000 and again in the 2005 World Summit Outcome. In 2017 the Food and Agriculture Organization of the UN (FAO) issued a set of guidelines for gender mainstreaming as a human rights–

based approach for its technical officers. The introduction captures the main argument for gender mainstreaming, notably that "it is, therefore, crucial that everyone benefits equally from the development gains provided by FAO programmes and projects. To ensure this aim, gender mainstreaming and the human rights-based approach (HRBA) underpin all of FAO's interventions" (FAO 2017, 1).

However, there are also benefits to having a dedicated section or programmatic area focusing on gender concerns and women's rights due to the unique nature of some of these issues, such as reproductive rights, or the specific kinds of discrimination faced by women and LGBTQI communities in various cultures, religious communities, and societies around the world. We expect that NGOs with a broad human rights agenda will be likely to have a dedicated section on women's and/or gender concerns because of the UN-directed efforts at raising the profile of women's rights on the international stage. However, given that the UN has focused on gender mainstreaming, in which every program engages with a gender analysis to some degree, organizations might also not have gender-specific sections. Although the data collected for this project do not examine gender mainstreaming per se, it is worth noting that several organizations we interviewed suggested the practice can be problematic in terms of addressing gender issues. Specifically, gender mainstreaming does not require a definitive focus on gender concerns per se, and if an organization has many foci, the gender lens may be assumed away to other aspects of programming such that no one gives it adequate attention. For example, gender mainstreaming has meant some NGOs have lacked a definitive plan of action on gender issues within former Soviet states because framing women's rights as human rights does not provide a specific enough agenda to deal with women's discrimination in society, which exists even though there is equality on paper (Tsetsura 2013). A one-size-fits-all approach to women's rights may not work, particularly since cultural and political elements can affect the success of such women's rights efforts. Thus, we expect that women's-only organizations and those with stand-alone gender sections are more likely to have a focus on gender-specific issues than organizations with no such dedicated focus.

State of the Literature on Religion and Women's Rights

A review of the literature suggests that nearly every religion has at some point supported policies that some might consider antithetical to women's rights. Further, religious views differ regarding whether gender equality implies the *same* or *complementary* roles and responsibilities between the genders and whether women's rights need to be explicitly addressed beyond basic human rights issues (Al-Hariri 1987; Saleh 1972). Space does not allow a full consideration of the history of women's rights throughout world religions or the various nuances that might be found within different strands of religious doctrine. As Moghadam (2004) has noted, patriarchy results not only from religion but also from interactions with a number of social, economic, and political issues. However, there has been ongoing tension within the international arena between the codification of women's rights and the right to the freedom of religion (Brandt and Kaplan 1995). Some have argued that "when freedom of religion conflicts with women's rights to equality and the question is which should take precedence, many would intuitively respond that the right to religious freedom should prevail" (Ross 2008, 115). While it is important to consider how key religious leaders have framed women's rights, since this may impact the mission and actions of FBOs, each FBO also has its own identity and may adhere to and support alternative approaches to women's rights than those articulated by these leaders. Thus, this chapter focuses on how human rights groups in our sample frame women's rights and the extent to which religious groups use their faith to justify their actions.

The Declaration of Human Rights by the World's Religions at the 3rd Conference on World's Religions after September 11, which took place on September 15, 2016, demonstrates the complexity of the relationship between religion and human rights, particularly women's rights. The Dalai Lama, Archbishop Desmond Tutu, Madam Shirin Ebadi, Bishop Belo of Timor-Leste, and professor Elie Wiesel, all Nobel Peace Prize laureates and adherents to various world religions, were patrons of the document and generally supportive of the collaborative declaration. Article 16 of the declaration specifically mentions that women have full equality with men and also deals with the issues of violence against women, marriage rights, and motherhood. This declaration demonstrates that at least certain elements within many world religions are increasingly concerned about women's rights (Third Global Conference on World's Religions 2016).

Christianity

Scholars have noted Christianity has an uneven record regarding the treatment of women and that the writings of early church leaders included prejudice against women (Sumner 2003; Rump 2008). Many Protestant denominations are supportive of women in all leadership roles, including as ministers. However, there are also many denominations that do not permit women to hold all leadership positions, with some being more restrictive than others (Christians for Biblical Equality 2007). Currently, some Christian fundamentalists see Western culture as weakening due to the decline of the "traditional family" as the basic unit of society (Ross 2008). In 1995, on the eve of the Fourth World Conference on Women, Pope John Paul II issued a Letter to Women in which he expressed his support for the conference and for the church's desire "to contribute to upholding the dignity, role and rights of women." He uses his letter as an opportunity to speak directly to women about "the problems and prospects of what it means to be a woman in our time" and focuses more specifically on women's dignity and rights in relation to "the word of God." He thanks women for all the roles they play in society (as mothers, wives, daughters, sisters, working women, and consecrated women) and then goes on to recognize some of the church's unfavorable history: "Unfortunately, we are heirs to a history which has *conditioned* us to a remarkable extent. In every time and place, this conditioning has been an obstacle to the progress of women. Women's dignity has often been unacknowledged and their prerogatives misrepresented; they have often been relegated to the margins of society and even reduced to servitude. This has prevented women from truly being themselves and it has resulted in a spiritual impoverishment of humanity" (Pope John Paul II 1995). However, while Pope John Paul II expressed the importance of women and the need for recognition of women's dignity and rights, women's rights activists have criticized church policies, such as the exclusion of women from priesthood. Pope Francis, often noted to be more progressive than many previous popes, has asserted that the Catholic Church will likely continue to ban women from becoming priests (Zauzmer 2016).

The Catholic Church has consistently opposed the use of artificial contraception, an issue many women's rights advocates view as an important part of women's health, on the grounds that the primary purpose of sexual activity is procreation (Pinter et al. 2016). Not surprisingly, the church also staunchly opposes abortion, viewing the practice as a sin, even if the mother's life is in danger. However, Pope Francis did announce in November 2016 that the Roman Catholic Church will allow priests to grant absolution for abortion (Hume 2016). The Eastern Orthodox Church views sexual intercourse as a reflection of marital unity used not only for procreation and thereby allows for contraceptives for birth spacing as well as for love and health. Like in Catholicism, abortion is prohibited, except for cases in which the mother's life is threatened (Pinter et al. 2016). Protestant faiths vary widely in their teachings but overall tend to support the use of contraceptives by married women and tend to consider abortion a sin, except, for most denominations, when the mother's life is threatened. A number of liberal Protestant denominations support the woman's choice to decide in the case of an unwanted pregnancy (Pinter et al. 2016).

Catholic women have been active agents even as Catholic teachings have restricted women's reproductive rights and limited women's ability to become priests or leaders with decision-making authority in the Roman Catholic Church. For example, sisterhoods provide institutions where women's leadership is nurtured and strengthened as the nuns perform good works in society (Hunt 2010). This contrasts with some fundamentalist Christian denominations where women are seen as subservient to men and where women's role at home is ordained by God and oriented toward supporting her husband's work (Alexander 2010, 535). Within Protestantism, teachings and practices regarding the role of women vary widely. Women in the Episcopal church of the United States are able to serve as priests and even bishops, but some Anglican communities in other parts of the world, including Africa, the Middle East, and Southeast Asia, forbid women's ordination. Similarly, Baptist denominations vary on their stance vis-à-vis women's ordination, and while the Presbyterian Church in America does not allow women's ordination, the Presbyterian Church (USA) is highly egalitarian and does (Weatherby 2010).

Islam

Islam is often cited as having incompatibilities with some rights of women as proposed in documents such as the UDHR, although authors have been quick to point out that many of these incompatibilities may lie more with social, cultural, or political circumstances than with Islamic principles. On the other hand, some Muslim-majority countries have suggested these international documents are culturally relative and promote Western ideas (Johnston 2015). Still, some human rights issues specific to women have been more objectionable to Muslim-majority countries, such as Article 16 of the UDHR, which discusses equal rights for spouses in marriage. Islamic law is generally viewed to prohibit women from marrying non-Muslim men, and historically many Islamic countries have not allowed women to initiate divorce. While this doctrine has changed in countries such as Morocco and Tunisia, initiating divorce is often more difficult for women than for men (Johnston 2015).

Other scholars, however, have pointed out that modern human rights doctrine, such as those principles contained in the UDHR, ICCPR, and CEDAW, is not necessarily inconsistent with Islamic law and that with suitable changes Islamic law can conform to these human rights standards for women (Chishti 2012). Like Christianity, Islam varies substantially across countries and legal schools in its interpretation of shari'a, or the religious law of Islam that includes interpretations of the Qur'an and Sunna of the prophet (An-Na'im 2008, 3). Shari'a also informs family law in many Muslim-majority states, which directly affects the rights and status of women. Although several Muslim-majority countries noted reservations to their ratification of CEDAW that are based on shari'a law, notably the argument of ensuring the right to freedom of religion (Brandt and Kaplan 1995), scholars have suggested that the interpretation of shari'a law is shaped by numerous forces, including the colonial history of a country, and is not monolithic (Saleh 1972; Glaze 2018). In fact, often culture (see chapter 2), more than Islam per se, accounts for what many Westerners assume is an antifeminist stance within the religion (Levine and Raghavan 2012).

Islamic tradition calls for a complementary approach to equality, where men and women may have separate and distinct rights but "God commands us to treat women nobly," which includes educating women, albeit in same-gender groupings (Al-Hariri 1987, 52). Some misunderstanding of what Islam says about women's rights stems from a lack of Arabic literacy in Muslim-majority countries, which gives certain religious elites a monopoly over translation and interpretation of religious teachings in a way that may reinforce patriarchal structures (Feldman 2011). Much of the literature on inequality in Islam examines laws surrounding marriage, divorce, and polygamy, topics that, apart from early or forced marriage (see chapter 5), are not often central to the work of human rights organizations, in part due to the personal and religious (as opposed to civil/public) nature of many marriage laws (Nicolau 2014; Feldman 2011; Glaze 2018). However, historical readings of Islamic teachings regarding marriage, divorce, and inheritance demonstrate that at the time Muhammad's teachings brought a complete change of status for women, shifting them from the equivalent of male property to equal footing with men (Balhera and Kumar 2017).

Birth control, particularly framed in terms of birth spacing, has always been accepted within the majority of schools of Islamic law, due in part to the belief within Islam that women have the right to complete sexual fulfillment as well as the importance of ensuring maternal health (Musallam 1981; Pinter et al. 2016). Islam does not completely ban abortion, although the Qur'an emphasizes the principle of the sanctity of life. Further, a variety of legal, religious, and social factors interact in determining the availability of abortion in Muslim-majority countries, including the primacy of the mother's health over that of the fetus as well as the different status of a pregnancy before and after the 120 days postconception mark (Pinter et al. 2016). Differences in religious interpretations account for why abortion is permitted in some Muslim-majority countries but not others, with Tunisia and Turkey, ostensibly the most secular of the Muslim states, having the most permissive laws (Hessini 2007). Further, some argue that birth control and birth spacing within Islam cannot be understood apart from broader concerns governing the protection of human offspring and the quality of family life overall, including a prohibition of killing children out of fear that adding to family size will contribute to poverty, a prohibition on adoption within Islam, and a prohibition on incest (Yunus 2017). Yet some Muslims also argue that precisely because marriage, pregnancy, and childbirth are so highly valued in Islam, it is critical to recognize the flexibility of shari'a in terms of how contraception is viewed (Serour 2013).

In contrast to abortion, which is not as widely discussed, honor-related violence, most often resulting in violence toward women and girls, has emerged as a topic of focus in Muslim-majority states in the past decade. While some honor killings are rooted in culture more than in Islam, there are particular Qur'anic passages used to justify violence toward women (Abbas and Idriss 2011; Wenger and Kashani-Sabet 2015). Further, despite popular assumptions to the contrary, Islam does not endorse female genital mutilation (FGM), and the practice is not mentioned in the Qur'an; instead, it is a cultural practice that predates Islam (Rouzi 2013; Renard 2015).

The question of women's leadership, particularly in the context of religious leadership, is also prominent in many religious traditions. However, despite some male opposition, women's leadership in Islamic religious circles is growing, and women are increasingly serving as religious leaders around the Muslim world (Kalmbach and Bano 2012; Crandall 2011). Despite assumptions to the contrary from non-Muslim audiences, Muslim women serve as leaders in the public sector as well as in the domestic and civil spheres (Feldman 2011). A number of Muslim-majority countries, including Kuwait, Morocco, Tunisia, and Egypt, have gender quotas for elected leadership. Thus, there is nothing in Islam per se that prohibits women from being leaders, and the premise of women's equality in the early teachings of Islam encouraged women's leadership.

Judaism

Judaism, like Christianity and Islam, is diverse in its orientation to scriptural interpretation. Debate continues within Judaism regarding the role of women in religious activities and the role of women's rights vis-à-vis religious freedom. In particular, there is tension between traditional religious views on gender within the Orthodox community and those of secular Jews as well as debates surrounding religious single parents (Rosenberg-Friedman 2018). Some also suggest that religious Jewish women often rank their female identity lower than their religious and national identities (Schwartz and Baumel 2005). Within religious Zionist society, women's role is to be a faithful life partner and not to have a separate public identity in the workforce, for example. Religious Zionist women are expected to prioritize family life by marrying young and having many children (Schwartz and Baumel 2005, 194, 203). Jewish girls were allowed into religious schools only in the nineteenth century, and then for the purpose of becoming better religious wives and mothers (Neil and Joffe 2012). Jewish fundamentalism assumes an inferior position for the woman in marriage. This results in a series of practices including gender segregation and restrictions on women's public conduct (Radford 2000). There is a tradition of honor killings in Judaism as well, particularly when women's alleged misconduct violates communal norms of virtue (Wenter and Kashani-Sabet 2015).

Abortion is generally forbidden in Judaism and considered a form of murder (Nadler 2006, 46). The Torah emphasizes the importance of procreation as well as that pregnancy cannot be taken for granted, both teachings that run contrary to abortion (Schiff 2002). For this reason, contraception is considered an option for Orthodox Jewish couples only for medical reasons, notably when pregnancy could seriously harm the woman, and particular types of contraception are prohibited entirely, given biblical commandments including not spilling a man's seed (Barilan 2009; Pinter et al. 2016, 489).

Violence against women is generally condemned in Judaism and even seen as grounds for divorce (DaDon 2018). Women's leadership, however, remains constrained in Orthodox circles, and some rabbis have completely rejected the possibility of women as religious leaders (Feldman 2011). However, women serve as rabbis in the Reform and Conservative traditions (Weatherby 2010), a tension that has played out controversially with Israeli officials prohibiting female rabbis from praying at the Western Wall in Jerusalem due to the Orthodox monopoly over religious affairs in Israel.

Other Faith Traditions

Religious fundamentalism often limits the rights of women using "pro-family" rhetoric, not only in Christianity, Judaism, and Islam, but also in Hinduism, Sikhism, and Buddhism (Sjoberg 2011; Tanyag 2017). Some so-called new religions in Japan, which often follow a charismatic leader and blend elements of different religious traditions, seek to bring back the model of the patriarchal family life, and some Hindu fundamentalists are prone to treat women as property (Ross 2008). Hinduism has also been criticized for its treatment of women, particularly in relation to marriage, as women are not afforded an identity separate from their husbands (Weatherby 2010). Further, some of the eight different types of marriage within Hinduism consider women like property (Sharma 2010). At the same time, however, the Hindu God has both female and male aspects, which gives women supreme power in the divine and mythological realm (Weatherby 2010). Hinduism is a very pluralistic religion, and individuals have freedom in how they worship, although individuals are held accountable for their actions through the concepts of karma and reincarnation. Within Hinduism sex and sexuality are viewed as important for pleasure as well as procreation, and in contrast to other faith traditions, no forms of contraception are proscribed. Abortion is condemned since conception is seen as a divine act; however, there is some flexibility within Hinduism if a moral case can be made based on the possibility of greater harm to the mother or family (Pinter et al. 2016, 493).

The doctrines of some religions, such as Buddhism and Baha'i, appear consistent with ideas of women's rights and equality. Buddhism, for example, accepts a female monastic order and unequivocally affirms the intellectual and spiritual equality of men and women. Still, some have pointed to the patriar-chal elements of the religion (Sirimanne 2016). Further, some of the histor-ical texts suggest than only men can achieve the highest levels of enlighten-ment (Weatherby 2010). A representative from Baha'i International suggested that the faith does not really see the human soul as having a sex, and thus there should not really be any difference between men and women because gender is just a temporary difference on this planet.

LGBTQI Rights in Religious Traditions

Conservative political (and religious) forces often equate advocacy for wom-en's rights and LGBTQI rights with "Western interference" (Acharya et al. 2017, 20; Feldman 2011). However, anti-LGBTQI sentiment continues in the so-called Western world as well. In the United States, for example, two hun-dred anti-LGBTQI bills were introduced in thirty-four states in 2015 and 2016, many of which used religion as a justification for refusing goods or services to LGBTQI people (Henneberg 2016, 15).

CHRISTIANITY

Historically the church has "regarded homosexuality as morally wrong" (Sub-hi and Geelan 2012, 183). However, some Christians and Christian denomina-tions, including the Quakers and the United Church of Christ, adopt more lib-eral readings of scripture, "moving toward a nonjudgmental platform" based on the lack of discussion of homosexuality by Jesus and the biblical mandate not to judge (McAuliffe 2015, 70, 75). Generally speaking, however, conserva-tive and fundamentalist Christians hold a negative view of homosexuality, al-though such views are sometimes discussed in terms such as advocating for "family rights" where the family is strictly defined as a union between one man and one woman rather than speaking against LGBTQI rights. Religious views on homosexuality are not uniform across countries and cultures, however. For example, studies show Catholics in Poland are more hostile toward homosexu-als than are those in the United States (Izienicki 2017). Some research has sug-gested that within South Korea, Protestants were consistently less supportive of homosexuals as compared to Catholics, Buddhists, and the nonreligious, thereby suggesting a possible intersection between culture and religion (Rich 2017).

ISLAM

While the literature agrees that many Muslim-majority states condemn and even criminalize homosexuality, there is disagreement regarding the extent to which homosexuality is explicitly banned in the Qur'an versus other religious teachings, such as the *hadith* and *fiqh* (Kligerman 2007; Kugle 2010). "For many Muslims, dealing with homosexuality or transgender issues is a matter of sin and heresy, not difference and diversity" (Kugle 2010, preface). However, whereas Kligerman (2007) argues the Qur'an explicitly condemns homosexuality, Kugle (2010) asserts that this is only in cases where homosexuality is exploitative or violent, and thus the condemnation is on par with other acts of sexual violence. Further, as is the case with gender relations more broadly, Kugle notes that often it is misogynist and homophobic culture, rather than religious tradition, that contributes to stigmatization of homosexuality, while Kligerman observes that Western influence has contributed to the social stigma against homosexuality in the Muslim world. Gilad (2016), for instance, asserts that homosexuality was tolerated in the Arab world prior to European rule despite the explicit ban in the Qur'an.

JUDAISM

Within Orthodox Judaism homosexuality is condemned, and the homosexual is viewed as a sinner (Kahn 1989, 47). Academic literature on the topic is scant, but elsewhere discussion of the history of homosexuality in Judaism has been shown to be more complicated, such as the practice of male and female sacred prostitutes in the First Temple Period as well as other verses suggesting homosexual intercourse among the men of ancient Judah (Gilad 2016). Sodomy laws in Israel were not strictly enforced even as homosexuality remained illegal until 1988; the first gay synagogue in the world was created in 1972 in Los Angeles. The Reform movement officially accepted homosexuals in 1990, the Conservative movement in 2006; Orthodox Judaism still views homosexuality as a sin (Gilad 2016). A number of Jewish organizations, including Hinenini, JQ Youth, and Keshet (all based in the United States), advocate for and support LGBTQI Jews in Jewish life.

OTHER FAITH TRADITIONS

There is not much academic literature on LGBTQI rights in other faith traditions. Hindu views are diverse with individual ashrams sometimes varying in their views, although Hindu sacred texts do not differentiate between heterosexual and homosexual acts (Human Rights Campaign n.d.-a). Buddhism also has a range of views across its different types, with Theravada Buddhism emphasizing the monastic tradition and Zen Buddhists focusing on the lack of harm or exploitation in sexual relations regardless of whether they are same sex or opposite sex (Human Rights Campaign 2018). What literature exists on LGBTQI rights in the Hindu and Buddhist majority states tends to focus on culture and secular laws rather than religious teachings per se. Ancient Hindu texts include stories of lesbian lovemaking and are inclusive of homosexual and third sex individuals. However, during the Mughal and British periods, homosexuality was punished severely in what is now India. Although India is a secular state and thus its laws are not directly rooted in religion, it was only in 2009 that a Delhi high court declared same-sex, private, consensual acts to be legal (Bhattacharya 2016). There is a thriving queer culture in Thailand, but this is discussed in terms of cultural and transnational movements (Jackson 2011). Similarly, research suggests that China, which is officially without religion but has Confucian and other traditional religious views, is largely hostile to queerness (Miller 2016).

Secular Approaches to Women's and LGBTQI Rights

At times it is difficult to fully separate religious and secular approaches to human rights and/or distinguish where the religious ends and secular begins. The issue of wearing headscarves and burkinis in countries like France is one such example where secular laws impede upon the rights of religious women to choose their own clothing (Johnston 2015). In states where religious law is partially or fully integrated with civil law, the government may be relatively weak vis-à-vis the religious establishment, which may undermine state support for women's rights as citizens. To further compound this, both shari'a (Islamic law) and halakha (Jewish law) are seen as frameworks for political rule in addition to bodies of religious law (Feldman 2011, 13). The 2004 revisions to the Moroccan family code, or *moudawana*, for example, reflect a compromise between the demands of the largely secular women's movements pushing for the reforms and the religious party seen as a potential threat to the king's rule and thus did not go as far as desired by activists (Hallward and Stewart 2018). However, this tension also raises the question of how to allow women to be free to choose the religious rules they abide by, particularly when they are religious individuals living in a secular state with very different social customs than their own (Mullally 2005; De Kroon 2016).

Most countries around the world have a variety of women's organizations struggling for a wide array of women's rights, from specific concerns such as reproductive rights to broader socioeconomic issues including improving women's economic status or accessing water and health care (Ross 2008). From a more secular perspective, reproductive rights are seen in the context of women's rights to control their own autonomy and to reinforce women's ability to build their capacities. From a human development and capabilities approach, women's control over their reproductive autonomy impacts their freedom as well as their economic development (Gómez-Dávila 2018). Women's rights groups—both secular and religious—point to the impact of women's lack of access to contraception, including sexually transmitted infections and induced and unsafe abortions, on women's health (Serour 2013). A number of countries around the world have reformed laws to be more accepting of abortion when it relates to the health and lives of women, particularly in response to the consequences of unsafe abortion (Ngwena 2010, 815). The question of reproductive rights is complex in many ways, not only between religious and secular groups but also because it is intertwined with issues of racism and population control; white women have often dominated the movement for reproductive rights, and at times such movements have had racist overtones (Silliman et al. 2016).

Combatting gender-based violence has been of increasing concern for human rights organizations and is targeted in CEDAW (Paludi 2010). Gender-based violence is evident domestically as well as in community and international settings, as women are targeted for rape and other forms of sexual assault in wartime (Walters 2011; Sjoberg 2011). CEDAW has sought to combat gender-based violence in part by targeting practices that describe women's roles as inferior to men and by creating opportunities for women's roles to be respected and valued (Hellum and Aasen 2013). The Beijing Declaration and Platform for Action also speaks extensively of the role of women in power and decision making as a mechanism for improving the status of women, thereby making women's leadership a key goal of many organizations (UN 2014). Struggles against gender-based violence take many forms, from state-level quotas for elected officials to grassroots activism by women's civil society groups around the world aimed at targeting gender-based violence and changing society's views of women (Cosgrove and Lee 2015).

Much LGBTQI activism has been done through a secular framework, particularly through the universalist-oriented human rights networks of Amnesty International (Linde 2018). The Western/universal approach has proven limiting for LGBTQI activists in other contexts, such as Russia, where the minority rights framework is not as salient (Rivkin-Fish and Hartblay 2014). Attacks on LGBTQI rights stem from secular as well as religious sources. Thirty-six African states, for example, have laws that criminalize same-sex sexual acts, and homosexuals achieved rights under the European Convention on Human Rights only in 1953 (Johnson 2013). However, despite this convention, some European states continued to legislate against homosexual acts, even when they were consensual and private (Johnson 2013, 252). Nearly two-thirds of LGBTQI Americans have also experienced some kind of discrimination, even after the landmark 2015 Supreme Court ruling concerning the right to same-sex marriage (Henneberg 2016, 14). The secular literature suggests that perhaps culture (see chapter 2) as much as religion impacts views on LGBTQI rights in various parts of the world (Lee and Ostergard 2017).

Hypotheses

Based on the literature, we offer specific hypotheses regarding the differences between religious and secular approaches to women's and LGBTQI rights. In general, we anticipate that religious organizations will be less likely than secular groups to discuss a myriad of women's issues since they are often considered controversial within and among many faiths. Specifically, we examine the following hypotheses:

1. Secular organizations will be more likely than religious groups to have specific sections on their websites dedicated to women and/or women's rights.
2. Religious organizations will be less likely to support and more likely to oppose reproductive rights, including abortion and family planning, than secular organizations.
3. Muslim organizations will be more likely than other religious organizations to support reproductive rights.
4. Religious organizations will be less likely to promote LGBTQI rights and more likely to actively oppose these rights than secular organizations.
5. Muslim organizations will be less likely than other religious organizations to discuss LGBTQI rights.
6. Secular organizations will be more likely than religious groups to discuss CEDAW on their websites.
7. Secular organizations will be more likely than religious groups to support women's training and women's leadership.
8. Secular and religious organizations will be equally likely to discuss gender-based violence.
9. Organizations in the Global North and the West will be more likely than those in the Global South and non-West to support reproductive rights, including abortion and family planning.
10. Women's organizations will be more likely than non–women's organizations to support reproductive rights, including abortion and family planning.

Findings

Despite expectations to the contrary, the differences between how religious and secular organizations approached gender on the items coded in the dataset are generally not great enough to meet the threshold for significance using chi-square tests. While there are multiple reasons that could explain this lack of significant difference, one factor might be the lower number of FBOs, which is simply part of the global organizational landscape. Of the 333 organizations coded in the dataset, 68 are FBOs and 265 are secular.

Extent of Specific Attention to Gender Concerns

Despite, or perhaps because of, the international efforts to mainstream gender sensitivity into programming, fewer than half of the organizations examined have a section specifically devoted to gender and/or women on their websites. Secular organizations have a slightly higher percentage of gender-specific sections (42 percent) than do FBOs (38 percent). FBOs varied by religion, with 35 percent of Christian organizations, 29 percent of Muslim organizations, 25 percent of Jewish organizations, and 67 percent of other religious organizations having a stand-alone section on gender and/or women. Thus, while overall there is little difference between the religious and secular organizations in terms of percentage with stand-alone sections focusing on gender and/or women's issues, the numbers do seem to indicate variance within the category of FBOs, although the number of organizations is too small to determine significance. In particular, Jewish and Muslim organizations seem least likely to have a gender-specific section, while non-Abrahamic and/or multifaith organizations seem most likely to have one. More research is needed to explore why this may be the case, but the historically patriarchal nature of the Abrahamic faith traditions could be one component.

The probability of patriarchal tendencies explaining the difference between the number of gender-specific sections on the websites of FBOs is further supported by the difference between the percentage of women's organizations with gender and/or women's sections, 77 percent (24 out of 31), compared with the percentage of non–women's organizations, 37 percent. This difference is significant at the $p < .001$ level, indicating a difference perhaps because women control the agenda in women's organizations. Many of these women's organizations have mandates that include issues facing the population at large, not only those concerning women and girls, yet they also include a special focus on gender issues specifically in addition to their broader mandate. Overall 13 percent of religious groups were women's organizations, compared with 8 percent of secular organizations. This variance, while not statistically significant, may reflect the fact that some religions separate male and female, taking a complementary approach to gender equality, as is prevalent in Catholicism, for example, where a number of groups are run by Catholic sisters.

CEDAW

As noted earlier in this chapter, CEDAW is the most comprehensive international treaty on women's rights, signed, albeit occasionally with reservations, by most countries in the world. Despite this, very few organizations in our sample mention CEDAW: 9 percent of religious organizations and 8 percent of

secular ones. While there does not appear to be much difference between secular and religious organizations more generally, all six of the religious organizations that mention CEDAW are Christian, indicating some interreligious
and perhaps cultural differences in support for CEDAW. This is not particularly surprising given that CEDAW specifically targets culture and tradition as
potentially problematic for women's rights.

When focusing on women's organizations, 32 percent mention CEDAW on
their website, in contrast to 6 percent of non–women's organizations. This difference is statistically significant at the $p < .001$ level, demonstrating that wom-
en's organizations are much more likely to emphasize CEDAW. This may be
due to the fact that CEDAW is a more distinct reference point for those working on women-specific rights-based activities, or it could also be that women's
organizations are more likely than other organizations to take the more radi-
cally feminist approach of CEDAW, which may be more reluctant to sign on to
some of the provisions in CEDAW that are seen as more contentious, such as
the affirmation of women's reproductive rights and the targeting of culture and
tradition as forces shaping gender roles.

The qualitative data reflect similar trends to the quantitative data, with
very few of the interviewees mentioning CEDAW. In fact, only one interview
subject, from WILPF, discussed CEDAW in the course of the interview, and
the interview guide included a question specifically asking interviewees about
their organization's work in terms of women's rights. A women's organization,
WILPF discussed their work with the CEDAW committee and the "excellent
relationships" they have with their members.

A few additional organizations mentioned CEDAW on their websites.
The Global Initiative for Economic, Social, and Cultural Rights is one of these,
and Adalah: The Legal Center for Minority Rights in Israel is another, suggesting a link between a focus on social and cultural rights and CEDAW-
related advocacy for non–women's groups. On the whole, however, CEDAW
was rarely mentioned on organizational websites, suggesting that the treaty
does not have a great deal of legitimizing power discursively in the field or that
sufficient numbers of countries either have reservations or have not signed
(e.g., the United States) or that women's rights efforts are deemed more effective in the absence of mention of CEDAW. Additional research is needed to answer these questions.

Women's Training and Leadership

Our expectation that secular organizations would be more likely than religious
groups to focus on women's training and leadership was not substantiated by
the dataset (see Table 4.1). In fact, a higher proportion of religious (25 percent)
than secular organizations (18 percent) discussed women's training or lead-

TABLE 4.1

Efforts on Gender Violence and Women's Leadership (in percentages)

	Women's training and leadership	Gender-based violence work
Religious organizations	25	22
Secular organizations	18	29
Women's organizations	65	68
Non–women's organizations	17	24
Organizations with women's section	43	57
Organizations without women's section	3	8

ership, and different religions appeared similarly likely to consider the issue. However, this difference is not statistically significant. Women's organizations, however, displayed a much greater focus on women's training and leadership (65 percent). Of the women's groups, 78 percent of the secular ones focused on women's training and leadership while 33 percent of the religious ones did, thereby suggesting this was not a factor of religious women's orders alone, with secular women's organizations actually being more likely than religious women's groups to focus on this topic. The groups with a women's section displayed a higher than average percentage focusing on women's training and leadership, at 43 percent of the total organizations with women's sections. In contrast, only 3 percent of the organizations without a woman's section discuss women's training and leadership. This finding, significant at the $p < .001$ level, suggests that gender mainstreaming efforts absent dedicated individuals and programmatic sections simultaneously and specifically focusing on gender concerns may have limited impact regarding gender equality.

Many of the organizations interviewed highlighted training and empowerment efforts related to women's rights and leadership. Le Réseau des Éducateurs, aux Droits de l'Homme, à la Démocratie et Genre (REDHG), for example, shared that they integrate efforts to promote and protect these three issues in combination. Graduate Women International sponsored teacher trainings for women to increase the number of women teachers, a factor in whether or not girls attend school. The organization also provided sponsorships to help train refugee women to enter the workforce. Organizations from a range of geographical locations discussed their efforts to target women directly, such as through the women's empowerment program run by BADIL in Palestine or the efforts of the Informal Sector Service Center (INSEC) in Nepal to push for a quota for women at various levels of government. Interestingly, these illustrative examples highlight the importance of dedicated programs focused on advancing gender equality; Graduate Women International is a women's organization, REDHG has an explicit gender focus, BADIL created a specific women's empowerment program when they realized through an internal audit that this need was not being met, and INSEC pushed for a dedicated quota of seats for women to ensure that their voices were heard. The lack of discussion of women's training and leadership from other groups where gender efforts were more mainstreamed highlights the importance of dedicating efforts to women's leadership.

Gender-Based Violence

A substantial portion of both types of organizations—22 percent of religious and 29 percent of secular—had a focus on gender-based violence (see Table 4.1). While secular and religious organizations were not substantially different in whether they considered gender-based violence, there were some differences between different types of religious groups, with Muslim and Jewish organizations the most likely to discuss gender-based violence on their websites. Around 19 percent of Christian, 43 percent of Muslim, 50 percent of Jewish, and only 11 percent of other religious organizations discuss gender-based violence. While the sample size is too small for these differences to be statistically significant, there does appear to be a difference in approach and discussion of gender-based violence among religious organizations. More research is needed to investigate this difference, but one possible explanation may be the existence of honor killings within both Islam and Judaism, an issue of concern to human rights organizations, as well as the fact that many contemporary armed conflicts are in regions of the world with Muslim and Jewish populations, and therefore gender-based violence, often highly correlated with wartime, may be of higher overt concern.

While there is no statistically significant difference between religious and secular groups in terms of a focus on gender violence, there are statistically significant differences between the percentages of women's organizations (68 percent) and general organizations (24 percent) working on gender violence and between those groups with a dedicated women's section (57 percent) compared to those without (8 percent) working on gender violence. This finding, which is similar to the findings regarding women's leadership and training previously discussed, suggests that having a dedicated focus on gender issues matters more than whether a group is religious or secular in orientation when it comes to gender violence. However, when looking specifically at the women's organizations, 82 percent (18 of 22) of the secular women's organizations focus on the issue of gender violence, compared to 33 percent (3 of 9) of religious women's organizations. This finding is statistically significant at the $p < .01$ level. Thus, religion does seem to play a significant factor when comparing women's organizations, with religious women's organizations being significantly less likely than secular ones to consider gender violence.

Gender violence was mentioned explicitly by eighteen of the organizations we interviewed. At times, organizational efforts to address gender violence were linked rhetorically to capacity building and training efforts either of women or of institutional actors such as police or Civil Society Organization members, as was the case for the Commonwealth Human Rights Initiative and the Lebanese Center for Human Rights. In discussing violence against women, those interviewed primarily mentioned direct violence, including sexual violence, child marriage, and honor killings. However, some organizations, such as the Comisión Jurídica Para el Autodesarrollo de los Pueblos Originarios Andinos and Djazairouna, also identified structural forms of violence against women, notably the need for women's socioeconomic empowerment in order to improve women's conditions and for women's nutritional and water needs.

A similar array of issues related to gender-based violence was mentioned by both religious and secular organizations interviewed. Islamic Relief, for example, noted they have "done some work with FGM in Sudan" and would like to do more work on "FGM, domestic violence, and early enforced marriage." This list is not significantly different from that of the secular Femmes Développment et Droits Humains en Guinée in Guinea, which stated that they "focus on women's rights, the struggle against violence against women, especially sexual violence and child marriage." However, some religious organizations also expressed hesitation regarding the sensitivity of issues surrounding gender-based violence. As noted by Dominicans for Justice and Peace, a Catholic order, such topics raise "big theological questions" and "gender and sexual related issues, which of course there's a big debate around even within the church, they are very delicate questions." Mazlumder, a Muslim group, also noted the challenges of furthering women's rights and the need to create special institutional structures to allow such work to continue unimpeded by elements within the organization who were more conservative when it came to women's issues than with other human rights topics.

Sampled organizational websites reflected similar themes, apart from a lack of discussion on the sensitivity of gender violence. For example, Arigatou International's website notes the connection between poverty and gender-based violence, reflecting the connection between gender violence and structural violence. Al Hakim Foundation's website points to the religious obligation to dignify and honor women and to fight against gender-based violence.

Abortion and Reproductive Rights

The assumption that reproductive rights remain contentious is affirmed by the data on abortion and reproductive rights found in our sample (see Table 4.2). Among the religious organizations, only 12 percent mentioned abortion, and all of these opposed it. Only 5 percent of secular organizations supported the

TABLE 4.2

Approaches to Reproductive Rights (in percentages)

	Support abortion rights	Oppose abortion rights	Support family planning rights	Oppose family planning rights
Religious organizations	0	12	3	4
Secular organizations	5	1	8	0
Women's only organizations	6	6	13	0
Organizations with women's section	7	2	15	1
Organizations without a women's section	2	4	2	<1

right to have an abortion, and around 1 percent opposed it. Although it is clear that more secular than religious organizations support abortion rights, this difference is not quite significant, although the differences in opposition to abortion rights are significant the $p < .001$ level, with religious groups much more likely than secular groups to oppose abortion rights.

Women's groups are not much more likely to focus on abortion, with only 13 percent even mentioning abortion (only four organizations). Of these, half support abortion rights and half—both religious—oppose them, thereby indicating an even divide among the women's groups in terms of abortion rights and a clear distinction between religious and secular women's groups. A similar pattern was found for groups with a women's section, with 91 percent of the organizations not mentioning abortion at all and only 7 percent of those with a women's-only section supporting abortion rights, in contrast to 2 percent opposing abortion rights. While organizations with a women's section are slightly more likely than those without a women's section to support abortion rights, a finding significant at the $p < .01$ level, on the whole abortion is rarely discussed on websites in our sample. Further, with the exception of one organization in the Global South (1 of 100), the overwhelming majority of the groups supporting abortion rights are based in the Global North (11 of 243), as are all of the organizations opposing abortion (11 of 243). Similarly, all of the organizations discussing abortion are based in the West. This reflects divides in global women's movements regarding issues of concern to different constituencies highlighted at the Beijing Conference and beyond, as women in the Global South were less likely to focus on reproductive rights and more likely to emphasize broader patterns of social, economic, and political inequity.

TEXTBOX 4.1

Comparisons of Reproductive Rights

Family Health International

FHI360 envisions a world in which all individuals and communities have the opportunity to reach their highest potential. FHI360's discussion of family planning is located in their section on Maternal and Child Health: Gender and thus is not distinctly focused on reproductive rights; sexuality is not mentioned. FHI360 notes, "When women can decide how many children to have and when, they are better able to maintain their health and provide for their families. Our programs encourage healthy birth spacing and empower couples to make shared and informed decisions about family size and contraception." One of their current projects in sub-Saharan Africa seeks to control the HIV epidemic and integrate family planning through integrated approaches at the health facility level, working with the government of Tanzania, international donors, and local civil society partners.

FHI 360. 2020. "Maternal and Child Health: Gender." https://www.fhi360.org/expertise/maternal-and
    -child-health-gender.
FHI 360. 2020. "USAID Boresha Afya Southern Zone." https://www.fhi360.org/projects/usaid-boresha
    -afya-southern-zone.

World Council of Churches

The World Council of Churches (WCC) is the only general religious organization in the dataset that overtly promotes family planning rights on their website. Their work is explicitly grounded in Christian teaching and theology, and one of their four aims is to "engage in Christian service by serving human need, breaking down barriers between people, seeking justice and peace, and upholding the integrity of creation." To this end, the WCC explicitly advocates for building a just community of women and men and is committed to supporting women's sexual and reproductive health and rights. The WCC cohosted a UN symposium titled "Keeping the Faith in Development: Gender, Religion and Health" that included a focus on the WCC-published "Dignity Freedom and Grace: Christian Perspectives on HIV, AIDS and Human Rights," which includes a discussion of reproductive rights for women and girls.

Gillian Paterson and Callie Long, eds. 2016. "Dignity, Freedom, and Grace." World Council of Churches. https://
    www.oikoumene.org/en/resources/publications/DignityFreedomandGracesample.pdf.
World Council of Churches. 2020. "Programme for Women in Church and Society." https://www.oikoumene
    .org/en/what-we-do/women-and-men/history/women-in-wcc-history.
World Council of Churches. 2020. "What Is the World Council of Churches?" https://www.oikoumene.org/en
    /about-us.

None of the organizations we interviewed discussed abortion rights when asked about their work with women's rights, and only one organization mentioned abortion at all, in the context of their ability to criticize extreme anti-abortion groups. The British Humanist organization noted that their unique position of being not really secular and not really religious allowed them the space to "be that critic" of "the smaller religious groups that are misbehaving" in terms of extreme positions vis-à-vis antiabortion activism. While not mentioning abortion explicitly, T'ruah, a US-based rabbinical association for hu-

TEXTBOX 4.2

Women's Organizations and Reproductive Rights

Plan International

Plan International is a development and humanitarian organization focusing on children's rights and equality for girls. It is one of four women's organizations in our sample that supports reproductive rights. In their section on sexual health and rights, they declare, "Gender equality and discrimination against girls mean they are often robbed of the right to make their own life decisions—from what happens to their bodies, to when and to whom they marry. Teenage pregnancy can rob girls of their potential by ceasing their education and giving them adult responsibilities. . . . Ensuring girls and young women realise their right to sexual and reproductive health and have control over their lives and bodies are critical to achieving gender equality." To address these goals, Plan International works with civil society groups to help young people access youth-friendly health services, correct reproductive health information, and modern contraceptives, among other services.

PLAN International. n.d. "Sexual Health and Rights." https://plan-international.org/sexual-health.

World YWCA

The World YWCA is a global women's rights movement that works across faith, culture, and region. They believe that when women rise to leadership they transform power structures and policies around human rights, gender equality, peace, and justice. Excerpts from their "Sexual and Reproductive Health and Rights" fact sheet include the following: "Access to information on sexual and reproductive health, rights and services enables women and young women to make decisions about their bodies and claim their rights. Every human being has a fundamental right to access the highest attainable standard of health. . . . Through its training programmes, [the World YWCA] equips young women and girls with the knowledge, skills, attitudes and values they need to determine and enjoy their sexuality. The World YWCA views sexuality holistically and within the context of emotional and social development."

World YWCA. 2016. "Sexual and Reproductive Health and Rights." https://www.worldywca.org/sexual-and
    -reproductive-health-and-rights-srhr-fact-sheet/.
World YWCA. n.d. "Our Work." https://www.worldywca.org/our-priorities/.

man rights, noted that they have leeway to sign on to human rights statements dealing with "the war on reproductive rights . . . because they're so important to who we are as an organization."

Similar to the data regarding abortion rights, few organizations in our sample discuss reproductive rights in terms of contraception and family planning. However, in contrast, 3 percent of religious organizations and 8 percent of secular organizations express support for family planning rights. Around 4 percent of religious organizations explicitly oppose such rights, whereas no secular organizations do. Overall, the differences between religious and secular organizations are slight in this regard and do not reach statistical significance. Of the women's groups, 13 percent support family planning and none oppose it. Looking at organizations with a stand-alone women's section, 15 percent support family planning, in contrast to 2 percent of organizations with-out a women's section, significant at the $p < .001$ level. Opposition to family planning is relatively consistent across those groups, suggesting limited differ-ence in this regard. As seen in Table 4.2, there appears to be a significant dif-ference in treatment of reproductive rights issues, including abortion, among those groups that have a special focus on gender and women's rights, both at the level of a stand-alone section and in terms of women's groups. This differ-ence between groups with and without dedicated women's sections reflects ear-lier patterns identified in this chapter. It also suggests that gender mainstream-ing efforts (absent dedicated staff members to focus on gender concerns) may result in pushing aside more controversial issues, such as reproductive rights.

When breaking down the data in terms of Global North and Global South, 4 percent of the organizations in the Global South support the right to fami-ly planning and/or contraception and none oppose, indicating that this issue is not pivotal in the Global South. In contrast, 8 percent in the Global North support rights to family planning and/or contraception and 1 percent oppose. Thus, while all of the organizations opposing family planning are found in the Global North, the differences between South and North are not statistically sig-nificant. Likewise, most of the organizations discussing rights for family plan-ning and/or contraception are based in the West, with 9 percent supporting these rights and 1 percent opposing. Out of the non-Western organizations in the sample, 2 percent support the right to family planning and/or contracep-tion. The difference between Western and non-Western organizations in terms of support for the right to family planning and/or contraception is statistically significant at the $p < .05$ level, but overall it seems that family planning rights are not an important issue for organizations based outside of the West and are of limited importance even for those groups based in the West.

Several of the groups that do mention reproductive rights on their web-sites have mandates that focus specifically on this issue, such as the Center for Reproductive Rights, whose mission includes creating a world "where every woman is free to decide whether or when to have children and whether to get married; where access to quality reproductive health care is guaranteed." So-roptimist, a secular group focused on women and girls specifically, does men-tion reproductive rights, but does so specifically in the context of population growth and climate change rather than in the abstract sense of women's rights over their bodies. Their website states, "Much of the population growth will be in developing countries where reproductive rights are sorely lacking, which also happen to be areas that are highly vulnerable to climate change. An un-stable climate coupled with a lack of reproductive rights threatens future gen-erations and puts countless lives at stake." Other organizations, such as Plan International, the Human Rights Law Centre, and Amnesty International, con-nect their reproductive health advocacy to issues such as gender-based violence, including practices like virginity testing and FGM. Such linkage suggests that perhaps support for reproductive rights is not as strong as that for gender-based violence more broadly, and thus activists link issues as a way of providing additional legitimation and support for their work in these areas. In contrast, FIDH does not link their support of abortion rights explicitly to child marriage or gender-based violence, although on their website they do mention that the prohibition of abortion can have "violent and sometimes deadly" consequences. While FIDH lists violence against women as a key issue area, it is not discursively linked to abortion the way it is in other cases.

LGBTQI Rights

Overall, LGBTQI and abortion rights were mentioned the least of any gender-related topics surveyed in the dataset, affirming the assumption that they are deemed more controversial for religious and secular organizations alike and suggesting that even if organizations support work on these issues, they do not publicly broadcast it on their websites. The vast majority of FBOs—88 percent—made no mention of LGBTQI concerns on their websites. As shown in Table 4.3, 9 percent of religious organizations openly discussed support of LGBTQI rights and 3 percent of the religious organizations openly opposed LGBTQI rights. Of the FBOs supporting LGBTQI rights, three were Christian, two were Jewish, and one (International Fellowship of Reconciliation) was originally Christian but is now open to all faiths. Both of the organizations opposed to LGBTQI rights are Christian. No Muslim organizations in our sample mentioned LGBTQI rights, which is consistent with our expectations. This finding suggests that most FBOs do not broach this topic publicly, likely due to its controversial nature or due to internal divisions within the faith community that may prevent them from reaching a common position on the topic.[3] Further, given that this research is based on what organizations choose to showcase on their website, the mere absence of the mention of a topic does not mean that the entity does not have a position one way or another on the issue.

The majority of secular organizations, 82 percent, also do not discuss LGBTQI rights on their websites, and only 17 percent openly support LGBTQI rights; less than 1 percent of the secular organizations oppose LGBTQI rights. While a larger percentage of secular organizations support these rights as compared to religious organizations, the difference is not statistically significant. However, the findings do suggest that even among the FBOs, very few human rights organizations openly oppose LGBTQI rights.

When comparing the general population of organizations to women's organizations, we do not see statistically significant differences, in contrast to the results for gender violence and women's training and leadership. Notably, the vast majority of women's organizations do not mention LGBTQI rights. A

TABLE 4.3

LGBTQI Rights (in percentages)

	Support LGBTQI rights	Oppose LGBTQI rights
Religious groups	9	3
Secular groups	17	<1
Women's organizations	6	3
Non–women's organizations	16	2
Groups with women's section	25	<1
Groups without women's section	8	2

small portion—6 percent—of the women's organizations openly support these rights, which is comparable to that of religious groups, but lower than that of secular groups. Opposition to LGBTQI rights among women's organizations is 3 percent, which is higher than the opposition of secular groups and comparable to the opposition of religious organizations. Notably, the one women's organization opposed to LGBTQI rights is the Worldwide Organization for Women, a Christian organization. Considering groups with a women's section, however, tells a different story. Of these groups, 74 percent do not mention LGBTQI issues at all, as compared to 90 percent of groups without a women's section. Further, 25 percent of the groups with a women's section support LGBTQI rights, in contrast to only 8 percent of groups without such sections, and these differences are significant at the $p < .001$ level. Only one organization with a women's section—the secular Institute for Family Policy—opposes LGBTQI rights, in contrast with 2 percent of organizations without a women's section.

These data suggest that organizations with a dedicated section on women or gender pay more attention to LGBTQI issues, although women's organizations do not illustrate this same pattern. Instead, women's organizations follow the pattern of religious organizations, with roughly comparable percentages supporting and opposing LGBTQI rights. This may be due to the fact that a higher percentage of religious organizations—13 percent—are also women's organizations, as compared to 8 percent of secular organizations, and that 29 percent of women's organizations in the sample are religious, as compared to 20 percent of the non–women's organizations. In contrast, the percentage of religious organizations with a women's section—38 percent—is slightly lower than the 42 percent of secular organizations with a women's section. The relative overrepresentation of religious women's organizations may account for the difference in views between women's organizations and organizations with a women's section and likely stems from the separation of genders found in some religious traditions, such as the Catholic sisterhoods and some Muslim women's organizations found in our sample.

Religion alone may not explain variance in views on LGBTQI issues. Given that views toward LGBTQI rights can be mediated by socioeconomic and cultural factors in addition to religion, we examine how support for LGBTQI rights differs between organizations based in the Global North and the Global South. Although 196 of 243 organizations in the Global North do not mention LGBTQI rights, 18 percent of the organizations support LGBTQI rights, in contrast to 2 percent that oppose them. Only 9 percent of organizations based in the Global South support LGBTQI rights, with none openly opposing them; 91 percent of these organizations do not mention LGBTQI rights at all. This variance between Global North and Global South is statistically significant at the $p < .05$ level; the possible reasons for this difference are discussed in the next section. Similarly, organizations based in the West display different views toward LGBTQI rights than non-Western organizations, with 18 percent of the Western-based organizations supporting LGBTQI rights in contrast to 7 percent of the non-Western organizations, and this difference is significant at the $p < .01$ level. Further, 2 percent of organizations based in the West oppose LGBTQI rights, in contrast to none of the non-Western organizations. The fact that all of the organizations that oppose LGBTQI rights are also in the West may simply suggest that LGBTQI concerns are more publicly discussed in the West and/or that LGBTQI movements are more developed and/or have different aims in those countries.

Around 15 percent of the organizations interviewed explicitly discussed work with the LGBTQI community during their interviews, including religious and secular organizations as well as groups from the Global North and Global South and from the West and outside the West. The Commonwealth Human Rights Initiative, headquartered in India, for example, mentioned a new program on antidiscrimination on the grounds of sexual orientation, and the Lebanese Center for Human Rights also noted that LGBTQI rights is a main focus of their work. A few religious organizations, including T'ruah and Soka Gakkai, noted their active support for LGBTQI rights, although World Council of Churches shared that LGBTQI concerns are "certainly still unfinished business within the religious sector."

The global International Service for Human Rights, a secular group, identified the challenges of integrating concerns for sexual orientation and gender identity into broader resolutions on gender and women's rights at the UN General Assembly, observing that "it might have jeopardized the entire resolution." However, the representative from the group also observed that their efforts to promote LGBTQI rights were significantly enhanced by a recent organizational shuffle whereby individuals were assigned target issues instead of a more general gender mainstreamed approach: "Whereas before I was doing a bit of the LGBTI work . . . it was a small part of my more general human rights defender work, whereas now I feel the main focus of my work is the LGBTI work. . . . I suppose, obviously, when you are given an issue to work on you want to know where you're going with it, so you have to come up with some sort of goals and then try to achieve them. So I would definitely say that re-structuring has focused us." This last point highlights the question of whether a targeted or mainstreamed approach to gender issues bears greater results, a topic discussed further in the conclusion.

Conclusion

Overall, despite expectations that significant differences would be visible on women's rights issues between religious and secular human rights organizations, such divides are not evident in the data. While there are observed differences between the groups in terms of abortion rights, with more secular than religious organizations mentioning support for abortion rights, this difference does not reach the level of significance. However, differences in the extent of opposition to abortion rights are significant at the $p < .001$ level, with religious groups showing more open opposition. There is no significant difference between religious and secular organizations in terms of support for or opposition to family planning. Likewise, there is little significant difference between the religious and secular organizations in terms of work on gender violence or women's training and leadership. Overall, CEDAW and LGBTQI rights are rarely mentioned by either religious or secular groups, although secular groups are slightly more likely (although not statistically significantly so) to support LGBTQI rights. On the whole, very few statistical differences are evident between religious and secular organizations as such in terms of the gender variables of interest in this study. The primary differences observed lie between general and women's organizations as well as between general organizations and those with specific sections focused on gender issues.

One of the major findings in this chapter is that while gender mainstreaming has been a key approach encouraged from the top as international organizations and donors have sought to integrate gender throughout their organizational cultures, those organizations with separate sections dedicated to gender issues tended to focus more on key gender issues such as gender violence and women's leadership. While several organizations stated they do not do any specific work on women's rights, at least one organization differentiated women's rights work from that of human rights, suggesting that women's rights were different (as opposed to simply not working on that aspect of human rights).

However, a number of organizations, such as the Mauritanian Association for the Rule of Law, emphasized their "inclusive" approach to gender. Similarly, B'Tselem noted that they ensure women's inclusion: "We are collecting testimonies from women, that when we employ field researchers, that we have women among those collecting stories and telling the stories of women under occupation. . . . Everything we do has built in gender perspective." Equitas similarly noted that they "have content around gender equality and include gender perspectives in all our programs." Catholic Relief Services shared that because donors have been insisting on gender-responsive approaches, they no longer have stand-alone gender projects. The World Council of Churches has a "transversal" on gender issues that cuts across all of their work, and both T'ruah and Soka Gakkai emphasized the importance of women in their organizations: "We think of [women's rights] as part of everything we do" and "the real power of the Soka Gakkai around the world lies with its women," although neither has dedicated programs focusing on gender issues. In contrast, the Lutheran World Federation has a commitment to have at least 40 percent women and at least 40 percent men participating in all of their governance bodies to ensure neither group dominates.

Such findings may be of interest to international donors considering how to best advance SDGs related to women's equality. The Development Assistance Committee of the Organisation for Economic Co-operation and Development (OECD), for example, includes gender as a cross-cutting theme in their development assistance projects (OECD 2014). This is mirrored in the US Agency for International Development's gender equality and women's empowerment website materials, which say, "Building on this critical foundation and decades of experience, we're ensuring all our strategies and programs are shaped by a gender analysis, and establish metrics that measure the gender impact of our programs." The International Human Rights Funders Group does include women's rights as one of their funded areas, but it is one of thirty-two areas. At the same time, a number of the religious groups report that they receive their funds primarily from their constituents or religious bodies, most of which do not have the same funding requirements as international donors.

Although it exceeds the scope of this current project, future studies should consider examining the approach organizations take to conceptualizing and achieving women's rights. Notably, a few of the organizations interviewed, including the secular WILPF and the religious Baha'i, among others, emphasized the importance of transformation in their approach to gender as a means to achieve greater equality. For the Baha'i, the human soul has no sex, and thus the goal should be "a more fundamental transformation about one's approach to one's role in contributing to the betterment of society." As noted by WILPF, "Just doing a comparative between the roles of men and women . . . includes women into an existing system which doesn't change the system." These two quotes suggest a quest for more than equality of rights between genders and instead a reformulation of how women's rights are conceptualized.

CHAPTER 5

Children's Rights

This chapter compares how religious and secular human rights organizations conceptualize, frame, and operationalize children's rights. The issue of children's rights is embroiled in conflict, particularly because some argue that certain children's rights directly conflict with the rights of parents and the rights of children are often closely shaped by religious and cultural norms. For example, one of the Ten Commandments in Christianity is to "honor thy father and mother," while other traditions have important ceremonies, such as bar and bat mitzvahs in Judaism, that mark the transition from childhood to adulthood. A parent may view that they have a right to discipline their child using corporal punishment, and cultural norms might suggest this is the most appropriate method of discipline. On the other hand, a children's rights activist might argue that children have rights to be protected from physical harm. As such, it becomes important to clearly define the rights of children in a way that both protects children but also accounts for religious and cultural norms related to child-rearing. Further, the discussion of who constitutes a child and which rights they may be entitled to also varies religiously and culturally.

Although there are disagreements on how to frame children's rights, there are also key international agreements in this area. This chapter begins with a discussion of the various international agreements and international laws related to children's rights and then explores the broader literature on children's rights, specifically focusing on the ways that the rights of children may be framed differently by various religious traditions. Finally, the chapter provides a discussion of the trends from the dataset and interviews, comparing religious and secular human rights organizations and their approaches to children's rights.

History of International Law as It Relates to Children

While there are certainly cultural dimensions and variations to discussions of what constitutes a child and what rights children may have, the international community has generally agreed that children do have rights and deserve special protection, and as early as 1924 the League of Nations adopted the Geneva Declaration of the Rights of the Child. This declaration asserts children's rights to normal development (including material and spiritual development), to be fed, to be cared for when sick, to be helped when in need, and to be sheltered. Further, the declaration suggests that children should be the first aided by relief efforts, that they "must be put in a position to earn a livelihood," and that they should be "protected against every form of exploitation" (League of Nations 1924b). The UDHR specifically mentions some rights of children. Article 25 grants children the right to special care, assistance, and social protection. Further, Article 26 of the UDHR states that everyone has the right to an education and that education should be free (at the elementary and fundamental stages), compulsory, and equally accessible to all. In 1959, the UN adopted a more extensive Declaration of the Rights of the Child that serves as the basis for the 1989 Convention on the Rights of the Child (CRC). The CRC has four guiding principles focused on children. First is the idea of nondiscrimination, that all state parties should respect and ensure children's rights without any discrimination based on "the child's or his or her parent's or legal guardian's race, colour, sex, language, religion, political or other opinion, national, ethnic or social origin, property, disability, birth or other status" (UN 1989). Further, states must take measures to protect children from all forms of discrimination. Second, laws and state actions affecting children should have the best interests of the child in mind. Third, the government must protect children and ensure not only their survival but their physical, spiritual, moral, and social development. Finally, the convention holds that children have the right to participate in the decisions that affect them. As part of the CRC, children are also granted similar basic freedoms granted to adults in other human rights laws, including freedom of expression and freedom of thought, conscience, and religion. At the time of this writing, 196 countries were party to the 1989 convention—every eligible party except the United States. Though the United States initially signed the convention, Congress never ratified it. In addition to the convention, there are two optional protocols, one related to children's involvement in armed conflict and another related to the sale of children, child prostitution, and child pornography.

The ICCPR, signed in 1966 and entering into force in 1976, specifies the need for states to ensure the protection of children following the divorce of the child's parents, affords children special protection as minors, affirms that children should be registered and given a name after birth, and grants all children the right to a nationality. The ICESCR also specifically mentions some rights of children. Again, children are offered special protection, and the covenant protects them from economic and social exploitation and declares that children's "employment in work harmful to their morals or health or dangerous to life or likely to hamper their normal development should be punishable by law." States are further required to set age limits for work. The ICESCR also recognizes the importance of a high standard of physical and mental health and notes that states party to the covenant should attempt to reduce infant mortality and work toward providing the "healthy development of the child" (UN 1966b). In addition, the covenant, similar to the UDHR, recognizes the right to an education—a key right for children. CEDAW also considers some rights relevant to children, particularly female children. Child marriage is prohibited, and states are instructed to set a minimum age for marriage.

The United Nations International Children's Emergency Fund (UNICEF) was created after World War II to help affected children. Since then, the organization has expanded efforts to protect children across the globe and works to implement and maintain children's rights as passed in the Declaration of the Rights of the Child and the CRC. In addition to UNICEF, many NGOs working on human rights also deal with children's rights. Some organizations specialize in them, while others may only implicitly consider these rights within their work.

Parents' Rights as an Obstacle to Children's Rights

While most countries recognize the importance of protecting children and children's rights, the rights of parents are sometimes seen as competing with those of children and have become a potential obstacle to the realization of children's rights. As Normand and Zaidi (2008) discuss, there was an inherent tension between parents' and children's rights in drafting the CRC. This tension is seen in other human rights documents as well. For example, the UDHR and the ICESCR, in addition to discussing the right to an education, also explicitly grant parents the right to choose the type of education their children will receive. This could lead to potential clashes between the rights of parents, who might argue their child does not need an education, and the rights of children for an education. This is further complicated when gender issues enter the mix. The ICCPR and the ICESCR grant parents and legal guardians the rights "to ensure the religious and moral education of their children in conformity with their own conviction" (UN 1966a, 1966b). International law has generally recognized the rights of parents to decide on what types of medical care and procedures their children will have, yet at the same time most Western countries have legally limited parents' rights to fully determine a child's medical care, including a consideration of the general welfare of the child (Woolley 2005). For example, parents may not be able to refuse lifesaving medical treatment for their children, as the welfare of the child may override the parents' right to determine medical intervention.

In fact, many individuals within the United States do not support the CRC because it challenges parents' rights. Further, there has been some support for a Parental Rights Amendment to the US Constitution, which would more specifically codify and enhance parents' rights related to issues like children's health care (Dailey 2019). Some worry about the potential for health care providers to offer abortion and contraception services to children without their parents' consent, one of the key motivations behind this amendment. This example demonstrates that religious beliefs and political views play a role in support for certain children's rights.

Who Is a Child?

Before we can discuss the rights of children, we must determine who constitutes a child, which is an area of dispute within the international community. The CRC defines a child as anyone under the age of eighteen "unless, under the law applicable to the child, majority is attained earlier" (UN 1989). Thus, countries are permitted to set their age of majority lower than eighteen. The Optional Protocol to the CRC on the involvement of children in armed conflict generally establishes eighteen as the age for which people can be recruited into the armed services, though there is an allowance for recruitment of people under that age as long as it is voluntary and with the consent of the person's parent or legal guardian, another illustration of the interaction between parental and child rights. Further, the Rome Statute of the International Criminal Court made it a war crime to conscript or enlist children under the age of fifteen. CEDAW prohibits child marriage but does not specify an age at which individuals become eligible to marry. By instructing states to provide legislation to specifically address child marriage, CEDAW allows states to set the age below eighteen. As these examples demonstrate, international law is not definitive on the definition of a child and provides certain allowances for cultural and religious variations. Defining a child is complicated by the idea of the unborn child. As Normand and Zaidi (2008) point out, there has been differences and conflict over the issue of the "rights of the unborn child" when discussing international human rights laws, like the CRC. In particular, these differences are found between prochoice and antiabortion groups, and religion is certainly a part of this discussion. In the end, the CRC does not specifically mention rights of the fetus, and this issue remains controversial. Organizational views of abortion and reproductive rights are discussed in greater detail in chapter 4.

Which Rights?

Three general themes related to children's rights are evident in the relevant UN documents. First is the right of children for basic survival and physical protection from violence, which also includes health-related issues. The second theme focuses on the right of children to normal development. This includes the right to an education as well as protection from child labor and other activities that would prevent children from reaching their full potential. Third is the idea that children should have some agency and should participate in the decisions that directly affect them.

These specific themes can also be seen in the Strategic Plan of UNICEF, which breaks its work into similar categories and goals (UNICEF 2018). The first goal is for every child to survive and thrive. In this area, UNICEF takes a broad approach focused on child survival, growth, and development. This goal focuses on heath, immunizations, nutrition, HIV and AIDS prevention, early childhood development, and capacity building. The second goal area is for every child to learn and is focused on equitable access to education and skills development. The third goal area is for every child to be protected from violence and exploitation and includes child marriage and FGM. The fourth goal is for every child to live in a safe and clean environment. The fifth and final goal is an equitable chance in life for every child (UNICEF 2018).

NGOs and Children's Rights

NGOs have played a major role in promoting international laws related to children's rights. In fact, thirty NGOs formed an Ad Hoc Group on the Drafting of the CRC, making recommendations regarding the text and serving as a bridge between states in the East and West (Becker 2017). While NGOs were important in the foundational stage of the CRC, they have a less clear role regarding children's rights outcomes in countries around the world (Türkelli, Vandenhole, and Vandenbogaerde 2013). Polonko and Lombardo (2015) found that most states that are party to the CRC do not actively encourage NGOs to take a child rights focus in their work, though at the same time nearly all states party to the treaty have at least one NGO involved in children's rights activities and more than 50 percent have NGOs that are members in the Child Rights Information Network, a major think tank that brings together organizations to fight for children's rights. Overall, NGOs continue to be involved in promoting children's rights, and approaches to children's human rights appear to follow along closely with international human rights laws and the work of UNICEF.

State of the Literature on Religion and Children's Rights

Since every country in the world except the United States has signed and ratified the CRC, there is some global consensus regarding children's rights. In fact, the CRC is the mostly widely ratified international treaty in history. However, there is still disagreement about what these rights might look like, particularly related to religious and cultural norms.

Controversies about children's rights in various religions often focus on the tension between the rights of the child versus the rights of the parents. The CRC, which is the most widely accepted international convention, has faced some opposition and reservations among countries based on religious arguments. When ratifying the CRC, the Holy See provided a series of reservations and declarations, including "that the application of the Convention [should] be compatible in practice with the particular nature of the Vatican City State and the sources of its objective law" (Schabas 1996, 478–79). Similar to the Holy See, when ratifying the CRC, many Islamic states stated that the provision of the convention should be interpreted in light of Islamic law and values (Schabas 1996).

Christianity

Witte and Browning (2012) argue that family rights, and as an extension children's rights, are rooted in Christian and Western traditions. The authors declare that much of what we think about as modern children's rights were part of medieval law, promoted by the Catholic Church and thinkers like Aquinas. Such rights included "rights to life and the means to sustain life; the rights to care, nurture, and education; the later rights to contract marriage or to enter into a religious life; and the rights to support and inheritance from his or her natural parents" and special rights for poor and abused children (Witte and Browning 2012, 1009–10). These rights are related both to children's physical security and protection as well as to their development and can be seen clearly within the CRC.

Further, children's agency and participation exhibit elements consistent with Christianity, like free will. Free will is a central part of Christianity and is important in relation to freely accepting God into one's life (Frede 2011). While Christianity has many different sects, in some children choose to be baptized, indicating their agentic decision to live their lives according to Christian thought. In the Catholic Church, children are generally baptized shortly after birth, but their confirmations occur later, typically between sixth and tenth grades (Allen 2014). Confirmation takes a long time and involves a lot of education related to the Catholic faith. In addition to the agency expressed in the confirmation process, children are often strong participants in the Christian church, taking on various tasks, such as becoming youth deacons, participating in choir and other organized activities, collecting tithes, and attending youth groups.

While there are clear examples from Christianity supporting children's agency and participation in religious activities, parents are still viewed to have a lot of control over and responsibility for their children. Further, some of the critiques of the CRC by Christians relate to the idea of agency and participation of children in making decisions about their own lives. The CRC has specifically suffered opposition in the United States, even though many American human rights lawyers and NGOs were part of the process of drafting this document (Witte and Browning 2012). However, observers have noted that the primary opposition to the CRC in the United States comes from conservative Christians, largely Evangelicals, though also some Catholic and Orthodox Christians as well as other Protestants and Mormons (Butler 2000; Witte and Browning 2012). The objections from US conservative and Evangelical Christians take a few different forms. First, some oppose the very idea that children have rights and instead argue that rights are something that an individual gains only upon adulthood. This argument suggests that children are the responsibility of their parents until they have reached the age of legal majority (Witte and Browning 2012) and provides opposition for all three of the types of children's rights previously discussed.

A second critique of the CRC relates to its international standing. Some conservative Christians do not necessarily oppose the idea of children having rights more generally, but they do not believe that children's rights should be internationally mandated. These individuals tend to support a federal system where states make laws regarding matters related to the family; thus, children's rights should be decided by individual US states (Witte and Browning 2012). Finally, some US Christian conservatives have argued that the CRC directly opposes the rights of parents to raise their children the way they see fit—and particularly in alignment with their own religious beliefs. Issues related to education, corporal punishment, the right of children to form and express their own views, and the right to freedom of thought, conscience, and religion have been particularly contentious, as individuals worry that these rights would directly impact parents' ability to raise their children in accordance with their own views and religion (Witte and Browning 2012). One specific example is the issue of medical care, where parental "medical neglect" has been a key issue for many Christians for more than a century, as parents argue that decisions regarding their children's medical care should be theirs, alone, to make, while children's rights advocates argue that children have the right to lifesaving medical care (Curry 2017). Such arguments have been particularly pronounced among Jehovah Witnesses. The Holy See provided a reservation to the CRC, stating that they interpret the convention in a way that safeguards the rights of the parents, particularly related to education and religion. These arguments, together, suggest less support for children's agency and participation as a right and give more weight to parents' rights.

As chapter 4 notes, Christianity has an uneven record regarding support for the rights of women and girls. The phrase "children should be seen and not heard" has its origins in the work of fifteenth-century Augustinian clergyman John Mirk, who wrote about this old English Proverb in his *Mirk's Festial* from the 1400s. The actual proverb cited in Middle English is "A mayde shuld be seen, but not herd," which specifically translates to "a young girl should be seen, but not heard" (Apperson 2006). Although this phrase has become more gender neutral over time, the fact that it was originally about girls specifically illustrates historical differences between girls and boys in Christian thought. Further, the proverb illustrates that although the idea of children's rights is consistent with Christianity, these rights have not always been treated as a high priority. For example, the Catholic Church has been criticized for covering up the sexual abuse of children by priests (Tzouvala 2015). Overall, there are elements of Christianity that suggest children's agency and participation are important, but there are also reasons to believe that Christian groups may be more reluctant to fully embrace the idea of children's agency.

Islam

While all Muslim-majority countries have signed the CRC, there are some key areas of contention. One area of difference relates to the definition of a child. For the CRC, children are generally considered those under the age of eighteen. In Islamic law, age is only one factor, with the concept of maturity being another that marks the move toward adulthood. Signs of maturity might include menstruation, pubic hair, and so forth—much of which would place the age at which an individual becomes an adult much earlier than eighteen (around fifteen for boys and between nine and thirteen for girls). Using the age of maturity to differentiate children from adults can have gendered effects since for some countries, and under some interpretations of Islamic law, age of maturity for girls is set lower than that for boys, and some Muslim-majority countries allow parents to marry girls even before the age of maturity (Hashemi 2007). Related, several Muslim-majority countries expressed reservations about Article 16 of CEDAW, which provides equality in marriage for women and men and prohibits the betrothal and marriage of a child. These reservations indicated that countries would follow this article only insofar as it is compatible with Islamic law (UN Committee on the Elimination of Discrimination against Women 2006). These reservations and the various laws defining age of maturity suggest less support for girls' rights more specifically.

Similarly, since the age of adulthood may be lower than eighteen in some Muslim-majority countries, it follows that certain punishments, including capital punishment, may be applied to individuals deemed children under international law. Another area of contention relates to children's right to religious freedom. Like arguments made by some Christians, some Muslim-majority states, including Iraq, Jordan, Morocco, Algeria, Syria, and Bangladesh, have suggested that children having freedom of religion conflicts with Islamic law (Hashemi 2007; LeBlanc 1996; Veerman and Sand 1999). This also conflicts with support for children's agency.

While there are areas of tension, there are also clear consistencies between Muslim traditions and laws and broader international human rights norms related to children's rights. For example, the 1981 Universal Islamic Declaration of Human Rights states that parents should provide for their children based on their means and provide material support for their care and declares that it is "forbidden that children are made to work at an early age or that any burden is put on them which would arrest or harm their natural development" (Islamic Council 1981). The declaration also indicates that parents have the right to raise their children in conformity with their religious beliefs, traditions, and culture. These ideas are similar to those found in the UDHR and other international laws and seem to particularly emphasize the importance of child development. Further, in 1994, at the Twenty-Second Conference of Foreign Ministers from the Organization of Islamic Conferences (now known as the Organisation of Islamic Cooperation), Muslim-majority countries made specific declarations regarding children's rights and called upon members to ratify the CRC. However, this conference also placed some constraints on the idea of a child's right to religion, one of the key elements of contention previously noted (Saeed 2018).

Judaism

Similar critiques of the CRC are also found in Judaism, particularly as they relate to children's freedom of religion. Like Christianity and Islam, Judaism views religious education of children as a responsibility of parents and the Jewish community more broadly (Dorff 2012). In this way, religious education is a part of the daily life of families, including children, who study the Torah. During early childhood, the responsibility for this religious teaching falls on the parents. However, when children reach thirteen, they are considered old enough to take individual responsibility for their faith and decisions, and this milestone is marked through the bar mitzvah and bat mitzvah preparation and ceremonies (Pace 2012). These ceremonies clearly indicate a move toward a mature child attaining greater agency. Further, Israel did not submit any reservations to the CRC, and its state laws are consistent with the tenets of various international conventions and treaties related to children (Library of Congress 2015).

Other Religions

Religious practice and traditions are a key part of the upbringing of children of a variety of faiths, including Hinduism and Buddhism (Langlaude 2007; Thomas 2017). The idea that parents are responsible for the religious education of their children again creates some potential tensions between parents' rights and religion, on the one hand, and children's rights, like freedom of religion and children's agency, on the other. At the same time, these various religions also emphasize the importance of the parents in protecting children and thus support many of the general principles of international human rights law related to children.

Overall, there are some key similarities across the religions surveyed here. Most religions support the general idea of protecting children from harm and promote the broader development of children through education. At the same time, most religions recognize that parents play a key role in the upbringing of children, particularly in relation to religion, though some faith traditions also support the idea of children's agency vis-à-vis active acceptance of religious views.

Cultural Differences and Children's Rights

While religion is one area that may impact attitudes related to children's rights, cultural differences are also relevant. For example, Windborne (2006) considers indigenous resistance in Ghana to the CRC and the various laws that the country enacted to support these child rights. Others have noted that some African countries felt the needs of Africa, including the social, economic, and cultural issues on the continent, had not been adequately and fully addressed by the CRC (Becker 2017). One area of contention is the legal age for marriage, particularly for girls. While the CRC defines a child as younger than eighteen, it does allow for state laws to define the age of majority differently. This is particularly important for determining the legal age to marry. At the same time, international organizations such as UNICEF define child marriage as marriage "between a child under the age of 18 and an adult or another child," suggesting that many in the international community do not fully support the exceptions provided for states to define the age of majority lower than eighteen (UNICEF n.d.). Mwambene and Mwaodza (2017) discuss child marriage in Malawi and argue that these marriages are largely a result of cultural practices. While Malawi has made strides to implement international laws related to child marriage into their national laws, current laws define children as those younger than sixteen, which has created tensions between those promoting these cultural norms related to defining a child for the purposes of marriage and the international norm that would place this age of majority at eighteen. Mutyaba (2011) notes how early marriage of girls in Africa is a fundamental violation of their rights, and Verner (2015) discuses child marriage in Yemen and how the country's failure to set a minimum age for marriage is a violation of international law.

Hypotheses

Given that children's rights are a small subset of human rights, we expect that most organizations will spend little time explicitly addressing them. In terms of religious and secular differences, we do not necessarily expect any key differences between these groups in terms of whether they are likely to consider children's rights more explicitly. However, we do expect some differences in relation to religious and secular approaches to specific children's rights. In addition, we expect some differences in relation to children's organizations or those with children's sections and approaches to children's rights. Specifically, we investigate the following hypotheses:

1. Most human rights organizations (both secular and religious) will not specifically discuss children's rights.
2. Secular organizations will be more likely than religious groups to mention children's physical well-being.
3. Religious organizations will be more likely than secular groups to mention child development.
4. Religious and secular organizations will be equally likely to mention child agency.
5. Fewer organizations (overall) will discuss child agency than the physical well-being and development of children.
6. Religious organizations will be less likely than secular groups to focus on girls' rights, including girls' education and child marriage.
7. Organizations in the Global North and West will be more likely than those in the Global South and outside of the West to focus on girls' rights.

Findings

Given that children's rights are but a subset of human rights, we expect that a minority of organizations will include a specific focus on children's rights.

Further, we expect to find some differences between religious and secular organizations in their approach to various types of children's rights. While we do find that children's issues are not a key consideration for most of the organizations in our study, we also find that there are fewer differences between secular and religious organizations' approaches to children's rights than we anticipated.

Programmatic Area Focused on Children

The overall sample includes 333 organizations, 68 faith-based and 265 secular human rights organizations. To measure whether NGOs in our sample have a major focus on children's rights, we consider whether the organizations have a specific programmatic area on their websites focused on children's issues and rights. We find that indeed only 66 of the 333 organizations in our sample, or 20 percent, have specific sections dedicated to children's rights. When comparing religious and secular human rights organizations, we find that 24 percent of religious and 19 percent of secular organizations have sections on their websites dedicated to children's issues and rights; this difference is not statistically significant.

When considering a breakdown of specific religious organizations, we find that Muslim organizations appear to be the least likely, compared to other religious human rights NGOs, to have sections dedicated to children's rights on their websites. Only one Muslim organization (out of seven in our dataset)—Al-Khoei Foundation—has a programmatic section on children. While these differences are not statistically significant due to the lower numbers of religious organizations in our sample, they are worth note noting. Similarly, only one Jewish organization (out of four), B'nai B'rith, has a section focused on children. Further, it appears religious organizations outside of the Abrahamic faiths, or that include multiple faiths, are more likely to have sections specifically focusing on children's rights. The three other religious organizations to include a children's section are the Brahma Kumaris World Spiritual University, the World Barua Organization (a Buddhist organization), and Arigatou International (an interfaith children's organization in Japan).

The findings above suggest that there may be further cultural dimensions to the consideration of children's rights. When examining North-South differences, we find that 21 percent of the organizations in the Global North include children's sections on their websites, while 18 percent of those in the Global South include them. This represents only a small difference and is not statistically significant. On the other hand, 18 percent of the organizations in the West and 26 percent of the organizations in the non-West have separate sections on children's rights, though this difference is significant only at the $p < .10$ level.

Physical Well-Being of Children

Though religious and secular organizations appear, overall, similarly likely to focus children's rights, there is still a question as to whether secular and religious organizations frame children's rights in similar ways. We identify three different approaches to children's rights: focusing on the physical well-being of children, child development, and child agency (see Table 5.1). One way to consider children's rights is to focus on the physical well-being, basic needs, and survival of children.

Organizations focusing on the physical well-being of children may consider problems of children living in poverty and having access to food and water. Further, they may focus on the right of children to live and be free from physical (and sexual) harm or on providing emergency relief or immunizations to children. Overall, each of these examples demonstrates a focus on the physical needs and well-being of children. Since organizations without specific children's sections do not generally provide enough information to assess their approach to children's rights, we consider only those with children's sections when discussing specific approaches to children's rights.

The results indicate that overall most organizations with children's sections also emphasize the physical well-being of children but that secular organizations are slightly more likely than religious groups to place emphasis on the physical well-being of children. In our sample, 75 percent of the religious organizations with a children's section also focus on the physical well-being of children, while 87 percent of the secular organizations do so. While these differences do not attain statistical significance due to the small sample size, we believe this difference is worth noting. The four religious organizations that do not discuss physical well-being are B'nai B'rith (Jewish), Brahma Kumaris

TABLE 5.1

Organizations with Children's Sections and Approaches to Children's Rights (in percentages)

	Physical well-being of children	Child development	Child agency
Religious organizations	75	82	47
Secular organizations	87	79	43
Global North organizations	82	80	44
Global South organizations	88	81	50
Western organizations	79	79	45
Non-Western organizations	91	83	48

TEXTBOX 5.1

Comparisons of Children's Rights

Human Rights Education Associates (HREA)

Human Rights Education Associates (HREA) is a secular organization that primarily focuses on human rights training and education as well as on training for human rights defenders and professional groups. The organization "is dedicated to quality education and training to promote understanding, attitudes and actions to promote human rights, and to foster the development of peaceable, free and just communities." The organization has a program specifically designed to discuss children's rights and child protection with the aim to "ensure that children and youth across the globe are able to realize their human rights" and that key individuals within society, such as social workers and law enforcement, "have the knowledge and skills they need to promote and protect children's human rights." HREA offers a variety of training workshops "on children's rights, child development, participation and protection."

HREA. 2020. "About Us." http://www.hrea.org/about-us/.
HREA. 2020. "Children's Rights and Child Protection." http://www.hrea.org/programs/childrens-rights-and
-child-protection/.

Daughters of Charity of Saint Vincent de Paul

The Daughters of Charity of Saint Vincent de Paul "are called to serve Jesus Christ in the person of those who are poor and marginalized with a spirit of humility, simplicity, and charity." The organization has a special section on "Ministry to Children" where they emphasize the importance of the rights of children to their childhood, and that "children have . . . a central place in our outreach to the poorest." In particular, the organization focuses on promoting the "well-being of children" through things like providing parenting and family support programs and nutrition programs for the malnourished as well as by working with schools and child care, adoption, and foster agencies.

Daughters of Charity of St. Vincent de Paul. 2020. "Ministry to Children." http://filles-de-la-charite.org
/who-we-are/our-ministry/ministry-to-children/.
Daughters of Charity of St. Vincent de Paul. 2020. "Who We Are." http://filles-de-la-charite.org/who-we
-are/.

World Spiritual University, Al-Khoei Foundation (Muslim), and Alliance Defending Freedom (Christian). As such, there does not appear to be much difference in relation to which religions do not discuss physical well-being.

Further, organizations in the Global South and outside of the West appear more likely than those in the Global North and West to consider the physical well-being of children. Of the organizations in the Global North with a children's section, 82 percent focus on children's physical well-being, while 88 percent of similar organizations in the Global South do so. Similarly, 79 percent of the Western organizations with a children's section focus on children's physical well-being, compared to 91 percent of the organizations in the non-West. Again, due to the small sample size, these differences are not quite statistically significant, but the differences are notable. The issue of poverty appears to be particularly important for these Global South and/or non-Western organi-

zations. For example, Arigatou International, a religious children's organization headquartered in Japan, specifically focuses on ending child poverty and
has an interfaith initiative to deal with this issue (Arigatou International 2017).
Similarly, the InnerCity Mission for Children, a Christian children's organization in Nigeria, also focuses on children living in poverty.

Several of the organizations we interviewed also emphasized the importance of the physical well-being of children, particularly in protecting them
from violence. The Federation of Environmental and Ecological Diversity for
Agricultural Revampment and Human Rights (FEEDAR & HR), a secular organization in Cameroon, focuses on FGM as one of its key areas. Public Foundation, Center for Human Rights Defenders "Kylym Shamy," an organization
in Kyrgyzstan, also mentioned their work related to violence against children,
including rape. B'Tselem, a Jewish organization in Israel, also focuses on violence against children, particularly within the occupied territories of Palestine. Similarly, Djazairouna, an organization in Algeria, considers violence
against children and Femmes Développement et Droits Humains en Guinée
(F2DHG), a secular organization in Guinea, focuses on sexual violence against
minors, including child marriage (discussed below) and FGM. Islamic Relief
Worldwide also emphasized their work against FGM.

Child Development

While one way to consider the rights of children is to focus on their physical
needs and well-being, another is to consider their human development. In this
regard, organizations might focus on education or promote the flourishing and
thriving of children. Organizations may emphasize building children's capacity
for their future or preventing child labor to help children reach their full potential. As mentioned previously, since organizations without a special children's
section do not generally have enough information on their website to access
their approach to children's rights, this section considers only those organizations with such specialized sections.

Similar to rights related to the physical well-being of children, we generally find that most organizations with children's sections explicitly discuss
rights related to child development. While secular organizations were more
likely than religious organizations to consider physical children's rights, we
find the opposite in relation to children's development. Around 82 percent of
religious organizations with children's sections considered children's development, while 78 percent of secular organizations with a children's section did.
While this difference is not statistically significant, it does suggest that religious
and secular organizations may sometimes have slightly different approaches
to children's rights. If we look a little closer at the data, we find that the only
three religious organizations that do not consider children's development are

TEXTBOX 5.2

Children's Organizations and Children's Rights

Arigatou International

Arigatou International is a faith-based children's organization that brings together people from diverse cultural and religious backgrounds. The organization "is dedicated to securing the well-being and rights of children and advancing the culture of peace through interreligious dialogue and cooperative action" and "draws on the universal principles of common good . . . to address children's issues." Arigatou International has four major initiatives: the global network of religions for children, ethics education for children, prayer and action for children, and an interfaith initiative to end child poverty. In their campaign to end child poverty, Arigatou International specifically states that their project "will actively engage children as active actors."

Arigatou International. 2019. "Interfaith Initiative to End Child Poverty." https://arigatouinternational
    .org/en/what-we-do/end-child-poverty.
Arigatou International. 2019. "What We Do." https://arigatouinternational.org/en/what-we-do.
Arigatou International. 2019. "Who We Are." https://arigatouinternational.org/en/who-we-are.

Save the Children International

Save the Children International is a secular children's organization consisting of twenty-eight member organizations working around the world. The organization uses a holistic and sustainable approach to children's rights. Their vision is for "a world in which every child attains the right to survival, protection, development and participation." They "fight for children's rights and help them fulfil their potential" through a variety of programs and campaigns focusing on health and nutrition, education, protection for the most vulnerable children (including those affected by natural disasters, war, extreme poverty, and exploitation), and child poverty.

Save the Children. 2020. "About Us." https://www.savethechildren.net/about-us.
Save the Children. 2020. "What We Do." https://www.savethechildren.net/what-we-do.
Save the Children. 2020. "Who We Are." https://www.savethechildren.net/about-us/our-vision-mission-and
    -values.

all Christian: Alliance Defending Freedom, Latter-day Saint Charities, and the Teresian Association. While these three organizations are quite different and represent various strands of Christianity, it is worth noting that aside from these three Christian organizations, all other religious organizations with children's sections in the sample emphasized child development on their websites.

In relation to potential cultural differences, organizations in the West seem slightly less likely than those in the non-West to consider child development, though again the difference is not statistically significant. Around 79 percent of Western organizations in the sample with a children's section focus on child development, while 83 percent of non-Western organizations do. There does not appear to be much difference between organizations in the Global South and Global North.

During the interviews, one of the primary children's issues discussed by organizations was education and its importance for child development. In particular, several organizations in Africa emphasized their work on education. For example, FEEDAR & HR emphasized their advocacy for children's right to education, at least elementary education, and that they "try to make sure that every school is not created just on paper but that resources should be used for the purpose it is given," such as libraries, toilets, and playgrounds. Human Rights Observatory in Rwanda, Association Africaine d'Éducation pour le Développement, and the Mauritanian Association for the Rule of Law also discussed their advocacy for education. Other organizations also mentioned an emphasis on education, including Graduate Women International, Equitas, Islamic Relief Worldwide, and Informal Sector Service Center in Nepal. Child labor was also an issue mentioned by some of the organizations we interviewed. For example, the Human Rights Commission of Pakistan said that they have focused on child labor issues, particularly work in hazardous industries like mining. The emphasis on dangerous industries also relates to children's physical well-being. Similarly, one of the religious organizations we interviewed that wished to remain anonymous discussed their work on child soldiers.

Child Agency

A third approach to children's rights emphasizes child agency. Organizations with a focus on children's agency may specifically discuss the promotion of children's participation in governance and decision making. They might also consider the importance of training programs—particularly in relation to helping children learn how to exercise and promote their own rights. In each of these examples, the focus moves beyond external actors promoting children's well-being and development on their behalf and becomes more inclusive of children as agents in exercising and promoting their own rights. As expected, fewer organizations with children's sections specifically promote child agency as compared to those promoting child development and physical well-being.

In general, and contrary to our expectations, religious organizations appear slightly more likely than secular organizations to focus on child agency. When considering those organizations with children's sections, around 47 percent of religious organizations focus on child agency, while 43 percent of secular organizations do so, though this difference is not statistically significant. When we consider the seven specific religious organizations that focus on child agency, we see some patterns. In the sample, eleven total Christian organizations have a separate section for children's rights, but only three of these (International Catholic Child Bureau, the InnerCity Mission for Children, and the Alliance Defending Freedom) consider child agency. For example, the website of InnerCity Mission of Children, a Christian children's organization, mentions one of their core values as "children must be active participants in their own change."

The one Jewish organization that has a children's section considers child agency, and all three of the religious organizations categorized as other consider child agency. In addition, one organization that would also be categorized as other, Aliran Kesedaran Negara National Consciousness Movement, also clearly mentions child agency on its website, even though it does not have a specific section on children. If we consider all four of these other religious groups, one is Buddhist (World Barua Organization), one is Brahma Kumaris (Brahma Kumaris World Spiritual University), and two do not specify a religion, though both are located in Asia (Aliran Kesedaran Negara National Consciousness Movement and Arigatou International).

The one Islamic organization with a children's section did not have enough data to code child agency. These data suggest that Christian organizations may be less likely than other religious organizations to consider the agency of children—though given the small sample size, only the difference between the other religious organizations and Christian organizations is statistically significant (at the $p < .05$ level). Although these differences are interesting, more research is needed to more fully explore the distinctions between various religious approaches to human rights and children's agency.

Organizations in the Global South and those in the non-West are slightly more likely to consider child agency, but these differences are not statistically significant. When considering those organizations with children's sections, around 44 percent of the organizations in the Global North and 50 percent of those in the Global South have a focus on child agency. Similarly, around 45 percent of Western and 48 percent of non-Western organizations with children's sections consider child agency. However, none of these differences are statistically significant.

As in the dataset, child agency was mentioned far less frequently than child physical well-being and child development in the interviews. Equitas, a secular organization, noted that in Syria they work on "creating spaces for children to be able to participate and identify what are some of the challenges they're facing as refugees, what can be done about it, and making sure that there's some space for child participation."

Girls' Rights

In addition to children's rights more broadly, some organizations also consider girls' rights more specifically. However, their number is small, with only 7 percent of organizations in the sample mentioning girls' rights. Around 9 percent of the secular organizations in the sample mention girls' rights, and only 3 percent of religious organizations mention girls' rights. Both of the religious organizations that mention girls' rights are Christian (World Young Women's Christian Association and World Vision). Thus, it appears that religious organizations are generally less likely than secular groups to consider girls' rights, though these differences are not statistically significant. If we consider only those organizations with dedicated sections for children's rights (Table 5.2), we find more interesting patterns. Around 30 percent of the secular organizations with children's sections also focus on girls' rights while only 6 percent of religious organizations do, though this difference is significant only at the $p < .10$ level. Thus, though religious organizations seem slightly more likely to consider children's rights more generally (or at least do so at the same rate as secular organizations), these organizations are significantly less likely to consider girls' rights specifically. Further, the only religious organization with a children's section that considers girls' rights is World Vision, which is also a children's organization, which increases the likelihood that it would consider broader rights.

Cultural differences are also shown when we consider North-South and West/non-West differences. Of the fifty organizations in the Global North with children's sections, around 28 percent consider girls' rights, compared to 11 percent of organizations in the Global South. Though this difference is not quite statistically significant due to the small sample size, it still suggests some potential differences between these organizations. Similarly, 30 percent of the organizations in the West with children's sections consider girls' rights, while only 12 percent of organizations in the non-West do, though this difference is significant only at the $p < .10$ level. These results suggest that organizations in the Global South and non-West may be less likely to consider girls' rights, even when they are focused on children's rights more broadly.

In the interviews, a few key themes emerged related to girls' rights: gender-based violence (including FGM) and rape, education, and child marriage. Public Foundation, Center for Human Rights Defenders "Kylym Shamy," in Kyrgyzstan, discussed a couple of cases they had worked on related to children, and both involved rape and/or violence. The Human Rights Commission of Pakistan also discussed their work on the sexual abuse of children. F2DHG, in Guinea, mentioned that they are "particularly engaged in the struggle against

TABLE 5.2

Organizations with Children's Sections and Girls' Rights (in percentages)

	Girls' rights	Girls' education	Child marriage
Religious organizations	6	19	19
Secular organizations	30	10	18
Global North organizations	28	16	22
Global South organizations	11	0	8
Western organizations	30	19	23
Non-Western organizations	12	0	8

sexual violence against minors." FGM, or female circumcision, was also specifically mentioned by some groups we interviewed, including F2DHG and Islamic Relief Worldwide. Girls' education and child marriage are discussed below.

Girls' Education

As discussed above, education is a key part of child development and something that many organizations specifically mention. Girls' education has increasingly become a focus in the international community, particularly giv-
en that there is a gap between the education levels of boys and girls in many
countries. Though girls' education is increasingly important within the international community, few of the organizations in the sample explicitly consider it: around 10 percent of religious and 6 percent of secular organizations. As
we would expect, women's organizations are more likely than non-women's
groups to focus on girls' education, 32 percent versus only 4 percent—and this
difference is significant at the $p < .001$ level. Given that many human rights organizations do not specifically focus on education, it is not surprising that girls'
education might not be a large focus for many organizations.

If we consider only those organizations with children's sections, we find
that around 19 percent of religious organizations consider girls' education,
compared to 10 percent of secular groups. While this difference is not statistically significant due to the small sample size, it does seem that religious organizations are more likely to consider girls' education. This finding is consistent
with the history of Christian missionary work, often focused on education and
building schools, throughout the world, especially in the Global South. When
looking at other differences, we find that organizations in the Global North and
West are more likely than organizations in the Global South and non-West to
consider girls' education rights. Around 16 percent of the organizations in the
Global North with children's sections also consider girls' education, compared
to none of the organizations in the Global South (though this difference is significant only at the $p < .10$ level). Similarly, 19 percent of Western organizations
with children's sections consider girls' education, while none of the organizations in the non-West consider these rights (and this difference is significant at
the $p < .05$ level). Similar to the discussion above about Christian missionary
work, there has been significant efforts in the West and Global North to help
provide schools and promote education in the Global South, though these efforts can also be criticized as being imperialist.

In the interviews, a few organizations mentioned girls' education or equality of education. For example, Human Rights Observatory in Rwanda works on
"equality of opportunity in access to schooling" but does not specifically mention girls, though they are implied. Graduate Women International emphasizes their work on removing barriers to education and specifically mentions the

issue of preventing girls from staying at school. Islamic Relief Worldwide similarly mentioned their work in Nigeria to deal with the issue of many girls not being educated due to the lack of schools. OIDEL, a Geneva-based organization, also discussed the problem of some parents not wanting their female children to attend school.

Child Marriage

Child marriage can affect the physical well-being of girls as well as their development and ability to reach their full potential. Most of the organizations with children's sections that consider child marriage do so in a way that is consistent with child development, though one organization, Refugees International, focuses more on the physical well-being of girls, particularly following humanitarian crises due to conflict. For this organization, child marriage is framed as a type of gender-based violence (along with rape, sexual assault, domestic violence, and FGM). Still, child marriage is also connected to children's development—as girls who are married very young are less likely to be able to pursue a full education and choose the path of their lives.

Child marriage is an issue that several organizations consider even if they do not have a specific section dedicated to children, though overall very few organizations in the sample specifically mention the practice. Given that the appropriate age for marriage may vary culturally and that marriage is very important within various religious traditions, we might expect religious human rights organizations to shy away from discussions of child marriage, though we do not necessarily find this to be the case. Around 9 percent of religious and 7 percent of secular organizations consider child marriage as a human rights issue. Thus, there is little difference between the percentage of secular and religious human rights organizations addressing the issue. When we consider the six religious organizations that consider child marriage, we find some patterns. Of these six organizations (Edmond Rice International Limited, International Catholic Child Bureau, Lutheran World Federation, World Vision, World Young Women's Christian Association, and Islamic Relief Worldwide), five are Christian and one is Muslim. No other religious organizations specifically mention child marriage. Though we expected religious organizations to be less likely to discuss child marriage, due to the fact that there is some variation among various cultures and religions in terms of the age of adulthood and not everyone within each religious tradition may agree, we do not find this to be the case. However, we do see that aside from Islamic Relief Worldwide only Christian organizations focus on child marriage and that three of these, Edmund Rice International Limited, International Catholic Child Bureau, and World Vision, are also children's organizations. This finding suggests that child marriage is something that is primarily considered by organizations that work specifically on children's rights rather than by those that consider human rights more broadly.

Given that child marriage is often considered an issue primarily for girls' rights, it is not surprising that women's organizations in the sample were also more likely than non–women's organizations to focus on child marriage, 26 percent versus only 6 percent (significant at the $p < .001$ level).

If we consider only those organizations with children's sections, 18 percent consider child marriage, compared to 5 percent of organizations without a children's section. Thus, organizations that are more likely to consider children generally are also more likely to focus on child marriage, and this is significant at the $p < .001$ level. Further, we find little difference between religious and secular organizations with children's sections in terms of their likelihood of discussing child marriage (see Table 5.2).

While there appears to be little difference between religious and secular organizations that have children's sections in relation to child marriage, there are some key differences between those organizations in the Global North and West and those in the Global South and non-West. Around 22 percent of the organizations in the Global North with children's sections also consider child marriage, compared to only 6 percent in the Global South. Similarly, 23 percent of Western organizations with children's sections also mention child marriage, while only 8 percent of such organizations in the non-West do. While these differences are not quite statistically significant (due to the small sample size), the numbers indicate a potential difference between those organizations in the Global North and West and those in the Global South and non-West, with those in the Global North and West being more likely to consider child marriage when considering children's rights. Given that countries within the Global South and outside of the West tend to have more variation in terms of how they define the age of adulthood for marriage, it is logical that organizations in these areas may be less likely to discuss child marriage as an issue, as there may be less agreement on how child marriage is defined and as to whether it is a problem.

Several of the organizations we interviewed mentioned the issue of child marriage, and contrary to the dataset, many of these organizations were in the Global South. Femmes Développement et Droits Humains en Guinée mentioned that they were "engaged in the fight against child marriage." Graduate Women International discussed their work in Turkey raising the national child marriage age, particularly so girls could stay in school. Further, the Ivorian Observatory for Human Rights said they specifically worked on the problem of girls being forced to marry. Thus, while the website data suggested that organizations from the Global South were less likely to discuss child marriage, during interviews multiple organizations from the Global South mentioned such work.

Conclusion

This chapter has illustrated some interesting trends related to children's rights. However, what is immediately evident is that few of the human rights organizations in the sample pay close attention to children's rights, with only 66 of the 333 organizations in the sample, or 20 percent, having specific sections dedicated to children's rights. Religious organizations appear slightly more likely than secular groups to have children's sections on their websites, though this difference is not statistically significant; Muslim organizations were the least likely.

In this chapter we identified three different approaches to children's rights: focusing on the physical well-being of children, on child development, and on child agency. Generally, we found that most organizations with children's sections focus on both the physical well-being of children and child development, with fewer than half of organizations with children's sections considering child agency. We found that religious organizations are less likely to focus on the physical well-being of children and are slightly more likely to focus on child development and child agency than secular organizations. While there does not appear to be any religious pattern in focusing on children's physical well-being, the only religious organizations with children's sections that do not consider children's development are all Christian. Thus, Christian organizations seem less likely to consider children's development. Further, we found that Christian organizations are less likely than the other religious groups in the sample to consider child agency (though we did not have enough data to consider the Muslim groups). One potential explanation for this finding is that many Christian organizations focus on issues like poverty and meeting the immediate needs of people. As such, many of these groups may focus more intently on issues related to children's well-being and physical safety than on children's development. Further, many Christian organizations categorize children as particularly vulnerable individuals in need of special protection. This categorization may also encourage a greater focus on well-being but also may create a paternalistic focus that discourages a promotion of children's agency.

While girls' rights were not a focus for most of the organizations in the dataset, religious organizations were much less likely to mention them. In fact, only two religious organizations in the sample, both Christian, mentioned girls' rights. However, religious organizations were slightly more likely than secular ones to consider girls' education. This may be because education is one of the issues related to girls' rights where there is greater agreement among different religious sects. Contrary to our expectations, religious organizations were not less likely than secular ones to discuss the issue of child marriage; however, we also found that of the six religious organizations that consider child marriage, five of these are Christian and one is Muslim. One potential explanation for this finding is that there is more variation outside of Christianity in terms of how adulthood is defined for marriage, perhaps making these religious organizations less likely to specifically broach the issue of child marriage in their work.

We should note, however, that while there are some differences between secular and religious organizations in terms of their approach to children's rights, many of these differences do not reach the level of statistical significance. One potential reason for this is the small number of organizations that consider children. Another interpretation is that secular and religious organizations do not vary dramatically in their approach to children's rights and that differences are really more marginal.

In addition to the results related to religious and secular groups, we found some interesting trends comparing organizations in the Global North and Global South and those in the West and outside the West. Non-Western organizations in the sample were more likely than those in the West to have a separate section on children's rights, though this difference was significant only at the $p < .10$ level. In addition, organizations in the Global South and in the non-West appear more likely than those in the Global North and West to consider the physical well-being of children and child development, and slightly more likely to emphasize child agency, and there were also differences in approaches to girls' rights. Overall, these findings suggest the need for further research on how cultural differences outside of religion impact approaches to children's rights. In particular, considerations of how the age of majority is defined across cultures and how this affects approaches to children's rights and especially girls' rights would be useful. Further, given the North-South differences illustrated by the data, the potential interaction between socioeconomic development and children's rights would also be an interesting area for further exploration.

CHAPTER 6

Peace, Conflict, and Rights

The general idea that human rights are interrelated with peace and conflict seems, at first glance, to be uncontroversial. Armed conflict and war often lead to human rights violations, and significant human rights violations can also lead to armed conflict and war (Isakovic 2001). It is also hard to imagine real peace being attained in the presence of human rights abuses. The experiences of World War II, and the gross human rights violations that were perpetuated during that war, made it clear that human rights violations threatened world peace. Based on these experiences, the UN was established in 1945 in an attempt to create and maintain a more peaceful world (McGuinness 2011). Shortly thereafter, in 1948, the UDHR was proclaimed, specifically stating a connection between human rights and peace. While there are clear connections between war and peace on the one hand and human rights on the other, in practice these ideas are often considered separately. While scholars studying conflict may consider the problem of human rights and how human rights violations perpetuate conflict, the connection between the promotion of human rights and peace is often a source of contention among scholars. This chapter considers the ways that peace and conflict overlap and intersect with human rights and how religious and secular divisions affect approaches to these issues.

History of International Law as
It Relates to Peace and Conflict

World War I (1914–18) devastated many countries, particularly in Europe, and left much of the world ready to commit to a more peaceful way of resolving disputes. The League of Nations was created in 1924, spearheaded by US president Woodrow Wilson, in an attempt to prevent another world war. The Covenant of the League of Nations (1924a) stated its aims "to achieve international peace and security," and the signatories agreed to avoid resorting to war and to reduce arms. While Wilson was instrumental in drafting the treaty, the US Senate failed to ratify it, and the United States never became a member of the League of Nations, which undermined its authority. A few years later, in 1928, the Kellogg-Briand Pact was signed by most of the major powers (including the United States), with signatories agreeing to the "renunciation of war as an instrument of national policy" (Kellogg-Briand Pact 1928). However, peace would prove to be short-lived, and neither of these agreements prevented World War II.

Similar to the League of Nations, the UN was created to maintain international peace and security. The UN charter clearly connects the ideas of conflict, peace, and human rights. The preamble to the charter begins, "We the peoples of the United Nations determined to save succeeding generations from the scourge of war, which twice in our lifetime has brought untold sorrow to mankind and to reaffirm faith in fundamental human rights" (UN 1945).

As Chapter I, Article 1, Section 1, of the charter states, the first purpose of the UN was "to maintain international peace and security, and to that end: to take effective collective measures for the prevention and removal of threats to the peace, and for the suppression of acts of aggression or other breaches of the peace, and to bring about by peaceful means, and in conformity with the principles of justice and international law, adjustment or settlement of international disputes or situations which might lead to a breach of the peace" (UN 1945). Section 2 further emphasizes that the UN has the purpose "to develop friendly relations among nations based on respect for the principle of equal rights and self-determination of peoples, and to take other appropriate measures to strengthen universal peace" (UN 1945). By signing the charter, states agree to "settle their international disputes by peaceful means in such a manner that international peace and security, and justice, are not endangered" and "shall refrain . . . from the threat or use of force against the territorial integrity or political independence of any state" (UN 1945). What is clear is that the primary purpose of the UN is to maintain peace, or at least prevent war, throughout the international system.

Much of the document of the UN charter is dedicated to helping states peacefully settle their disputes and outlining when war might be justified. Chapter VI outlines the pacific settlements of disputes between countries and encourages countries to seek out negotiation, enquiry, mediation, conciliation, arbitration, judicial settlement, and other peaceful means in order to settle their disputes. While peaceful settlement is preferred, the UN charter also recognizes that sometimes states may cause threats to peace and that these acts may need to be dealt with through force. However, Chapter VII of the charter is clear that such force must be authorized by the UN Security Council, which would initiate such a peace enforcement measure. However, the charter does recognize a state's right to self-defense against an armed attack, in Chapter VII, Article 51. Further, the Security Council can authorize peacekeeping missions, typically with the consent of all the parties involved, to help maintain peace during cease-fires. However, in practice peacekeeping has been associated with both respect for and increased violations of human rights (Murdie and Davis 2010). Further, UN peacekeepers have been accused of committing rape and sexual abuse during their peacekeeping missions, illustrating that those acting on behalf of the UN itself also perpetuate human rights abuses (O'Brien 2011).

Human Rights Laws, War, and Peace

While the charter of the UN clearly demonstrates a connection between human rights, conflict, and peace, various international laws directly related to human rights also illustrate these links. The UDHR, passed by the UN General Assembly in 1948, begins its preamble by stating that "recognition of the inherent dignity and of the equal and inalienable rights of all members of the human family is the foundation of freedom, justice, and peace in the world," clearly making the connection between human rights and peace (UN 1948). The ICCPR and the ICESCR, both signed in 1966 and entering into force in 1976, reiterate these ideas in their preambles. Further, the ICCPR prohibits propaganda for war.

Humanitarian Law, War, and Peace

Aside from international human rights law, there are also international laws of war that primarily deal with issues related to the conduct of war and directly relate to human rights. The idea that there should be rules for how wars are fought is not necessarily new, but the idea that civilians should be protected from the harms of war became a more prominent part of international law in the late nineteenth and early twentieth centuries and became codified in the Hague Conventions (1899 and 1907) and Geneva Conventions (1949).

The First Conventions at both of the Hague Conferences (1899 and 1907) discussed the pacific settlement of international disputes and the importance of maintaining peace and provided various rules of war and limitations on weapons with the intention of "laying down certain limits for the purpose of modifying their severity as far as possible" in "the interest of humanity and the ever increasing requirements of civilization" (Hague Convention 1899). Thus, the idea was to limit the destructive capacity of war and to make it easier for countries and people to move forward following a war. The ideas of the Hague Conventions were further solidified and codified in the Geneva Conventions

(1949) and the Additional Protocols that followed. In relation to human rights, the Geneva Conventions provide protections for wounded, sick, and ship-wrecked military personnel and prisoners of war (Geneva Conventions I, II, and III; International Committee of the Red Cross 1949a, 1949b, 1949c). The idea was that once a person was no longer able to participate in combat, even if they were military personnel, they were afforded protections, including freedom from continued attack and protection from torture and ill treatment. Perhaps most importantly, the Fourth Geneva Convention grants protection to civilians (noncombatants not involved in the conduct of war), including those in occupied territory (Geneva Convention IV; International Committee of the Red Cross 1949d). Overall, protecting the human rights of those either no longer able to participate in conflict and those civilians who are not part of the conflict is a key part of the Geneva Conventions and demonstrates a clear link between human rights and conflict.

While international law long held only states accountable for human rights abuses, since states were the primary actors in international law, increasingly measures have been taken to hold individuals accountable for violations of human rights, particularly in relation to war crimes, crimes against humanity, and genocide. Following World War II, the Nuremberg and Tokyo War Crimes Tribunals were implemented to provide justice for the crimes perpetrated during the war. More recently, the International Criminal Court was established in 2002 to investigate, charge, and try individuals accused of genocide, war crimes, crimes against humanity, and the crime of aggression (International Criminal Court n.d.). The International Committee of the Red Cross is an independent international organization that bases their work on these Geneva Conventions. They provide "humanitarian protection and assistance for victims of armed conflict and other situations of violence" and promote "respect for international humanitarian law and its implementation in national law" (International Committee of the Red Cross n.d.). Overall, these organizations work to ensure that countries follow the Geneva Conventions and provide assistance to individuals, including civilians, affected by war. Through these mechanisms, the international community and international law clearly link conflict with human rights abuses.

Right to Peace

The connections between conflict and human rights violations have been clearly noted in international law—and much of international law, including the charter of the UN, is founded on the idea of creating a more peaceful world. More recently there has been movement promoting a "right to peace" within the international community, though this idea has not been without controversy.

In November 1984, the Declaration on the Right of Peoples to Peace was approved by the General Assembly. The short document "proclaims that the peoples of our planet have a sacred right to peace" and that "the preservation of the right of peoples to peace and promotion of its implementation constitute a fundamental obligation of each State" (UN 1984). In order to ensure this peace, states are encouraged to direct their state policies toward the elimination of the threat of war, especially nuclear war, and to settle their disputes peacefully.

Beginning in 2005, the Asociación Española para el Derecho Internacional de los Derechos Humanos (AEDIDH), or the Spanish Society for International Human Rights Law, led a global campaign for an updated declaration on the right to peace. This campaign specifically targeted civil society organizations throughout the world, attempting to gather support for such a declaration. In 2010, the work of the AEDIDH and its president, Carlos Villán Durán, along with a coalition of other civil society organizations, resulted in the Santiago Declaration on the Human Right to Peace being adopted by the International Congress on the Human Right to Peace (Durán 2011). This conference was organized by AEDIDH and the World Council of Churches. The ultimate objective was to introduce a Declaration on the Human Right to Peace to the Human Rights Council. The Santiago Declaration on the Human Right to Peace was submitted to the Advisory Committee of the Human Rights Council in 2011 for consideration (Durán 2011).

The Human Rights Council Advisory Committee approved the Santiago Declaration in 2012, paving the way for further discussion in the Human Rights Council and movement to the UN General Assembly. In July 2016, the Human Rights Council approved a Declaration on the Right to Peace (Resolution 32/28) based on the Santiago Declaration (though including only around 85 percent of the provisions of the document)—the vote was thirty-nine in favor, nine against, and four abstentions. North-South divisions were evident in the voting, with all countries in the Global South supporting the declaration and all those in the Global North (with the exception of the Russian Federation) voting against or abstaining (UN 2016; Public Service International 2017). In December 2016, the General Assembly adopted the Declaration on the Right to Peace with Resolution 71/189 (UN 2017). While this was considered a win by many, the 474 civil society organizations that had originally signed the Santiago Declaration criticized the UN declaration for not fully adopting the ideas set forth in the Santiago Declaration (Public Service International 2017). The debate over an updated Declaration on the Right to Peace continues.

Many civil society organizations spoke in favor of the proposition. For example, prior to the February 2013 meeting of the Human Rights Council, several NGOs submitted statements in favor of the right to peace, including secular organizations such as the Women's World Summit Foundation, United Network of Young Peacebuilders, International Movement ATD Fourth World, Japanese Workers' Committee for Human Rights, Nonviolent Peaceforce, Zonta International, Make Mothers Matter International, International Association of Democratic Lawyers, and Initiatives of Change International. FBOs such as the United Religions Initiative, Associazione Comunità Papa Giovanni XXIII, Istituto Internazionale Maria Ausiliatrice delle Salesiane di Don Bosco, and the Institute for Planetary Synthesis also gave their support for a right to peace, and as noted before, the World Council of Churches helped organize the conference that brought about the Santiago Declaration.

While many civil society organizations and countries around the world support the idea of a right to peace, at least in principle, the concept is not without critics. As previously mentioned, many countries in the Global North, including many EU countries, have opposed the right. It has not been fully cemented in the international community, and the 2016 Declaration on the Right to Peace (General Assembly Resolution 71/189) does not fully address the concerns of civil society organizations promoting the right to peace. Further, some civil society organizations are staunchly against the idea, arguing that it could protect dictators and allow them to commit human rights abuses. The controversies surrounding the right led to a broader discussion of the tensions between peace and human rights and the debates surrounding the relationship between these two ideas.

The Peace versus Human Rights Debate

While the connection between armed conflict and human rights is fairly straightforward and international law clearly links human rights and peace and conflict, in practice human rights and peace are often treated as conflictual concepts. Before more fully discussing this tension, it is important to define peace. In particular, two types of peace are important to distinguish: negative peace and positive peace. Negative peace is simply the absence of violence and war. During a violent conflict, negative peace, or stopping the violence, is likely the immediate goal. However, as Galtung (1964, 1969) argues, violence includes more than direct, physical violence, and consequently a society might achieve peace in the negative sense without necessarily attaining greater peace, especially due to structural and cultural violence. Galtung (1969) asserts that structural violence is built into systems of inequality and manifested in unjust and unrepresentative social structures that prevent people from reaching their full potential. Because such conditions can (and do) exist in places without manifest physical violence and can contribute to the eruption of armed conflict, Galtung argues that scholars and policy makers should pay attention to both forms of violence. He suggests the term "positive peace" to refer to the absence of structural violence and the presence of social justice (Galtung 1969). This chapter conceptualizes peace in both ways, as the absence of physical violence or war and more broadly as positive peace.

Many scholars have discussed the intrinsic relationship between human rights and peace, with one author noting that "there is no short cut to peace without human rights" (Hoole 2009, 136) and another stating that "there cannot be a real peace in a society in which human rights and the fundamental freedoms are mass-violated" (Lopatka 1980, 364). Physical integrity rights, or those that focus on bodily harm and death, should be associated with negative peace since these rights are directly related to physical violence. Some political and civil rights, such as electoral self-determination, might also be associated with negative peace, but others begin to move into the realm of positive peace. Economic and social rights and those promoting equality for groups of people based on characteristics such as race, ethnicity, and gender, for example, fall under a broader understanding of positive peace that looks toward greater equality.

The one area that seems to provide the greatest division between those focusing on peace and those focusing on human rights is the settlement phase of conflict; scholars point to a disconnect, or even tension, between peace negotiators and human rights advocates (Hannum 2006). On one side of the debate are those who prioritize human rights and equate protecting human rights with war crimes prosecutions and legal justice. They argue that the prosecution of abusers of human rights is important and creates a deterrent to future violators of rights; as such, legal justice mechanisms should be incorporated into any type of postconflict peace agreement. These groups are specifically concerned with physical integrity rights and move to hold human rights violators accountable through tribunals or human rights commissions (Anonymous 1996; Gaer 1997; O'Flaherty 2004). On the other side are those who argue that efforts to prosecute human rights violators will make it more difficult to reach a peace agreement, that conflict parties will not come to the negotiation table if there is the threat of criminal prosecutions, and thus a focus on legal justice can impede peace settlements and ultimately lead to greater conflict and human rights violations (Akhavan 2009; Williams 2014, 135). Armstrong (2014, 590) notes that the International Criminal Court's decision to investigate the government of Uganda and the Lord's Resistance Army "was considered a direct challenge to local peace efforts." This view is also largely focused on negative peace—as the peace agreement itself is primarily meant to end armed conflict.

Despite the apparent challenge of reconciling these two viewpoints, there is space for agreement, particularly when groups begin to more clearly and broadly define human rights and peace. For example, Saliternik (2015) promotes the "justice" side of this debate by arguing that peace agreements have the potential to undermine the principles of justice and human rights norms, since agreements might lead to more oppressive regimes, generate additional human rights abuses, or fail to deal with issues such as "representation deficits" and "biased or corrupt decision making" (Saliternik 2015, 181–82). Saliternik pits peace against justice—but how he conceptualizes justice and peace is important for this discussion. While some authors consider justice in purely legal terms, Saliternik includes references to social justice principles, including ideas of equality and reconciliation. Saliternik generally agrees with the argument of many peace scholars, that both negative and positive peace are important. Many peace scholars see peace settlements not only as a means of ending physical violence but also as important steps toward positive peace. For example, Kumar (2010, 317–18) suggests that the very act of coming to the negotiating table "is a step towards recognition of the entitlement of the rights of the citizens."

Scholars also point to the relationship between human rights and peace in the establishment of postwar institutions (McGuinness 2011), noting that the mere existence of peacetime institutions intended to provide justice is not the same as building institutions that promote human rights (Cooper 2002, 13; Llewellyn 2012, 296; Reuter 2012, 364). Others stress the need to integrate human rights into peacekeeping operations and the various components of postconflict peacebuilding, including disarmament, demobilization, and reintegration (Alston and Asbjorn 1980; Gaer 2003; Waldorf 2013). In each of these examples, we see human rights as an integral part of establishing positive peace.

Yet there remain many practical challenges to linking peace and human rights because of the complexity, internal contradictions, and variation within and between peace and human rights movements (Mertus and Helsing 2006; Kinderman 2009). The differentiation between the concepts by the UN—with human rights defined at the individual level and delegated to the Human Rights Council and peace and security defined at the state level and under the purview of the Security Council—also adds to the challenges (Donnelly 2006, 155; Durán 2011; McGuinness 2011). However, Butcher and Hallward (2017) argue that it is possible to bridge these gaps. Still, the authors find that few organizations specifically associated with the Human Rights Council explicitly link human rights and peace but that religiously affiliated organizations are more likely than secular organizations to discuss peace and to connect peace to human rights.

State of the Literature on Religion and Peace and Conflict

As Butcher and Hallward (2017) find, faith-based NGOs are more likely to discuss peace, and this section focuses on the various connections between specific religious traditions and the concepts of conflict and peace. Most major religions have been tied to conflict at some point in history, just as most have elements that promote peace. Mark Juergensmeyer (2003) argues that religion has often provided power to violent extremism, particularly though claims of moral justification and religious symbolism. At the same time, as Cortwright (2006) and Barash and Webel (2009) note, most major world religions, including Christianity, Islam, Judaism, Buddhism, and Hinduism, have nonviolence as a core tenet. Similarly, Braungart (2019) notes that many RNGOs support the International Criminal Court, though they largely favor a restorative approach to justice and promote reconciliation among parties involved in conflict. Marshall (2013) discusses how many religious actors call for peace and a just world order and how religion often has an untapped potential for peacemaking, particularly in areas where conflicts have religious dimensions, such as in Nigeria and Sudan.

Christianity

The Crusades, which occurred between 1096 and 1291, are probably the most infamous example of Christian religious conflicts. The Crusades began after Pope Urban called upon Christians in the West to rise up against Muslims and take back control over areas they viewed as holy. There were multiple Crusades, or "holy wars," all between Christians and Muslims and largely initiated by Christians and the popes in Europe (Claster 2009). The Spanish Inquisition of the twelfth century is another example of violence and conflict within Christianity. For more than two hundred years, Jews, Muslims, and other non-Catholics were persecuted and tortured for their religious (real or suspected) beliefs (Pérez 2005). In more recent times, individuals touting Christian ideology have bombed churches and abortion clinics in the United States and other countries around the world. Thus, the ties between Christianity and violent conflict have long historic roots.

While Christian history has included many examples of violence, there are also clear connections to peace and nonviolence. Volf (2008) argues that while the Christian faith may have at times been used to justify violence, the heart of the Christian faith is one that fosters a culture of peace. In Christianity, Jesus is seen as one of the primary examples of a figure promoting peace and nonviolence. There are also examples of conscientious objectors, individuals who refuse to fight in a war due to their religious convictions, within both Europe and the United States. Rev. Martin Luther King Jr. also promoted nonviolence and nonviolent resistance and connected these ideas to his religious views.

The idea of just warfare is one that can be found in the early religious scholarship of Saint Augustine (354–430), who promoted limited warfare, and then only in self-defense. He set forth criteria for just war—that it must be fought for defense purposes, be authorized by a legitimate authority, cause as minimal harm as possible, and have the right intentions (Duffey 2015). These ideas of just war are still promoted today as part of just war theory and can be found in international law. Thus, this tradition attempts to limit war to only self-defense and promotes limiting the negative effects of war.

Further, the Quakers and Mennonites, historic peace churches, identify the inherent connection between conflict resolution and human equality and rights (Quaker Council for European Affairs n.d.; Lampen 2015). These concerns for human rights and peace are found in the scholarship of several Mennonite and Quaker scholars such as Adam Curle (1971, 2000), John Paul Lederach (1997, 2014; Sampson and Lederach 2000), Ron Kraybill (1994, 2000), and Lisa Schirch (2005, 2006). The MCC, for example, connects peace and social justice, seeing these concepts "as one ideal rather than as separate goals" (Dicklitch and Rice 2004, 665).

Judaism

Like other religions, Judaism has had its share of violence, and violence is present in key Jewish religious texts. Various religious texts are important within Judaism, including the Torah and the Hebrew Scriptures, which are the equivalent to the Christian Old Testament. These religious texts discuss war and conflict and are relevant to the discussion here. For example, in Deuteronomy 7, when speaking to Israelites about how they should treat nonbelievers, it is said, "When the Lord your God brings you into the land you are entering to possess and drives out before you many nations . . . and when the Lord your God has delivered them over to you and you have defeated them, then you must destroy them totally. Make no treaty with them, and show them no mercy . . . break down their altars, smash their sacred stones, cut down their Asherah poles and burn their idols in the fire" (International Bible Society n.d.). However, it should also be noted that, at the same time, Deuteronomy "depicts God as advocating negotiated peace as a preferable alternative to war" (Burns 2015, 91). The point here is that religious scriptures often tell a nuanced story and that the interpretation of this story may vary or even be manipulated and utilized by those wishing for conflict. However, it does not follow that the religion itself is inherently conflict prone.

Burns (2015, 90) notes that "a major component of the contemporary Jewish agenda for social justice is peacemaking, fostering healthy relations between the Jewish people and their neighbors in the global community." These ideas can be seen in the Hebrew term *shalom*, which signifies peace in a variety of contexts, as well as the Hebrew phrase *tikkun olam*, which translates to "restoration of the world." Together, these concepts are often connected with the Jewish value of social justice and peacemaking (Burns 2015, 87–89). Nonviolence is also prominent within Judaism. Individuals such as Rabbi Lynn Gottlieb have discussed Jewish approaches to nonviolence, and groups like Shomer Shalom have used Jewish principles to support nonviolent actions (Abu-Nimer 2015, 41).

Islam

The Arabic root word for Islam, *silm*, "means reconciliation, peace, submission, and deliverance" (Pal 2011, 14). Thus, at its core Islam is connected to ideas of peace. At the same time, certainly Islam has been invoked to justify violence and conflict; this has been seen in the modern era by groups such as al-Qaeda, which was responsible for the September 11 attacks against the United States, and Daesh (ISIS) in Syria and Iraq. Omar (2015, 14) points out that violence is not necessarily contained within Islamic texts, such as the Qur'an, but rather that usually "religiously inspired violence is forced upon the text rather than the other way around." The issue is not necessarily what is actually written in religious texts but rather how these words are interpreted and utilized by some individuals, such as Muslim "fundamentalists."

One area that has led to misunderstanding about violence and Islam is the term "jihad." Many have incorrectly associated this word with war and conflict, and holy war in particular, but the word has its origins in "the Arabic root letters J H D, meaning 'to strive' or 'to exert' oneself, in the religious sense, in the service of God" (Omar 2015, 15). A better, and more general, interpretation of the term "jihad" is how one strives to fight against temptations and desires. As authors have noted, this term does not appear to be connected to the idea of a war, let alone a holy war, in the Qur'an. However, there are some Muslims who evoke the term in a way that is violent to further their own extremist agendas. In particular, Qur'an 22:39–40, which grants permission to fight against oppression and persecution, is often used to justify jihad against nonbelievers (Saeed 2018). However, these verses do not actually reference jihad and instead use the word *qitāl*, which means "to fight" (Saeed 2018). In general, most scholars would argue that the idea of jihad is not something that extends to offensive warfare and rather is manipulated to serve the agenda of specific people and groups (Omar 2015; Saeed 2018).

There are times when war and conflict are justified in the Qur'an, though this is generally for self-defense. A defensive war, which is permitted by the Qur'an, is referred to *harb qitāl* and not "jihad" (Omar 2015, 17). Qur'an 2:190 specifically states, "Fight in the way of God against those who fight against you but be not the aggressors. Surely God does not love aggressors" (quoted in Omar 2015, 24). Thus, defensive war is supported by the Qur'an, and authors have pointed out that this defensive war is broader than the defensive wars permitted by the UN, as it is not required to be authorized by any particular authority and does not necessarily require a formal armed attack by an enemy (Saeed 2018).

As scholars have noted, there are many references to peace in the Qur'an and far fewer references to defensive war (Omar 2015). Similar to other religions, such as Christianity and Judaism, Islam also emphasizes that all human beings are created in the image of God and that social empowerment leads to justice and peace (Abu-Nimer 2003; Abu-Nimer and Kadayifci-Orellana 2013, 11, 55; Johnston 2014). Furthermore, "justice is the essential component of peace according to the Qur'anic message, therefore it is the responsibility of all Muslims to work toward the establishment of justice for all, including social and economic justice" (Abu-Nimer and Kadayifci-Orellana 2013, 12). Moreover, Muslim religious scholars have actively participated in advocating for peace and nonviolence, including Mawlana Wahiduddin Khan, Shaykh Jawdat Sa'id, and Chaplain Rabia Terri Harris, who founded the Muslim Peace Fellowship and promotes nonviolence (Omar 2015). In addition, nonviolence has been promoted throughout the history of Islam, including by the Prophet Muhammad (Abu-Nimer 2015).

Other Religions

Similar to other religions, Hinduism can be linked to both conflict and peace. Hindu violence against Muslims has occurred multiple times within the current state of India as well as in previous historic periods. On the other hand, Hinduism encourages the pursuit of an inner peace, with this peace extending past the individual to their home, neighborhood, country, and beyond. Further, the sacredness of the sky, earth, river, and sun in Hinduism requires nonviolence in practice, as individuals should not harm their environment and should create harmony between themselves, others, and their environment through peaceful actions. However, violence and war are permitted within Hinduism and even encouraged, particularly to defend oneself and one's country. Still, Hinduism promotes nonviolence more generally, and there are traditional Hindu methods of peacemaking and conflict resolution, with Mohandas Gandhi being the most visible representative of this Hindu nonviolence (Mohanty 2015).

Peace and nonviolence are often considered cornerstones of Buddhist thought. Within Buddhism, peace is a state of being and is quite introspective. Generally, nonviolence is part of how to live one's life according to Buddhist teachings (in an effort to eventually find internal peace), and thus, particularly in early Buddhism, the recommendation was pacifism (Rosch 2015). However, Buddhism has also been interpreted as supporting violence and war, and war and violence have certainly been carried out by Buddhists, for example, by Japan during World War II and in Myanmar with violence against the Rohingya Muslims. Still, there have yet to be any Buddhist groups that have explicitly supported violence as a principle (Rosch 2015, 156).

Similarly, peace and harmony are key components of Confucianism, and many view the religion as promoting pacifism (Chan 2015). At the same time, violence is also sanctioned for punishment or for punitive war in a variety of ways, including "to remove tyrants and deter potential offenders," "to express or demonstrate the correct (moral) order of retributive justice," and "to educate or 'correct' the common people" (Chan 2015, 125). Further, Confucian societies such as China have often used violence against both internal and external populations.

Secular Approaches to Human Rights, Peace, and Conflict

Secular human rights groups often accentuate political and civil rights, emphasizing "neutrality" and "impartiality" over what some might interpret as religious or cultural relativism (Johnston 2014, 907). In the secular arena of large donors and UN peacebuilding missions, efforts to promote human rights and peace "have historically proceeded on separate tracks" (Sharp 2013, 195). Thus, contrary to religious organizations, which tend to espouse a more holistic view of "peace" that includes addressing systemic injustice and restorative processes of conflict resolution (American Friends Service Committee 2012; MCC n.d.), secular approaches to human rights appear more likely to differentiate between peace and human rights. At the same time, human rights abuses often occur during conflicts, and it would be difficult for human rights groups to ignore the role played by conflict in human rights abuses. However, given that peace is directly related to the idea of conflict, it is also likely that many organizations that are reluctant to mention peace will also shy away from explicitly discussing conflict in relation to human rights abuses.

Hypotheses

It is clear that religion has often been utilized to justify war and violence and that nearly every major world religion has been associated at one time or another with acts of war and violence. What is also clear is that all major world religions also support peace, and particularly link peace to social justice. Given the tensions between human rights discussed above, we expect that most human rights NGOs will not discuss peace, a right to peace, or conflict nor have sections on their websites dedicated to peace and/or conflict resolution. However, we also expect differences in religious and secular approaches to human rights and peace. In particular, we examine the following hypotheses:

1. Religious organizations will be more likely than secular groups to discuss peace.
2. Religious organizations will be more likely than secular groups to have a separate section on their website dedicated to peace and/or conflict resolution.
3. Religious organizations will be more likely than secular groups to focus on social justice.
4. Religious and secular organizations will be equally likely to consider a right to peace.
5. Organizations in the Global South will be more likely than those in the Global North to discuss a right to peace.
6. Organizations that focus on social justice will be more likely than others to discuss peace.
7. Organizations that focus on legal justice will be less likely than others to discuss peace.

Findings

The sample for this study includes 333 organizational websites, 68 FBOs, and 265 secular human rights organizations. In addition, we interviewed members of 47 human rights NGOs, some of which are also included in the website analysis.

Peace

Consistent with expectations, only 36 percent of the organizations in the sample mention peace in their mission statements, vision statements, about us sections, advocacy page, or other page directly related to their work at the UN (see Table 6.1). Considering religious and secular organizations more specifically, again, as expected, religious organizations were more likely than their secular counterparts to mention peace. Of the FBOs in the sample, 54 percent mention peace, compared to only 31 percent of secular organizations, and this difference is statistically significant at the $p < .001$ level. Of the FBOs in the sample, Muslim organizations were the least likely to mention peace, though the differences are not statistically significant.

TABLE 6.1

Comparisons of Approaches to Peace and Conflict (in percentages)

	Religious organizations	Secular organizations
Peace	54	31
Peace and social justice	50	28
Peace and/or conflict resolution programmatic area	33	17
Right to peace	2	2
War and armed conflict	29	22

Conceptions of Peace

Vivat International

Vivat International is an organization with more than twenty-five thousand members from various Catholic religious congregations. The organization's vision views "every human being as created in goodness and dignity" and is founded upon "believing, defending and proactively supporting the equality in rights and in dignity of all individuals, peoples and cultures." The organization further envisions that their presence at the United Nations will help attain "a world of equality, justice, reconciliation, peace and care of the environment." The organizations has a special section on their website focusing on a "Culture of Peace" where they promote non-violence as a "commitment to peace-building, mediation, conflict prevention and resolution, peace education, education for non-violence, tolerance, acceptance, mutual respect, intercultural and interfaith dialogue and reconciliation."

Vivat International. 2019. "Culture of Peace." https://vivatinternational.org/culture-of-peace-2/.
Vivat International. 2019. "Vision & Mission." https://vivatinternational.org/about/vision-mission/.

Committee on the Administration of Justice

The Committee on the Administration of Justice (CAJ) is a human rights organization that was established in response to the human rights violations committed during the conflict in Northern Ireland and "to ensure that the protection of human rights was at the heart of ending conflict and building a society based on the rule of law." The organization works to "combat impunity, promote a rights based framework for the exercise of the freedoms of expression and assembly, protect human rights and the peace settlement, advocate the application of the fundamental principles of equality and practice international solidarity." One of the primary concerns of the organization is "to protect peace through justice and equality." The organization has a specific section dedicated to "Protecting Human Rights and the Peace Settlement" surrounding the conflict in Northern Ireland.

CAJ. 2019. "Protecting Human Rights and the Peace Settlement." https://caj.org.uk/about/, https://caj
    .org.uk/about/our-work/protecting-human-rights-peace-settlement/.

When interviewing human rights organizations, we find that some groups more clearly connect peace and human rights—seeing these two concepts as closely linked—while others are reluctant to fully consider issues of peace within the framework of human rights. The World Lutheran Federation discusses how religion might play a role in peace, stating, "We are . . . mindful that this is a time in which religion is so often seen as a source of conflict in the world and we wanted to make witness that people of different faiths could collaborate together and try to make for peace."

Several organizations specifically link human rights and peace, and many are located in Africa. Le Réseau des Éducateurs, aux Droits de l'Homme, à la Démocratie et Genre (REDHG), a secular organization in Côte d'Ivoire, noted that "respect for human life is one measure of peace." The Organisation Guinéenne de Défense des Droits de l'Homme et du Citoyen, located in Guinea, similarly stated that "without human rights there would be no peace." "Our vision is peace, dignity and reconciliation of all Rwandan people living in harmony," said the Human Rights Observatory in Rwanda, and the Association Rwandaise pour la Défense des Droits de la Personne et Libertés Publiques (ADL) saw their work in postconflict Rwanda as being "a work of peace" and that "by organizing campaigns for tolerance and reconciliation we work for peace." The Association Africaine d'Éducation pour le Développement (ASAFED) mentioned that one of its aims was "to work for the promotion and protection of human rights and fundamental freedoms . . . and to promote education for peace and peaceful resolution of conflicts." The connection between peace and human rights is clear. Similarly, women's organizations also more explicitly linked peace and human rights. For example, WILPF noted that they "don't think that there is any possibility of peace without human rights," and Feminist Dalit Organization said that "human rights and peace [are] crosscutting." Overall, several organizations in Africa and two of the women's organizations discussed the inextricable link between peace and human rights.

Even some groups that did not explicitly frame their work in terms of peace, such as the International Service for Human Rights, asserted that "ultimately, most human rights defenders in pushing for human rights are ultimately pushing for peace." Several religious organizations made similar assertions. For example, while noting that they were not really a peacebuilding organization, Franciscans International stated that their "contribution to peace is really to look at peace from a human rights perspective," and T'ruah noted that they didn't really have a specific peace framing but that "building more on-the-ground rights for Palestinians, for Bedouin, will aid the work of peace."

Some of the organizations clearly connect peace with other issues and related all of these to human rights, for a comprehensive approach to human rights and peace. For example, the Lebanese Center for Human Rights discussed how they were doing peace work and service work, which "is life changing for people." This organization seemed to equate service work, particularly for refugees who have been displaced due to conflict, and peace work, demonstrating a much closer connection between broader human rights issues (like service) and peace. Similarly, Djazairouna (des Familles Victimes du Terrorisme Islamiste), an organization in Algeria, saw their work as being closely related to and entwined with peace. ADL, in Rwanda, noted that their aim is for "peace and development." Here, again, is a connection between peace and broader human rights issues, like development. Feminist Dalit also stated that they especially focused on human rights, peace, and development. They also noted that political participation was especially important for "sustainable peace." ASAFED stated that their work related to women's rights and violence against women, the fight against racism and racial discrimination, and other projects were "all different struggles [that] lead to the construction of peace in national and international societies." WILPF discussed the problem of trying to talk to people about peace when they felt there are more pressing needs: "You want to talk about peace in the middle of conflict, people look at you like, are you mad? We need other things right now, and they talk about health, they talk about food, they talk about water, they talk about housing . . . [and] missing persons. And each one has a different compelling need, and for each one of those, that's a component part of peace, but until you get all of it, you're not going to have peace." Several of the religious organizations interviewed exhibited similar themes during their interviews. The Baha'i International Community mentioned that they issued a "Peace Statement" that "explains that peace can only be achieved if some principle problems that society today faces are resolved," some of these issues being human rights, equality between women and men, the eradication of racism and poverty, and so on. Further, they noted that "there are a lot of aspects of human rights that have everything to do with peace." Similarly, Dominicans for Justice and Peace said of the work they do that "in some ways all of it is directed toward peace." They specifically mentioned economic issues, such as inequality and poverty, being closely tied with issues of peace and that they were using a broad definition of peace. One religious organization said "all of our work here is peace work" and that would include "work on food and sustainability . . . rights and refugees . . . peace and disarmament . . . and climate change."

The connections that many of these organizations, both secular and religious, made between issues like poverty, development, and others constitute positive peace, not just the absence of violence as peace. As the representative from Dominicans for Justice and Peace said, "Our Catholic social teachings spell it out quite significantly to say that it's [peace] not just the absence of war . . . peace is . . . for people to find peace in their hearts and to be at peace with themselves, and with others." The International Peace Bureau stated similarly that "peace is not only the absence of war, or violence, it's also to do with social justice, it's to do with democracy and human rights, it's to do with our relationship to the environment; it's a much more holistic concept, this idea of structural violence by Galtung."

"The absence of war is not peace," noted WILPF, and Catholic Relief Services stated, "Our first choice is to transform conflict, rather than just resolve it; moving beyond just the negative peace but to the positive peace." Looking at "peace in various dimensions . . . not only peace in terms of an absence of conflict, but also peace in terms of social justice, including respect for human rights, economic justice, environmental protection, and climate change" was important for the World Council of Churches.

Several secular organizations distanced themselves from the term "peace" because of their specific understandings of the term in their particular context. For example, B'Tselem, an Israeli human rights organization, was more skeptical of what they called "a peace industry" and noted that "peacebuilding . . . is not the focus of what we do" and that in terms of peace work, they have been "very skeptical of that." Rather, they stated, "We are against violence, we are committed to human rights, but not part of this peace industry." This conception of peace is more in line with negative peace—associated with lack of violence. BADIL, a Palestinian organization, stated that they "don't like to use the word 'peace,' . . . not because we don't want peace . . . we do want peace, but we want a just peace, and the peace that Israel is offering, and the international community, is not a just peace, it's not based on international law and human rights." BADIL clarified that they see their own approach as being "completely peace-based" but that because of the context within Israel, the term "peace" has been "mired or dirtied" by something that is not "rights-based" and thus they have reservations about using the term. In this context, peace is defined more in terms of positive peace and negative peace, without this more "just peace," may give the false impression of peace that would work against the human rights approach of the organization. A Geneva-based organization stated that they "never thought of [themselves] as a peace group" and associated peace with "hippies" and feminists from the sixties. Just as B'Tselem and BADIL sought to differentiate their work from so-called peace work in the context of Israel/Palestine, this organization made it clear that peace had a particular connotation that they did not want to be associated with.

Other organizations simply did not view their human rights work within the framework of peace. For example, the Helsinki Foundation noted, "We actually don't really think of ourselves this way" and that "peace groups" in Poland were different groups. At the same time, they did note, "We understand human rights are important for sustaining peace in the world . . . and we agree with that, but we . . . don't think in those terms, we'd rather think in the terms of human rights." This response suggests that the organization, while understanding that peace and human rights are linked at some level, finds it strategically useful to separate them both conceptually and in practice.

Peace and Justice

As discussed previously, there is tension within the literature between the ideas of peace and justice—particularly legal justice. Due to this, it is expected that organizations that focus on legal justice will be less likely to mention peace than those that do not. Further, since social justice efforts are often more consistent with the idea of peace, it is expected that organizations that focus on social justice will also be more likely to mention peace. The findings lend some support for these propositions. First of all, around 31 percent of the organizations that focus on legal justice also discuss peace, compared to 38 percent of the organizations that do not focus on legal justice. Thus, organizations with a legal justice focus are slightly less likely than others to discuss peace; however, this difference is very small and not statistically significant. In terms of social justice, 43 percent of the organizations that consider social justice also mention peace, compared to only 12 percent of others, and this difference is significant at the $p < .001$ level. These results suggest that a focus on legal justice has little impact on discussions of peace but that those organizations with a social justice orientation are more likely than others to mention peace. This is particularly important in that it suggests more common ground between human rights and peace than presented in the literature on these issues, especially in how human rights might relate to positive peace.

As expected, religious organizations (50 percent) also appear more likely than secular groups (28 percent) to discuss both peace and social justice, and this difference is significant at the $p < .001$ level. Thus, religious organizations appear more likely to work on both peace and social justice.

For example, in the interviews Catholic Relief Services, an FBO, connected social justice and conflict. They stated that their organization "seeks to alleviate poverty and address the root causes of social injustice in violent conflict throughout the world." They further noted that they work with those who have been "subjected to structural violence and often, for long periods, actual violent conflict." This demonstrates that the organization sees a close connection between peace and social justice. As mentioned previously, the World Council of Churches connected peace with various types of justice, including social and economic justice. Further, the group mentioned the potential difficulties in achieving peace when there is a strong focus on legal justice and holding people accountable for their crimes, saying that they had recently considered "the extent to which human rights, or . . . an unreflective approach to human rights, can actually be the enemy of a good outcome. For example, one case in the slightly more distant past was obviously the effort to hold leaders of the Lord's Resistance Army accountable for crimes against humanity, human rights violations . . . it actually undermined efforts to achieve peace and reconciliation in the communities concerned."

A few secular organizations emphasized the need for legal justice to take precedence over peace. FIDH stated "that there can be no sustainable peace without accountability for the most serious human rights violations." The Helsinki Foundation made this distinction even clearer when they noted, "The different divisions of justice, of course the idea of reparative justice, is close to us" and that their work is more focused on legal justice than the idea of peace. The Ivorian Observatory also framed peace in relation to legal justice. The representative from the organization said the transitional justice processes in Côte d'Ivoire were not yet working but that "their group is interested in enforcing the rule of law and promoting fair prosecutions for all sides," which he thinks "will bring about peace."

Peace or Conflict Resolution Programmatic Area

In addition to focusing on broad conceptions of peace and justice, this chapter also considers whether the human rights organizations within the sample have a specific programmatic area or section that is focused on peace and/or conflict resolution. This allows for a consideration of organizations that not only mention peace but are more committed to dealing with peace and conflict resolution issues and topics. As expected, a minority of human rights organizations in the sample (20 percent) have a specific programmatic area dedicated to peace and/or conflict resolution.

Also as expected, religious organizations (33 percent) were more likely than secular groups (17 percent) to have programmatic peace/conflict resolution sections on their websites, a difference significant at the $p < .01$ level. No Muslim organizations have peace-specific sections, but around 35 percent of the Christian organizations, 25 percent of the Jewish organizations, and 44 percent of the other religious organizations in the sample have them. These differences are statistically significant at the $p < .05$ level for the difference between Muslim and other religious organizations.

Though the interviews cannot clarify whether organizations have specific programmatic areas focused on peace or conflict resolution, some of the organizations we interviewed frame their work as part of a broader peacebuilding, conflict resolution, or transitional justice effort, similar to the programmatic areas of focus on the websites we analyzed. However, contrary to the sample, interviewed secular and religious organizations are equally likely to focus more fully on these efforts. For example, the representative from the Ivorian

Observatory said that they view a lot of their work as peace work and that because the country was coming out of a political crisis, they felt they could help bring peace and reconciliation to the country. The Public Foundation "Kylym Shamy," located in Kyrgyzstan, noted that "the organization is a peace maker" and is working to help various groups within the country. Djazairouna mentioned that a lot of their work is related to transitional justice and reconciliation, and Mazlumder mentioned their "conflict monitoring resolution committee" that sends teams to postconflict situations. In terms of religious organizations, Catholic Relief Services discussed their "People to People" peacebuilding projects as well as projects aimed to promote "higher level reconciliation between the different conflict groups," and the World Council of Churches said that "in the case of South Sudan . . . our role there has been to try and facilitate the engagement of religious leaders, church leaders from South Sudan and specifically of the ecumenical council, the South Sudan council of churches directly in the peace process negotiations and discussions." While these organizations do not necessarily mention specific programmatic sections related to peace and conflict resolution, they do indicate several examples of where their organizations are working to actively resolve conflict.

Right to Peace

We expected very few human rights organizations to mention the right to peace explicitly on their websites (in the about us section, vision statement, mission statement, advocacy page, or document directly related to their work at the UN), and as expected, only five (around 2 percent) of the organizations in the dataset mention the right to peace. There also appears to be no difference between religious and secular organizations.

However, contrary to expectations, most of the organizations that mentioned the right to peace were in the Global North; around 2 percent of organizations in the Global North mentioned the right to peace, compared to 1 percent of those in the Global South. However, these differences are not statistically significant. Given the small number of organizations that mention the right to peace, it is difficult to draw any conclusions regarding cultural differences.

The controversial nature of the right to peace is evident in the interviews. Dominicans for Justice and Peace noted that there was "a big debate at the moment, because there are a number of groups . . . that are advocating for the 'right to peace'" and that "it's becoming very polarized in this UN context, even among Catholic groups." The International Peace Bureau expressed some skepticism with the idea of a "right to peace," saying that this might allow states to say "Oh, we're for peace, we support the right to peace and we defend that peace with armed force." On the flip side, another secular international organization suggested that they oppose a right to peace because they view it as a negative response to the responsibility to protect (R2P). The organization suggested that in response to R2P, "the bad guys came up with the right to peace, to balance their [the West's] responsibility to protect" and that this right to peace basically meant that the West didn't "have the right to intervene" because the countries they would be intervening in "have a right to peace." This wide range of approaches to the right to peace illustrates the difficulties faced in attempting to make the right to peace more institutionalized in international human rights law.

Armed Conflict and War

As mentioned earlier, many human rights abuses take place within the context of armed conflict and war. From this perspective, it might be expected that human rights organizations would mention armed conflict or war as a human rights issue. However, this is not necessarily the case. Out of the organizations in the sample, only 23 percent mention armed conflict/war as an issue. This is fewer organizations than those that mention peace (36 percent). This finding is a bit perplexing at first glance. One potential explanation is the controversial nature of war and armed conflict in the international system. Major international actors, such as the United States, have initiated conflicts in the international system. There are likely significant reservations on the part of human rights organizations to make broad statements about the costs of war in terms of human rights. Furthermore, the UN and other international organizations, such as NATO and the African Union, have authorized the use of force to deal with states that are violating human rights. The use of force by major international actors is likely to have an impact on how international human rights organizations talk about armed conflict and war.

In the sample religious organizations (29 percent) are slightly more likely than secular organizations (22 percent) to mention war and/or armed conflict as an important issue. However, this difference is relatively small and not statistically significant. Jewish organizations are less likely than other religious organizations to discuss conflict and/or war as a human rights issue, with none of the Jewish organizations discussing this issue. Around 31 percent of Christian organizations, 29 percent of Muslim organizations, and 33 percent of other religious organizations discuss war or armed conflict as an issue. Though the difference between Jewish organizations and others does not reach the level of statistical significance, we believe this is an interesting finding and indicates the need for further research on the relationship between Jewish organizations and discussions of war and conflict.

When looking at the interviews, a few key themes emerge. First, many of the human rights organizations we interviewed discussed their humanitarian aid and emergency relief work during conflicts. The Federation of Environmental and Ecological Diversity for Agricultural Revampment and Human Rights, an organization in Cameroon, discussed their work providing food, salt, washing materials, soap, detergent, and so on to families affected by conflict. The organization further lamented the difficulty of providing for families due to lack of resources.

Second, and related to emergency relief and humanitarian aid, several organizations emphasized the issue of refugees and people displaced as a result of conflict as part of their work. For example, the Lebanese Center for Human Rights created a rehabilitation center to work with refugees from conflict zones. The Human Rights Commission of Pakistan mentioned the problems of internal displacement due to the conflicts in Pakistan. The Mauritanian Association for the Rule of Law discussed their projects in Mauritania and Senegal dedicated to helping refugees and internally displaced people. They stated, "We provide refugee camps with foods and water and also drugs" and that "trainings were also conducted in these camps" and that they work to "reinforce peace in these zones." BADIL was primarily concerned with issues of refugees and displaced people, particularly from Palestine. Equitas also mentioned their work with "Syrian children who are in refugee camps, or who were refugees in Jordan."

Third, several organizations noted the difficulty with accessibility in terms of conflict zones. The Human Rights Commission of Pakistan mentioned that the main conflict zones in Pakistan, such as the tribal zones, were not really accessible to the organization, making it difficult for them to help the situation. Mazlumder noted how they could not "send monitoring teams to conflict zones during conflict . . . the government doesn't let us do that." Islamic Relief Worldwide also emphasized that they were forced to withdraw from large areas of Syria and Iraq that were controlled by ISIS.

Fourth, a few organizations, both secular and religious, specifically mentioned the difficulty of ethnic and religious conflicts. For example, the Public Foundation "Kylym Shamy," an organization in Kyrgyzstan, discussed their work to bring ethnic minorities that have been in conflict in the country together to work toward peace. Equitas noted their work in Sri Lanka "promoting religious harmony, because one of the legacies of the civil war in Sri Lanka was the conflict among the different religious groups." Religious organizations in particular mentioned issues related to the root causes of conflict. The Lutheran World Federation discussed their work in ethnic conflict zones in Ethiopia.

Fifth, a few organizations suggested the importance of focusing on the root causes of conflict. For example, Franciscans International stated that they "really try to target the root causes of the conflict." Catholic Relief Services said that "one of our guiding principles when we're addressing violent conflict is to address root causes."

Finally, several organizations discussed the issue of arms control, disarmament, and nuclear weapons. Dominicans for Justice and Peace stated that "if we can get rid of the arms industry, I think that would be a major catalyst towards peace and human rights in the world." Similarly, much of the work of the International Peace Bureau is centered on the issue of disarmament, and one of their primary programs focuses on "disarmament for development." One religious organization also mentioned the importance of disarmament and arms control and were particularly interested in the humanitarian case for nuclear disarmament. WILPF also focused on disarmament, including nuclear disarmament, the arms trade, and the proliferation of weapons. In particular, they considered the "gender dimensions" of the impact of these weapons. Not all organizations we interviewed were supportive of disarmament, and one secular organization was more dismissive of the issue, suggesting that it wasn't really an issue that people in the human rights committee were working on. Overall, disarmament was a key theme in discussions of war and conflict and one that was equally discussed by religious and secular organizations.

Conclusion

This chapter has shown that most human rights organizations working closely with the Human Rights Council do not prominently mention peace or conflict on their websites. Further, most organizations do not have dedicated sections on peace and/or conflict resolution nor openly support a "right to peace." At the same time, FBOs are significantly more likely than secular organizations to discuss peace. Religious organizations are also more likely to mention both peace and social justice and more likely to have dedicated peace and/or conflict management sections on their websites.

Disaggregating the data into respective religious groups shows notable variance in several key instances. The Muslim groups included in the sample are the least likely to discuss peace. Further, none of the Muslim organizations in our sample have specific sections on their websites dedicated to peace and/ or conflict resolution. To be clear, this does not mean that Islam does not value peace but rather may reflect the organizational tendencies of the religion in terms of priority areas as they align with human rights activism. More research is needed to examine why this difference exists, as it could be terminological, could have to do with how peace work is conceptualized and categorized in websites, or may have to do with a division of labor between organizations as well as the small size of the sample of Muslim organizations.

Only five organizations within the sample mention a right to peace, and there was no significant difference between secular and religious organizations in their support for a right to peace. Contrary to expectations, organizations from the Global South are not necessarily more likely to discuss a right to peace, although it is difficult to draw many conclusions with such a small sample of groups. Some of the organizations we interviewed discussed their skepticism and uncertainty related to a right to peace; these responses, along with the small number of organizations openly mentioning a right to peace, indicate that this right has yet to be fully embraced by the international community.

Though war and armed conflict are clearly tied to human rights issues, only 23 percent of the organizations in the sample discuss this as an important issue. In fact, fewer organizations mention war/armed conflict than discuss peace. Religious organizations are slightly more likely than secular groups to mention war and armed conflict, but this difference is small and not statistically significant. Jewish organizations are the least likely to discuss conflict and war. Still, with only four Jewish organizations in our sample, it is difficult to fully analyze the differences between these and other types of religious organizations, and these results suggest a need for further research.

Overall, the results indicate that there is a clear difference between religious and secular organizations in how they approach peace and human rights. FBOs are significantly more likely to consider peace, to have peace and conflict resolutions on their websites, and to connect peace and social justice. The results also indicate that there may be key differences between different types of religious organizations and faith movements. More research is needed to more fully explore the ways that various religious traditions may differ in their approaches to peace and human rights.

CONCLUSION

This book set out to explore the question of whether and how religious and secular human rights organizations approach advocacy differently and to map out areas of convergence and divergence. Normand and Zaidi (2008, 7) observe that the human rights paradigm has "the capacity to mean different things to different people while retaining overall ideological coherence . . . [and yet] despite being highly contested, human rights are still widely considered to be the best, if not the only possible, universal global ethic." This book has explored many of the contradictions of the human rights paradigm laid out by Normand and Zaidi, including the extent to which they are rooted in religious traditions versus overturn traditional patterns of obedience as well as the extent to which human rights are universal or rooted in Western philosophy.

By empirically exploring the websites of 333 organizations affiliated with the UN Human Rights Council as well as interviewing members of 47 human rights organizations, we were able to identify areas where religious and secular human rights organizations pursue similar goals and objectives and therefore can work cooperatively for a common purpose. The goal of this project was to map out broad themes for initial comparisons and to pinpoint areas for further research. The large-N research design lays out the groundwork for future anthropological field work or analysis of select religious and secular organizations using a traditional comparative case study method. The preceding chapters have examined how religious and secular organizations engage with key themes and debates in the human rights arena, namely cultural rights, socioeconomic development rights, women's rights, children's rights, and rights related to peace and conflict. In the conclusion we emphasize the key takeaway points from the research and identify areas warranting further study and exploration.

Navigating the Boundary of Religion and Secularity

A key challenge in researching religious and secular human rights organizations is determining how those categories are defined, particularly since not all organizations are explicit in their orientation to religion. Some groups have quasi-cultural ties to a faith community, and others reflect the social mores of a country dominated by a particular religious group. Some human rights organizations are overtly secular but profess their mission and vision in ways that are almost religious in tone. While we coded groups as religious or secular based on established criteria determined at the beginning of the project, the dividing line between what makes a group religious as opposed to secular is often blurry, and religiosity and secularity may in fact be more aptly conceived as spectrums.

Another sampling and coding strategy might yield slightly different results than those found here since we narrowed the universe of human rights organizations by focusing on those affiliated with the UN Human Rights Council. This decision in and of itself yielded a particular population of organizations and does not account for all activism in particular issue areas or include all FBOs. Thus, some of the religious organizations in our sample may hold positions that differ considerably from the doctrinal views of more orthodox clergy in their given faith, and there is certainly a diversity of theological, social, and political perspectives within and across the faith groupings included here.

This project yielded a number of insights regarding the intersection of religious and secular human rights organizations and highlighted a number of areas worthy of further research. One of the topics repeatedly mentioned was how secular organizations navigate highly religious societies and what impact this has on the framing of their work. For example, a representative of the Human Rights Commission of Pakistan noted that their organization is "totally a secular organization, which is rare for Pakistan. . . . [We] believe in the equality of all people regardless of their faith. . . . A lot of Islamic organizations have the Muslim identity somewhat there." Due in part to their focus on rights for non-Muslims, this organization has sometimes had trouble with "the powers that be" but has persisted due to their commitment to the human rights framework. B'Tselem, an Israeli human rights organization, does not define itself as either religious or secular but noted that public opinion research in Israel shows that "support for human rights is very political and has to do with religiosity. The more religious a person is, the less likely they are to support human rights as a notion." At the same time, however, B'Tselem noted that although the religious community in Israel does not generally support their human rights work, they do have religious supporters—primarily Jews and Christians—from elsewhere in the world, evidence that religious views differ from place to place, even within the same religious tradition.

The funding of secular human rights organizations based in the Global South and/or outside the West by religious individuals and religious organizations from Europe and the United States also underscores divides between liberal and conservative elements within and between faith traditions as well as between human rights organizations and conservative and/or religious elements in their local society. BADIL, a secular Palestinian organization, for example, receives funding from church agencies but is not religious itself, and Catholic Relief Services supported Latin American human rights organizations during their struggles in the 1990s.

Further, our findings show that when religious organizations perform certain services in the international community, such as providing humanitarian aid, they are more likely to receive monetary support from state and local governments, the UN, and the EU than when they do not include these services. This illustrates how government funding, particularly for religious organizations, may be particularly tied to the provisions of services. It also suggests a way for religious organizations to potentially increase funding from governments by broadening their scope of human rights work to include humanitarian missions. Further research might look more closely at questions of funding for human rights organizations, differentiating types of grant-giving institutions, for example, based on degree of religious affiliation or where large churches, for example, use their funds. However, funding information for many organizations was missing or incomplete, and thus additional in-depth qualitative research would likely be needed to explore such questions.

Consistent with our expectations, we found differences in the motivations and reasons for religious and secular human rights organizations' unique framing of their work. As a member of the Baha'i observed, "We are an organization that represents a community of people who belong to the Baha'i faith, and so the approach [to human rights] is slightly different." The Dominicans identified that faith is their "starting point . . . where people are suffering or oppressed or afflicted. . . . If we ascribe to the full dignity and equal dignity of every individual, we have to be struggling for the acknowledgement of their human rights." The Lutheran World Federation observed, "We are motivated for doing this work because of our faith and because of our desire to serve. And in a way I suppose you could say obviously that many, many, many of the people working in the secular organizations also have quite strong and commendable motivations for being of assistance and many of them being individually doing that or as a result of their own faith commitments. But on an organizational level that is not the case."

As expected, religious human rights organizations often framed their work in terms of duties and obligations, in contrast to the more humanistic moral commitment to human rights found in secular organizations. This can translate into resilience for religious organizations in times of conflict, crisis, and/or funding cuts. Mazlumder, for example, spoke of their work in terms of a "Qur'anic duty to justice" and noted, "We try to expand the notion of human rights to include religious foundations . . . fulfilling [our] mission on earth to pursue justice." Islamic Relief Worldwide stated that "the shari'a is essentially a whole set of rights and obligations" to the family as well as the broader community. Religious organizations, as expected, also emphasized the divine mandate of human rights, often framed in terms of human dignity. The World Council of Churches stated that "human rights law is nothing more, but nothing less, than a set of tools and procedures for promoting and protecting God given human dignity." Likewise, T'ruah shared that the basis for their work is "the perspective that every human being is created in the image of God," and Soka Gakkai noted the importance of the daily Buddhist practices of "recognizing the inherent dignity of our own lives, and equally, the dignity inherent in other lives."

At the same time, however, religious organizations noted the challenges inherent within faith communities regarding the extent to which human rights are religiously mandated. The World Council of Churches identified the need to address "an increasing level of antagonism by religious leaders in different parts of the world against the language of human rights precisely because it is seen . . . as a post-religious secular religion." A representative from Islamic Relief Worldwide suggested that it could make a huge difference if secular human rights activists could join forces with religious human rights activists "in presenting a vision of how faith teachings supports human rights."

Although this project asked whether religious and secular human rights organizations were competitors or partners, differences within faith communities pose a significant challenge, such as those religious organizations that hold views on the composition of the family that directly contradict the views of other religious organizations; T'ruah noted, for example, that they are unique among rabbinical associations in using a human rights, as opposed to a social justice, framing for their work. Further, they suggested that in contrast with many secular Jews who might use social justice frameworks for justifying their human rights advocacy, many synagogues do not even have a social justice orientation. Though many casual observers might assume that various faith communities share a common belief regarding human rights, there are clearly divisions within faiths. Further, such divisions also occur between secular human rights organizations. Though secular organizations generally subscribe to the tenets of the UDHR and other international human rights laws, there is not necessarily a common ethical framework among these organizations. As the results from this study show, secular organizations often have divisions in their approaches to rights. Additional research is needed to more fully explore the variations within faith communities and within the secular community regarding their framing and conceptualization of human rights.

Areas of Complementarity and Divergence

In many areas, religious and secular human rights organizations appear to approach issues in a similar fashion. In terms of children's rights, for example, there were limited differences between religious and secular organizations in terms of the percentage approaching children's rights and in the types of children's rights that were considered. Overall, secular organizations were slightly more likely to consider the physical well-being of children, and religious organizations were slightly more likely to consider child development, but these differences were minor. Further, both types of organizations were equally likely to consider the importance of child agency. Thus, children's rights is one area where there appeared to be more convergence in terms of approaches to rights. Similarly, religious and secular organizations did not differ greatly when it came to a range of women's rights issues, although there were differences in terms of opposition to abortion, which came more from religiously oriented groups.

Differences between religious and secular organizations are notable in several key areas, including mentioning "rights" on their websites. While the organizations in the sample clearly identify with the broader human rights framework, not all of these organizations mention rights. Even though the vast majority of organizations do specifically mention "rights," 17 percent of the organizations in the sample do not mention rights prominently on their websites. However, secular organizations are significantly more likely to mention rights than FBOs. Consistent with previous research, we find that secular organizations are also more likely than religious organizations to consider political and civil rights, including democracy, and to discuss legal justice, while religious organizations are more likely to consider social and economic rights and issues of dignity and to emphasize social justice. At the same time, while there were differences between religious and secular organizations in terms of social and economic rights, it is worth noting that the vast majority of both types of organizations considered these rights. Thus, while religious organizations were more likely to focus on social and economic issues, these issues were also important for secular organizations, indicating areas of potential convergence and cooperation.

There are also differences in approaches to peace and conflict. Religious organizations are much more likely than secular organizations to mention peace, to have a programmatic area on peace and/or conflict resolution, and to connect peace and social justice. This finding may reflect an orientation toward peace found in the major world religions or a tendency among those religious organizations that work for human rights specifically, given that many of the religious justifications for human rights activism, for example that humans are made in the Divine's image, are also commonly cited reasons for peace activism, such as that every life is sacred because it is an image of the Divine. Similarly, and consistent with our expectations, religious organizations were found to focus more on issues of poverty and humanitarian efforts, perhaps because of the more holistic view of human rights found in some religions and/or the obligation of serving fellow humans in need. However, neither religious nor secular organizations engaged much with third-generation rights such as the right to peace and the right to development, indicating how these newer rights have not been fully institutionalized in the international system. Only four religious organizations, all of which were Catholic, mentioned the right to development. This finding is consistent with Catholic social teachings regarding economic development, which emphasize a concern for not only the poor but also economic equality.

The data do indicate that often differences *within* and *between* religious groups are more significant than those between the general categories of religious and secular. Although religious and secular groups did not show any significant differences in approaches to collective identity rights as a whole, when disaggregated into faith traditions, 100 percent of the Jewish groups and 44 percent of the other religious groups showed an emphasis on collective identity rights. Some of this may be an artifact of how culture and religion intersect given that Jewish is considered an ethnic as well as religious category and most of the other faith traditions were non-Western. Examples such as these indicate that further research is needed to explore the intersection of religion and culture in relation to human rights orientation. We also found differentiation between faith traditions when considering justice, with Christian organizations the least likely and Jewish organizations the most likely to consider legal justice. The strong tradition of Jewish law, the halakha, could account for this difference. Muslim organizations in the sample were the most likely to mention duties, which could be related to the Muslim obligation of giving alms to the poor, or zakat.

In another example of interreligious differences, the Muslim groups included in the sample were the least likely to discuss peace and, in contrast to the Christian, Jewish, and other religious groups, did not have any organizations with peace/conflict resolution sections. In addition, although some of the Jewish organizations mentioned peace and conflict resolution, none of them mentioned war or armed conflict, which suggests that perhaps their orientation to peace and conflict resolution may be at the interpersonal rather than the intergroup or international level. To be clear, such differences do not mean that Islam does not value peace or that Judaism is not concerned with armed conflict, but instead they reflect organizational tendencies in terms of priority areas as they align with human rights activism. More research is needed to examine why these differences exist, as they could be terminological or have to do with how peace and conflict work is conceptualized and categorized in websites since all of the Muslim organizations focus on social justice, suggesting a positive orientation to peace. Alternatively, some differences may have to do with a division of labor between FBOs (i.e., some focusing more on rights, some focusing more on peace/conflict) as well as the small size of the sample of organizations in any given religious tradition.

Competing Explanations

Analysis of the data shows that sometimes factors other than religion seem to influence approaches to human rights activism, most notably whether an organization is based in the Global South versus the Global North and whether the organization is Western or non-Western in orientation. While our categorizations of these organizations are approximations, based on website identification of the headquarters, these trends still provide material to guide further investigation, which may include a refinement of categorizations based on more nuanced case study data, such as funding sources, whether the organizational culture of the organization is in fact more "Western" or based on local customs, and whether the organizational budget or the GDP of the country in which an organization is based has more of an influence on how groups operate. Although this study did not examine differences in organizational budgets and staffing sizes due to the fact that many organizations did not have that information readily available, this is an important avenue for future research.

In several cases the data did not conform to expected patterns of difference between groups from the Global North / Global South or West/non-West. In particular, there is no significant divide between these groups in terms of work on socioeconomic rights, which were traditionally associated with the Soviet sphere during the Cold War. However, we found a significant difference between organizations from the Global South and non-West in terms of emphasis on collective identity rights; this difference likely interacts with religion to shape organizational approaches to collective identity rights. Groups in the Global South and the non-West are also more likely to promote democracy than those in the Global North or West, which contradicted our initial expectations. This result intuitively makes sense if one considers where democracy already exists and where prodemocracy activists would likely be struggling to achieve it, but more research is needed to explore this finding, particularly given trends of democratic decline and rising authoritarianism in many countries around the world.

Limitations

One of the limitations of this study is that it is largely based on organizational websites. This poses a particular challenge for capturing information from smaller, less well funded, and less tech-savvy groups as well as capturing information that may be deemed sensitive or considered illegal in the home country context (Acharya et al. 2017, 22). Thus, the data here may not fully reflect the full scope of work that is being conducted on gender rights in particular, given the sensitivity of those topics. While we attempted to mitigate this limitation by interviewing additional organizations outside the West and/or in the Global South, it is unlikely that we were able to completely avoid this bias. Furthermore, even in Western industrialized contexts, many organizations speak of controversial issues such as abortion in code such as "right to life" rather than making a statement against abortion. Organizations, particularly in oppressive contexts, mentioned that "we are not free in movement, we can't have normal meetings, we have to ask for permission all the time, even for meetings . . . it's always a struggle." In contexts where the government is hostile even to international organizations like International Crisis Group and Plan International, local groups such as the Human Rights Commission of Pakistan and other groups that wished to remain anonymous face particular challenges. Consequently, we can assume that organizations, particularly in the Global South and in authoritarian contexts, are selective in what they post on their websites regarding their areas of work.

Further, many organizations struggle with their budgets, with some focused on grants from Western donors and others largely volunteer run and funded by contributions, often in-kind, from their members. Some interview subjects shared that they have worked at a number of different organizations because funding would run out at one and they would have to move; at times the previous organization even became defunct. Even when projects were funded, this was on a short-term, one- to three-year project cycle that did not promote long-term social change. A related challenge is that, as observed by someone at Baha'i International, "Not everybody who says he or she is an NGO is a real NGO, and because some are funded by governments, some are actually created by governments, some have agenda that have nothing to do with NGO agendas." We selected organizations that were able to attain consultative status with the UN and participate in the UN Human Rights Council meetings because this provided a basic litmus test regarding the authenticity of the organizations in our sample. That said, the diversity of organizational mandates in the 333 organizations surveyed is dramatic, with quite disparate conceptions of rights.

Another limitation of this study is the inability to fully explore the ways that the variation in size and scope of organizations impacted their human rights advocacy and approach. This is a fruitful area for future research but was outside the scope of this current study.

Looking Ahead

The data collected for this book indicate that there are both similarities and differences between religious and secular human rights organizations and that in several key areas other factors, such as culture or position in the global economy, seem to matter more than religion in terms of how a group positions itself. In terms of similarities, one reason that religious and secular organizations may have similar approaches to human rights is that human rights discourse is often shaped by secular voices, and as such, in order to work within this arena, religious organizations assimilate their message to be more similar to secular organizations. Some scholars have even referred to these secular organizations as "gatekeepers" who shape the human rights agenda on the global stage (Kindornay, Ron, and Carpenter 2012). Another potential reason for such similarities is sampling; organizations that attend the Human Rights Council meetings may be more similar to each other in approach than those that do not—thus creating a selection effect. Regardless of the reasons, these similarities indicate common ground and areas where secular and religious human rights organizations can be partners. Still, there were several areas where religious and secular organizations differed in their approach to human rights, indicating competing views concerning international human rights. More research is needed to critically examine some of these areas of convergence and divergence in more depth, as the methodology in this study was designed to see the broader trends and significant themes differentiating religious and secular human rights organizations. In addition to the areas for further research already identified, a few major areas for future study warrant particular mention. First, a careful study of the discursive and programmatic differences between religious organizations falling on opposite sides of the same issue, such as those opposing and supporting reproductive rights, LGBTQI rights, or economic development. While a range of perspectives was found on these issues on organizational websites, the coding schema used here captures only support, lack of mention, or explicit opposition to a particular right. By looking specifically at areas with the broadest array of disparity, particularly within religious groups, one may be able to identify some of the more particular mechanisms affecting how religion interfaces with human rights activism.

A second area warranting further study involves the ways particular religious traditions are distinctive in their approach to human rights advocacy. In other words, not all religions approach human rights in the same manner, and the literature on religions and human rights does not deeply engage with how varying faith traditions approach specific topics and issues. More investigations are needed—whether theological or empirical case studies—to see how religion shapes approaches to a range of human rights topics, from women's rights to socioeconomic development and environmental activism. In an age of increasing attention to intersectionality in fields including women's studies and cultural studies, exploring how religion interacts with these other aspects of identity in shaping the human rights agenda is an important consideration. To do this we would need to expand the dataset using additional sampling strategies given the small number of non-Christian organizations affiliated with the UN Human Rights Council.

A third major area for additional research involves the 2030 Agenda for Development. While none of the SDGs explicitly engages with human rights, most of the goals implicitly focus on various components of the international human rights agenda, and most of the international organizations associated with the UN are actively integrating the SDGs into their work programs and advocacy efforts. However, the broad reach and imprecise nature of the indicators and plans for implementation of these goals make it difficult to define what development is and how it interacts with other rights-based goals and objectives. Notably, discussion regarding the right to development is markedly absent from the discourse surrounding the SDGs, and it is unclear how various political, social, and economic rights fit within the seventeen goals. Absent this, it is difficult to discuss how religious and secular organizations can cooperate in achieving collective goals.

Overall, this book has found areas of both convergence and divergence between secular and religious approaches to human rights. However, given the number of areas where similar approaches were found, we are hopeful that secular and religious organizations can find ways to cooperate, rather than compete, within the international human rights arena. Concentrating on areas where both secular and religious organizations have a high degree of synergy, such as social and economic rights and social justice, can help bridge any gaps that might exist between various human rights approaches. Further, recognizing areas where one type of organization might have an advantage, such as religious organizations in providing humanitarian aid, may also help groups find ways to collaborate by building on their respective strengths. Although important distinctions exist, there is clearly space for religious and secular organizations to partner in the quest for human rights.

Distribution of Organizations

Type	Number	Percentage of total
Secular organizations	265	80
Religious organizations	68	20
Christian organizations	48	14
Muslim organizations	7	2
Jewish organizations	4	1
"Other" religious organizations	9	3
Global North organizations	243	73
Global South organizations	100	30
Western organizations	244	73
Non-Western organizations	98	29
Women's organizations	31	9
Organizations with women's sections	136	41
Children's organizations	19	6
Organizations with children's sections	66	20

N = 333.

APPENDIX B

Human Rights Agreements

Agreement	Date signed	Effective	Web link
The Hague Conventions of 1899 and 1907	October 18, 1907	January 26, 1910	https://ihl-databases.icrc.org/ihl/INTRO/195
Kellogg-Briand Pact	August 27, 1928	—	https://history.state.gov/milestones/1921-1936/kellogg
Universal Declaration of Human Rights (UDHR)	—	December 10, 1948	https://www.un.org/en/udhrbook/pdf/udhr_booklet_en_web.pdf
First Geneva Convention	August 12, 1949	October 21, 1950	https://ihl-databases.icrc.org/applic/ihl/ihl.nsf/INTRO/365
Second Geneva Convention	August 12, 1949	October 21, 1950	https://ihl-databases.icrc.org/applic/ihl/ihl.nsf/INTRO/370
Third Geneva Convention	August 12, 1949	October 21, 1950	https://ihl-databases.icrc.org/applic/ihl/ihl.nsf/INTRO/375
Fourth Geneva Convention	August 12, 1949	October 21, 1950	https://ihl-databases.icrc.org/applic/ihl/ihl.nsf/INTRO/380
Convention Relating to the Status of Refugees	July 28, 1951	April 22, 1954	https://www.humanrights.ch/en/standards/un-treaties/further-conventions/refugee-convention/
Convention Relating to the Status of Stateless Persons	September 28, 1954	June 6, 1960	https://treaties.un.org/Pages/ViewDetailsII.aspx?src=TREATY&mtdsg_no=V-3&chapter=5&Temp=mtdsg2&clang=_en
Convention on the Reduction of Statelessness	August 30, 1961	December 13, 1975	https://treaties.un.org/pages/ViewDetails.aspx?src=TREATY&mtdsg_no=V-4&chapter=5
International Convention on the Elimination of All Forms of Racial Discrimination	December 21, 1965	January 4, 1969	https://www.humanrights.ch/en/standards/un-treaties/racism/
International Covenant on Economic, Social, and Cultural Rights (ICESCR)	December 16, 1966	January 3, 1976	https://www.humanrights.ch/en/standards/un-treaties/icescr/content-icescr/
International Covenant on Civil and Political Rights (ICCPR)	December 16, 1966	March 23, 1976	https://www.humanrights.ch/en/standards/un-treaties/iccpr/iccpr-content/
Optional Protocol to the International Covenant on Civil and Political Rights	December 16, 1966	March 23, 1976	https://www.ohchr.org/en/professionalinterest/pages/opccpr1.aspx
Convention on the Non-applicability of Statutory Limitations to War Crimes and Crimes Against Humanity	November 26, 1968	November 11, 1970	https://www.un.org/en/genocideprevention/documents/atrocity-crimes/Doc.27_convention statutory limitations warcrimes.pdf
Declaration of the United Nations Conference on the Human Environment	—	June 16, 1972	https://legal.un.org/avl/ha/dunche/dunche.html

Agreement	Date signed	Effective	Web link
Declaration on the Establishment of a New International Economic Order	—	May 1, 1973	https://legal.un.org/avl/ha/ga_3201/ga_3201.html
International Convention on the Suppression and Punishment of the Crime of Apartheid	November 30, 1973	July 18, 1976	https://treaties.un.org/doc/Publication/UNTS/Volume%201015/volume-1015-I-14861-English.pdf
Protocol Additional to the Geneva Conventions and Relating to the Protection of Victims of International Armed Conflicts (Protocol I)	June 8, 1977	December 7, 1978	https://ihl-databases.icrc.org/applic/ihl/ihl.nsf/INTRO/470
Protocol Additional to the Geneva Conventions and Relating to the Protection of Victims of Non-international Armed Conflicts (Protocol II)	June 8, 1977	December 7, 1978	https://ihl-databases.icrc.org/applic/ihl/ihl.nsf/INTRO/475
Convention on the Elimination of All Forms of Discrimination against Women (CEDAW)	December 18, 1979	September 3, 1981	https://www.humanrights.ch/en/standards/un-treaties/women/
The Declaration on the Right of Peoples to Peace	—	November 12, 1984	https://www.ohchr.org/EN/ProfessionalInterest/Pages/RightOfPeoplesToPeace.aspx
Convention against Torture and Other Cruel, Inhuman or Degrading Treatment or Punishment	December 10, 1984	June 26, 1987	https://www.humanrights.ch/en/standards/un-treaties/torture/
International Convention against Apartheid in Sports	December 10, 1985	April 3, 1988	https://treaties.un.org/Pages/ViewDetails.aspx?src=TREATY&mtdsg_no=IV-10&chapter=4&clang=_en
Convention on the Rights of the Child	November 20, 1989	September 2, 1990	https://www.humanrights.ch/en/standards/un-treaties/children/
Second Optional Protocol to the International Covenant on Civil and Political Rights, Aiming at the Abolition of the Death Penalty	December 15, 1989	July 11, 1991	https://treaties.un.org/Pages/ViewDetails.aspx?src=TREATY&mtdsg_no=IV-12&chapter=4&clang=_en
Rio Declaration on Environment and Development	—	June 14, 1992	https://legal.un.org/avl/ha/dunche/dunche.html

Name	Date Adopted	Date Entered into Force	URL
International Convention on the Protection of the Rights of All Migrant Workers and Members of Their Families	December 18, 1990	July 1, 2003	https://www.humanrights.ch/en/standards/un-treaties/migrant-workers/
Amendment to Article 8 of the International Convention on the Elimination of All Forms of Racial Discrimination	January 15, 1992	Not yet in force	https://treaties.un.org/Pages/ViewDetails.aspx?src=TREATY&mtdsg_no=IV-2-a&chapter=4&clang=_en
Vienna Declaration and Programme of Action	—	June 25, 1993	https://www.ohchr.org/en/professionalinterest/pages/vienna.aspx
Agreement Establishing the Fund for the Development of the Indigenous Peoples of Latin America and the Caribbean	July 24, 1992	August 4, 1993	https://treaties.un.org/Pages/ViewDetails.aspx?src=TREATY&mtdsg_no=IV-14&chapter=4&clang=_en
Rome Statute of the International Criminal Court	July 17, 1998	July 1, 2002	https://www.humanrights.ch/en/standards/un-treaties/further-conventions/icc/
Optional Protocol to the Convention on the Elimination of All Forms of Discrimination against Women	October 6, 1999	December 22, 2000	https://treaties.un.org/Pages/ViewDetails.aspx?src=TREATY&mtdsg_no=IV-8-b&chapter=4&clang=_en
The Earth Charter	March 2000	June 2000	https://earthcharter.org/about-eci/faqs/
Optional Protocol to the Convention on the Rights of the Child on the Sale of Children, Child Prostitution and Child Pornography	May 25, 2000	January 18, 2002	https://www.ohchr.org/EN/ProfessionalInterest/Pages/OPSCCRC.aspx
Optional Protocol to the Convention on the Rights of the Child on the Involvement of Children in Armed Conflict (Child Soldier Treaty)	May 25, 2000	February 2002	https://treaties.un.org/Pages/ViewDetails.aspx?src=TREATY&mtdsg_no=IV-11-b&chapter=4&clang=_en
Optional Protocol to the Convention against Torture and Other Cruel, Inhuman or Degrading Treatment or Punishment	December 18, 2002	June 22, 2006	https://www.ohchr.org/EN/ProfessionalInterest/Pages/OPCAT.aspx
Protocol Additional to the Geneva Conventions and Relating to the Adoption of an Additional Distinctive Emblem (Protocol III)	December 8, 2005	December 14, 2007	https://ihl-databases.icrc.org/applic/ihl/ihl.nsf/INTRO/615

Agreement	Date signed	Effective	Web link
Convention on the Rights of Persons with Disabilities	December 13, 2006	May 3, 2008	https://www.humanrights.ch/en/standards/un-treaties/disabilities/
Optional Protocol to the Convention on the Rights of Persons with Disabilities	December 13, 2006	May 3, 2008	https://treaties.un.org/pages/ViewDetails.aspx?src=TREATY&mtdsg_no=IV-15-a&chapter=4
International Convention for the Protection of All Persons from Enforced Disappearance	February 6, 2007	December 23, 2010	https://treaties.un.org/pages/ViewDetails.aspx?src=TREATY&mtdsg_no=IV-16&chapter=4
Optional Protocol to the International Covenant on Economic, Social and Cultural Rights	December 10, 2008	May 5, 2013	https://treaties.un.org/Pages/ViewDetails.aspx?src=TREATY&mtdsg_no=IV-3-a&chapter=4&clang=_en
Santiago Declaration	December 10, 2010	March 4, 2016	https://imadr.org/wordpress/wp-content/uploads/2013/01/No.-3-Feature-story.pdf
Optional Protocol to the Convention on the Rights of the Child on a Communications Procedure	December 19, 2011	April 14, 2014	https://www.ohchr.org/EN/ProfessionalInterest/PagesOPICCRC.aspx
Declaration on the Right to Peace (Resolution 32/28)	April 16, 2012	December 19, 2016	https://www.refworld.org/docid/589c72134.html
The Arms Trade Treaty	April 2, 2013	December 24, 2014	https://www.humanrights.ch/en/standards/un-treaties/further-conventions/att/

NOTES

Introduction

1. For the purposes of simplifying the language used in this book, we use the term "religious" NGOs or organizations to include all of these variations, conceptualizing this term broadly and inclusively.

2. The designation of countries as "developed" or "developing" can be found here: https://www.itu.int/en/ITU-D/Statistics/Pages/definitions/regions.aspx.

3. Kennesaw State University IRB Study Number 14-403.

Chapter 1. Religious and Secular Approaches to Human Rights

Portions from this chapter are taken from Butcher and Hallward (2018).

1. Additional discussion of democracy can be found in chapter 2.

Chapter 2. The Role of Culture

1. A handful of countries around the world have not signed and/or ratified the ICESCR, noteworthy among them the United States, which signed but never ratified the treaty, Saudi Arabia, Malaysia, Mozambique, and Botswana.

2. For more on Hofstede's dimensions, see his six-dimensional model, available on his website: https://geerthofstede.com/culture-geert-hofstede-gert-jan-hofstede/6d -model-of-national-culture/.

Chapter 3. Rights-Based Approaches to Socioeconomic Development

1. Appendix B has a full listing of all of the international human rights agreements and associated websites.

2. The full list of SDGs can be found at https://www.un.org/sustainabledevelopment /sustainable-development-goals/.

3. Structural adjustment programs (SAPs) were a type of conditional lending from the International Monetary Fund that involved a wide range of neoliberal policies, many of which were seen to perpetuate poverty and harm the environment. For more information, see https://ips-dc.org/structural_adjustment_programs_poverty _reduction_strategy/.

4. More explanation of the Human Development Index can be found on the United Nations Development Programme (UNDP) website: http://hdr.undp.org/en/content /human-development-index-hdi.

5. For illustrative quotes on Catholic teachings from a number of popes related to the right to development, see the website of Catholic Charities: https://www.cctwin cities.org/education-advocacy/catholic-social-teaching/notable-quotations /development-and-underdevelopment/.

Chapter 4. Exploring the Intersection of Gender and Human Rights in Religious and Secular Organizations

1. For a full listing of state reservations, many of which are also secular in nature, see "Meeting of States Parties to the Convention on the Elimination of All Forms of Discrimination against Women, Fourteenth Meeting, New York, 23 June 2006," https:// www.un.org/womenwatch/daw/cedaw/.

2. The Millennium Development Goals and Sustainable Development Goals are discussed in greater depth in chapter 3.

3. Several major Christian denominations in the United States have been examining their positions on LGBTQI members in the ministry in recent years. For example, in February 2019 the General Conference of the United Methodist Church voted 438–384 to reinforce a policy that states "the practice of homosexuality is incompatible with Christian teaching" (https://www.reuters.com/article/us-religion-lgbt-united -methodist/united-methodist-church-strengthens-ban-on-same-sex-marriage-lgbt -clergy-idUSKCN1QG022). The Presbyterian Church (USA) amended its constitution in 2015 to allow same-sex unions. In Judaism, the Reform community is openly supportive of LGBTQI rights (https://reformjudaism.org/jewish-views-lgbt-equality), although Torah law forbids male homosexuality (https://www.chabad.org/library /article_cdo/aid/663504/jewish/Judaism-and-Homosexuality-Do-Homosexuals-Fit -into-the-Jewish-Community.htm).

BIBLIOGRAPHY

Interviews

1. Anonymous. Interview by author. April 19, 2016.
2. Anonymous. Interview by author. May 20, 2014.
3. Anonymous. Interview by graduate assistant. January 29, 2019.
4. Association Africaine d'Éducation pour le Développement (ASAFED). Email correspondence with authors. January 25, 2019.
5. Association Rwandaise pour la Défense des Droits de la Personne et Libertés Publiques (ADL). Email correspondence with authors. March 5, 2019.
6. BADIL Resource Center for Palestinian Residency & Refugee Rights. Interview by author. February 23, 2016.
7. Baháʼí International Community. Interview by author. May 21, 2014.
8. British Humanist Association. Interview by author. March 1, 2016.
9. B'Tselem. Interview by author. January 29, 2019.
10. Catholic Relief Services (CRS). Interview by author. March 3, 2016.
11. Center for Prisoners' Rights Japan. Email correspondence with author. February 7, 2019.
12. Comisión Jurídica Para el Autodesarrollo de los Pueblos Originarios Andinos (CAPAJ). Email correspondence with author. May 10, 2016.
13. Commonwealth Human Rights Initiative. Interview by author. February 1, 2019.
14. Djazairouna (des Familles Victimes du Terrorisme Islamiste). Email correspondence with authors. March 28, 2019.
15. Dominicans for Justice and Peace. Interview by author. May 21, 2014.
16. Educatrice en Droits Humains; Women Network for Human Rights (WNHR). Interview by author. April 20, 2015.
17. Equitas. Interview by author. February 26, 2016.
18. Federation of Environmental and Ecological Diversity for Agricultural Revampment and Human Rights (FEEDAR & HR). Interview by author. February 5, 2019.
19. Feminist Dalit Organization (FEDO). Interview by author. April 15, 2016.

20. Femmes Développement et Droits Humaines en Guinée (F2DHG). Email correspondence with authors. February 25, 2019.
21. Franciscans International. Interview by author. May 20, 2014.
22. Graduate Women International. Interview by author. March 31, 2016.
23. Helsinki Foundation. Interview by author. March 3, 2016.
24. Human Rights Commission of Pakistan. Interview by author. January 22, 2019.
25. Informal Sector Service Center (INSEC). Interview by author. April 7, 2016.
26. International Association of Jewish Lawyers and Jurists (IAJLJ). Interview with author. March 31, 2016.
27. International Federation for Human Rights (FIDH). Interview by author. May 23, 2014.
28. International Peace Bureau (IPB). Interview by author. May 22, 2014.
29. International Service for Human Rights (ISHR). Interview by author. May 22, 2014.
30. Islamic Relief Worldwide. Interview by author. March 11, 2016.
31. Ivorian Observatory for Human Rights (OIDH). Interview by author. April 21, 2016.
32. Lebanese Center for Human Rights (CLDH). Interview by author. January 25, 2019.
33. Le Réseau des Éducateurs aux Droits de l'Homme, à la Démocratie et Genre (REDHG). Email correspondence with author. May 4, 2016.
34. Lutheran World Federation (LWF). Interview by author. March 7, 2016.
35. Mauritanian Association for the Rule of Law. Email correspondence with author. February 18, 2019.
36. Mazlumder. Interview by author. March 24, 2016.
37. Observatoire des Droits de l'Homme au Rwanda (ODHR). Email correspondence with authors. February 25, 2019.
38. OIDEL-Ignasi Grau. Interview by author. February 16, 2016.
39. Organisation Guinéenne de Defense des Droits de l'Homme et du Citoyen (OGDH). Email correspondence with authors. January 24, 2019.
40. Public Foundation, Center for Human Rights Defenders "Kylym Shamy." Email correspondence with author. February 8, 2019.
41. Quaker United Nations House. Interview by author. May 19, 2014.
42. Rescue Alternatives. Interview by author. April 19, 2016.
43. Soka Gakkai. Interview by author. February 24, 2016.
44. T'ruah. Interview by author. March 24, 2016.
45. Union for Civil Liberty. Interview by author. January 22, 2019.
46. Women's International League for Peace and Freedom (WILPF). Interview by author. May 20, 2014.
47. World Council of Churches (WCC). Interview by author. February 24, 2016.

Published Sources

Abbas, Tahir, and Mohammad Mazher Idriss. 2011. *Honour, Violence, Women, and Islam.* Abingdon: Routledge.

Abu-Nimer, Mohammed. 2003. *Nonviolence and Peace Building in Islam: Theory and Practice.* Gainesville: University Press of Florida.

———. 2015. "Spiritual and Religious Approaches to Nonviolence." In *Understanding Nonviolence: Contours and Contexts,* edited by Maia Carter Hallward and Julie M. Norman, 39–56. Cambridge: Polity.

Abu-Nimer, Mohammed, and Ayse Kadayifci-Orellana. 2013. "Understanding an Islamic Framework for Peacebuilding." https://jliflc.com/resources/understanding-an-islamic-framework-for-peacebuilding/.

Acharya, Bondita, Helene Kezie-Nwoha, Sondos Shabayek, Shalini Eddens, and Susan Jessop. 2017. "Standing Firm. Reclaiming Civic Space." *Sur—International Journal of Human Rights* 26: 17–26.

Advocates for Human Rights. n.d. "Human Rights Approach to Social Justice." http://www.theadvocatesforhumanrights.org/a_human_rights_approach_to_social_justice.

African Commission on Human Peoples' Rights. 1981. "African Charter on Human and People's Rights." https://www.achpr.org/legalinstruments/detail?id=49.

Agadjanian, Alexander. 2010. "Liberal Individual and Christian Culture: Russian Orthodox Teaching on Human Rights in Social Theory Perspective." *Religion, State & Society* 38 (2): 97–113.

Akhavan, Payam. 2009. "Are International Criminal Tribunals a Disincentive to Peace? Reconciling Judicial Romanticism with Political Realism." *Human Rights Quarterly* 31 (3): 624–54.

Alexander, Estrelda. 2010. "Women as Leaders in Pentecostal/Charismatic Religions." In *Gender and Women's Leadership: A Reference Handbook,* edited by Karen O'Connor, 533–43. Thousand Oaks, CA: Sage.

Al-Hariri, Rafeda. 1987. "Islam's Point of View on Women's Education in Saudi Arabia." *Comparative Education* 23 (1): 51–57.

Alldén, Susanne. 2007. "Internalizing the Culture of Human Rights: Securing Women's Rights in Post-conflict East Timor." *Asia-Pacific Journal on Human Rights and the Law* 8 (1): 1–23.

Allen, John L. 2014. *The Catholic Church: What Everyone Needs to Know.* Oxford: Oxford University Press.

Almqvist, Jessica. 2005. *Human Rights, Culture, and the Rule of Law.* Oxford: Hart.

Alston, Philip, and Eide Asbjorn. 1980. "Peace, Human Rights and Development: Their Interrelationship." *Security Dialogue* 11 (4): 315–18.

American Friends Service Committee. 2012. "American Friends Service Committee Mission Statement." http://www.afsc.org/mission-vision-and-values.

Amnesty International. "Gender, Sexuality, & Identity." http://www.amnestyusa.org/our-work/campaigns/my-body-my-rights.

An-Na'im, Abdullahi Ahmed. 2008. *Islam and the Secular State: Negotiating the Future of Shari'a.* Cambridge, MA: Harvard University Press.

Anonymous. 1996. "Human Rights in Peace Negotiations." *Human Rights Quarterly* 18 (2): 249–58.

Apperson, George Latimer. 2006. *Dictionary of Proverbs.* Hertfordshire: Wordsworth.

APRODEH. 2018. "Áreas." http://www.aprodeh.org.pe/areas/.

Arat, Zehra F. Kabasakal. 2006. "Forging a Global Culture of Human Rights: Origins and Prospects of the International Bill of Rights." *Human Rights Quarterly* 28 (2): 416–37.

Arigatou International. 2017. "End Child Poverty." https://arigatouinternational.org/en /what-we-do/end-child-poverty.

Armstrong, Kimberley. 2014. "Justice without Peace? International Justice and Conflict Resolution in Northern Uganda." *Development and Change* 45 (3): 589–607.

ATD Fourth World. n.d. "Who We Are." https://www.atd-fourthworld.org/who-we -are/.

Balhera, Anil, and Anand Kumar. 2017. "Right to Gender Equality and Muslim Laws of Divorce (Talaq-Ul-Bidaat): A Critical Study." *VIDHIGYA: The Journal of Legal Awareness* 12 (1): 66–70.

Banchoff, Thomas, and Robert Wuthnow. 2011. "Introduction." In *Religion and the Global Politics of Human Rights*, edited by Thomas Banchoff and Robert Wuthnow, 1–22. New York: Oxford University Press.

Barakat, Sultan, and Arne Strand. 1999. "When East Meets West: Clash of Civilisations or a New Islamic-Western Aid Culture?" *Humanitarian Affairs Review* (Summer): 30–36.

Barash, David P., and Charles P. Webel. 2009. *Peace and Conflict Studies*. London: Sage.

Barber, Benjamin. 1995. *Jihad vs. McWorld*. New York: Ballantine Books.

Barilan, Yechiel M. 2009. "Judaism, Human Dignity and the Most Vulnerable Women on Earth." *American Journal of Bioethics* 9 (11): 35–37.

Barton, Carol. 2004. "Global Women's Movement at a Crossroads: Seeking Definition, New Alliances and Greater Impact." *Socialism and Democracy* 18 (1): 151–84.

Baumgart-Ochse, Claudia, and Klaus Dieter Wolf, eds. 2019. *Religious NGOs at the United Nations: Polarizers or Mediators?* New York: Routledge.

Becker, Jo. 2017. *Campaigning for Children: Strategies for Advancing Children's Rights*. Stanford, CA: Stanford University Press.

Beinlich, Ann-Kristin. 2019. "'And You, Be Ye Fruitful, and Multiply.' Religious NGOs and the Struggle over Sexual and Reproductive Health Rights at the UN." In *Religious NGOs at the United Nations: Polarizers or Mediators?*, edited by Claudia Baumgart-Ochse and Klaus Dieter Wolf, 64–83. New York: Routledge.

Beinlich, Ann-Kristin, and Clara Braungart. 2019. "Religious NGOs at the UN: A Quantitative Overview." In *Religious NGOs at the United Nations: Polarizers or Mediators?*, edited by Claudia Baumgart-Ochse and Klaus Dieter Wolf, 26–46. New York: Routledge.

Benedetti, Carlo. 2006. "Islamic and Christian Inspired Relief NGOs: Between Tactical Collaboration and Strategic Diffidence?" *Journal of International Development* 18 (6): 849–59.

Benthall, Jonathan. 1997. "The Red Cross and Red Crescent Movement and Islamic Societies, with Special Reference to Jordan." *British Journal of Middle Eastern Studies* 24 (2): 157–77.

Berger, Julia. 2003. "Religious Nongovernmental Organizations: An Exploratory Analysis." *Voluntas: International Journal of Voluntary and Nonprofit Organizations* 14 (1): 15–39.

Bhattacharya, Pallavi. 2016. "Loud and Proud in India." *Herizons* 29 (4): 12–14.

BICE (International Cathothic Child Bureau). 2015. "Right to Development: From Rhetoric to Action." http://bice.org/en/right-to-development-from-rhetoric-to -action/.

B'nai B'rith International. 2019. "Home." https://www.bnaibrith.org/.

Bompani, Barbara, and James Smith. 2013. "Bananas and the Bible: Biotechnology, the Catholic Church, and Rural Development in Kenya." *International Journal of Religion and Society* 4 (1–2): 17–32.

Bonney, Richard. 2004. "Reflections on the Differences between Religion and Culture." *Clinical Cornerstone* 6 (1): 25–33.

Braaten, Daniel. 2017. "Walking a Tightrope: Human Rights, Basic Human Needs and US Support for Development Projects in the Multilateral Development Banks." *Human Rights Review* 18 (1): 45–66.

Bradley, Tamsin. 2009. "A Call for Clarification and Critical Analysis of the Work of Faith-Based Development Organizations (FBDO)." *Progress in Development Studies* 9 (2): 101–14.

Brandt, Michele, and Jeffrey A. Kaplan. 1995. "The Tension between Women's Rights and Religious Rights: Reservations to CEDAW by Egypt, Bangladesh, and Tunisia." *Journal of Law and Religion* 12 (1): 105–42.

Braungart, Clara. 2019. "Reconciliation versus Punishment: Religious NGOs and the International Criminal Court." In *Religious NGOs at the United Nations: Polarizers or Mediators?*, edited by Claudia Baumgart-Ochse and Klaus Dieter Wolf, 126–47. New York: Routledge.

Brems, Eva, Christophe Van Der Beken, and Solomon Abay Yimer. 2015. *Human Rights and Development: Legal Perspectives from and for Ethiopia*. Leiden: Brill Nijhoff.

Browne, Stephen. 2017. *Sustainable Development Goals and UN Goal-Setting*. Oxon, UK: Routledge.

Burns, Joshua Ezra. 2015. "Jewish Ideologies of Peace and Peacemaking." In *Peacemaking and the Challenge of Violence in World Religions*, edited by Irfan A. Omar and Michael K. Duffey, 83–106. West Sussex, UK: John Wiley.

Butcher, Charity, and Maia Carter Hallward. 2017. "Bridging the Gap between Human Rights and Peace: An Analysis of NGOs and the United Nations Human Rights Council." *International Studies Perspectives* 18 (1): 81–109.

———. 2018. "Religious vs. Secular Human Rights Organizations: Discourse, Framing, and Action." *Journal of Human Rights* 17 (4): 502–23.

Butler, Jennifer. 2000. "The Christian Right Coalition and the UN Special Session on Children: Prospects and Strategies." *International Journal of Children's Rights* 8 (4): 351–71.

Caldwell, Melissa L. 2012. "Placing Faith in Development: How Moscow's Religious Communities Contribute to a More Civil Society." *Slavic Review* 71 (2): 261–87.

Carr, Caroline. 2016. "Does the Dao Support Individual Autonomy and Human Rights?" *Stance* 9: 9–16.

Carrette, Jeremy, and Hugh Miall, eds. 2017. *Religion, NGOs and the United Nations: Visible and Invisible Actors in Power*. London: Bloomsbury.

Cavalcanti, Joabe G. 2007. "Development versus Enjoyment of Life: A Post-development Critique of the Developmentalist Worldview." *Development in Practice* 17 (1): 85–92.

Černič, Jernej Letnar. 2016. "The European Court of Human Rights, Rule of Law and Socio-economic Rights in Times of Crises." *Hague Journal on the Rule of Law* 8 (2): 227–47.

Chan, Sin Yee. 2015. "From Sincerity of Thought to Peace All Under Heaven: The Confucian Stance on Peace and Violence." In *Peacemaking and the Challenge of Violence in World Religions*, edited by Irfan A. Omar and Michael K. Duffey, 112–34. West Sussex, UK: John Wiley.

Cheru, Fantu. 2016. "Developing Countries and the Right to Development: A Retrospective and Prospective African View." *Third World Quarterly* 37 (7): 1268–83.

Chishti, Muhammad Naeem-ul-Haq. 2012. "Gender Equality: Human Rights versus Islam." *Pakistan Perspectives* 17 (1): 102–22.

Christians for Biblical Equality. 2007. "US Denominations and Their Stances on Women in Leadership." *E-Quality* 6 (2). http://www2.cbeinternational.org/new/E -Journal/2007/07spring/denominations%20first%20installment—FINAL.pdf.

Clarke, Gerard. 2006. "Faith Matters: Faith-Based Organizations, Civil Society and International Development." *Journal of International Development* 18 (6): 835–48.

Clarke, Gerard, and Michael Jennings. 2008. "Introduction." In *Development, Civil Society and Faith-Based Organizations: Bridging the Sacred and the Secular*, edited by Gerard Clarke and Michael Jennings, 1–17. New York: Palgrave Macmillan.

Clarke, Matthew. 2016. "Points of Equilibrium: Religious Beliefs and Economic Development Policy." *Sustainable Development* 24 (3): 181–89.

Claster, Jill N. 2009. *Sacred Violence: The European Crusades to the Middle East, 1095–1396*. Toronto: University of Toronto Press.

Clements, Kevin P. 2018. "Authoritarian Populism and Atavistic Nationalism: 21st-Century Challenges to Peacebuilding and Development." *Journal of Peacebuilding & Development* 13 (3): 1–6.

Cohen, Adam B., and Peter C. Hill. 2007. "Religion as Culture: Religious Individualism and Collectivism among American Catholics, Jews, and Protestants." *Journal of Personality* 75 (4): 709–42.

Cooper, Sandi E. 2002. "Peace as a Human Right: The Invasion of Women into the World of High International Politics." *Journal of Women's History* 14 (2): 9–25.

Cortwright, David. 2006. *Gandhi and Beyond: Nonviolence for an Age of Terrorism.* Boulder, CO: Paradigm.

Cosgrove, Serena, and Kristi Lee. 2015. "Persistence and Resistance: Women's Leadership and Ending Gender-Based Violence in Guatemala." *Seattle Journal for Social Justice* 14 (2): 309–32.

Cotler, Irwin. 1999. "Jewish NGOs, Human Rights, and Public Advocacy: A Comparative Inquiry." *Jewish Political Studies Review* 11 (3/4): 61–95.

Crandall, Barbara F. 2011. *Gender and Religion, 2nd Edition: The Dark Side of Scripture.* London: Continuum.

Curle, Adam. 1971. *Making Peace.* London: Tavistock.

———. 2000. "Obstacles to Peace: Peace and Conflict." *Journal of Peace Psychology* 6 (3): 247–52.

Curry, Lynne. 2017. "'A Sick Child Deserves Its Rights': Law, Religion, and Children's Medical Care in the United States, 1870–1910." *Journal of the History of Childhood and Youth* 10 (3): 313–38.

DaDon, Kotel. 2018. "Role of the Wife in the Jewish Marriage in Old Testament Scripture, in Jewish Law, and in Rabbinic Literature." *Kairos: Evangelical Journal of Theology* 12 (2): 129–49.

Dailey, Timothy J. 2019. "Battle for the Children: The Parental Rights Amendment versus the United Nations." Illinois Family Institute. https://illinoisfamily.org/federal/battle-for-the-children-the-parental-rights-amendment-versus-the-united-nations/.

Dargin, Justin. 2013. *The Rise of the Global South: Philosophical, Geopolitical and Economic Trends of the 21st Century.* Singapore: World Scientific.

Davis, Comfort, Ayodel Jegede, Robert Leurs, Adegbenga Sunmola, and Ukoho Ukiwo. 2011. "Comparing Religious and Secular NGOs in Nigeria: Are Faith-Based Organizations Distinctive?" Working paper, University of Birmingham.

Davis, Thomas W. D. 2009. "The Politics of Human Rights and Development: The Challenge for Official Donors." *Australian Journal of Political Science* 44 (1): 173–92.

De Feyter, Koen. 2015. "Right to Development in Africa." In *Human Rights and Development: Legal Perspectives from and for Ethiopia*, edited by Eva Brems, Christophe Van der Beken, and Solomon Abay Yimer, 23–50. Leiden: Brill.

De Kroon, Eefje. 2016. "Islamic Law, Secular Law, and Societal Norms: The Recognition of Islamic Legal Practices in the Netherlands and the Protection of Muslim Women's Human Rights." *Journal of Muslim Minority Affairs* 36 (2): 153–83.

Deneulin, Séverine, and Augusto Zampini-Davies. 2017. "Engaging Development and Religion: Methodological Groundings." *World Development* 99: 110–21.

Dicklitch, Susan, and Heather Rice. 2004. "The Mennonite Central Committee (MCC) and Faith-Based NGO Aid to Africa." *Development in Practice* 14 (5): 660–72.

Donders, Yvonne. 2016. "Cultural Diversity and Cultural Identity in Human Rights." In *Culture and Human Rights: The Wroclaw Commentaries*, edited by Andres Johannes Wiesand, Kaliopi Chainoglou, and Anna Śledzińska-Simon, 23–32. Berlin: De Gruyter.

Donnelly, Jack. 1984. "Cultural Relativism and Universal Human Rights." *Human Rights Quarterly* 6 (4): 400–419.

———. 1999. "Human Rights, Democracy, and Development." *Human Rights Quarterly* 21 (3): 608–32.

———. 2006. "Peace as a Human Right: Toward an Integrated Understanding." In *Human Rights and Conflict*, edited by Julie Mertus and Jeffrey Helsing, 151–58. Washington, DC: US Institute of Peace.

Dorff, Elliot. 2012. "The Concept of the Child Embedded in Jewish Law." In *Children, Adults, and Shared Responsibilities: Jewish, Christian and Muslim Perspectives*, edited by Marcia Bunge, 19–38. Cambridge: Cambridge University Press.

do Valle, Vanice Regina Lirio. 2016. "Enforcing Socio-economic Rights through Immediate Efficacy: A Case Study of Rio de Janeiro's Right to Housing." *Tulane Journal of International & Comparative Law* 25 (1): 1–44.

Duffey, Michael. 2015. "Christianity: From Peacemaking to Violence and Home Again."

In *Peacemaking and the Challenge of Violence in World Religions*, edited by Irfan A. Omar and Michael K. Duffey, 47–74. West Sussex, UK: John Wiley.

Du Plessis, Chrisna. 1999. "Sustainable Development Demands Dialogue between Developed and Developing Worlds." *Building Research & Information* 27 (6): 378–89.

Durán, Carlos Villán. 2011. "Civil Society Organizations Contribute to the Universal Declaration on the Human Right to Peace." *International Journal on World Peace* 28 (4): 59–126.

Ebaugh, Helen Rose, Paula F. Pipes, Janet Saltzman Chafetz, and Martha Daniels. 2003. "Where's the Religion? Distinguishing Faith-Based from Secular Social Service Agencies." *Journal for the Scientific Study of Religion* 42 (3): 411–26.

Edmund Rice International. 2017. "India—UPR Submission." http://www.edmundriceinternational.org/?page_id=3452.

Elliott, Michael A. 2007. "Human Rights and the Triumph of the Individual in World Culture." *Cultural Sociology* 1 (3): 343–63.

Fagan, Andrew, and Hans Fridlund. 2016. "Relative Universality, Harmful Cultural Practices and the United Nations Human Rights Council." *Nordic Journal of Human Rights* 34 (1): 21–39.

Feldman, Jan. 2011. *Citizenship, Faith, and Feminism: Jewish and Muslim Women Reclaim Their Rights*. Waltham, MA: Brandeis University Press.

Felter, Claire, and Danielle Renwick. 2019. "Same-Sex Marriage: Global Comparisons." https://www.cfr.org/backgrounder/same-sex-marriage-global-comparisons.

Ferguson, Kristin M., Qiaobing Wu, Grace Dyrness, and Donna Spruijt-Metz. 2007. "Perceptions of Faith and Outcomes in Faith-Based Programs for Homeless Youth." *Journal of Social Service Research* 33 (4): 25–43.

Ferris, Elizabeth. 2005. "Faith-Based and Secular Humanitarian Organizations." *International Review of the Red Cross* 87 (858): 311–25.

Fitzgerald, Timothy. 2011. *Religion and Politics in International Relations: The Modern Myth*. New York: Continuum.

Flanigan, Shawn Teresa. 2007. "Paying for God's Work: A Rights-Based Examination of Faith-Based NGOs in Romania." *Voluntas* 18 (2): 156–75.

Food and Agriculture Organization of the United Nations (FAO). 2017. "Gender Mainstreaming and a Human Rights-Based Approach. Guidelines for Technical Officers." http://www.fao.org/3/a-i6808e.pdf.

Forum-ASIA. 2019. "About FORUM-ASIA." https://www.forum-asia.org/?page_id=21481.

Frame, John. 2017. "Exploring the Approaches to Care of Faith-Based and Secular NGOs in Cambodia That Serve Victims of Trafficking, Exploitation, and Those Involved in Sex Work." *International Journal of Sociology and Social Policy* 37 (5/6): 311–26.

Frede, Michael. 2011. *A Free Will: Origins of the Notion in Ancient Thought*. Berkeley: University of California Press.

Freeman, Michael. 2004. "The Problem of Secularism in Human Rights Theory." *Human Rights Quarterly* 26 (2): 375–400.

Gaer, Felice D. 1997. "UN-Anonymous: Reflections on Human Rights in Peace Negotiations." *Human Rights Quarterly* 19 (1): 1–8.

———. 2003. "Human Rights NGOs in UN Peace Operations." *International Peacekeeping* 10 (1): 73–89.

Galtung, Johan. 1964. "An Editorial." *Journal of Peace Research* 1 (1): 1–4.

———. 1969. "Violence, Peace and Peace Research." *Journal of Peace Research* 6 (3): 167–91.

Gilad, Elon. 2016. "Judaism and Homosexuality: A Brief History." *Haaretz*. https://www.haaretz.com/jewish/.premium.MAGAZINE-judaism-and-homosexuality-a-brief-history-1.5390687.

Glaab, Katharina, Doris Fuchs, and Johannes Friederich. 2019. "Religious NGOs at the UNFCCC: A Specific Contribution to Global Climate Politics?" In *Religious NGOs at the United Nations: Polarizers or Mediators?*, edited by Claudia Baumgart-Ochse and Klaus Dieter Wolf, 47–63. New York: Routledge.

Glaze, Mackenzie. 2018. "Historical Determinism and Women's Rights in Sharia Law." *Case Western Reserve Journal of International Law* 50 (1–2): 349–76.

Gómez-Dávila, Joaquín Guillermo. 2018. "Abortion: A Look from the Perspectives of Public Health, Rights and Social Justice / El Aborto: Una Mirada Desde La Salud Pública, Los Derechos y La Justicia Social." *Revista Colombiana de Obstetricia y Ginecología* 69 (1): 53–64.

Goodman, Lenn Evan. 1998. *Judaism, Human Rights, and Human Values*. New York: Oxford University Press.

Graddy, Elizabeth A., and Ke Ye. 2006. "Faith-Based versus Secular Providers of Social Services: Differences in What, How, and Where." *Journal of Health and Human Services* 29 (3): 309–35.

Hague Convention. 1899. "Convention with Respect to the Laws and Customs of War on Land (Hague, II)." https://avalon.law.yale.edu/19th_century/hague02.asp.

Hallward, Maia Carter. 2008. "Situating the 'Secular': Negotiating the Boundary between Religion and Politics." *International Political Sociology* 2 (1): 1–16.

———. 2011. "International Law and the Case of Operation Cast Lead: 'Lawfare' and the Struggle for Justice." In *Nonviolent Resistance in the Second Intifada*, edited by Maia Carter Hallward and Julie M. Norman, 111–32. New York: Palgrave Macmillan.

———. 2013. "The Ramallah Friends Meeting: Examining One Hundred Years of Peace and Justice Work." *Quaker Studies* 18 (1): 76–95.

Hallward, Maia, and Cortney Stewart. 2018. "Challenges and Opportunities Facing Successful Women in Morocco." *Journal of North African Studies* 23 (5): 871–95.

Hannum, Hurst. 2006. "Human Rights in Conflict Resolution: The Role of the Office of the High Commissioner for Human Rights in UN Peacemaking and Peacebuilding." *Human Rights Quarterly* 28 (1): 1–85.

Harris-Curtis E. 2003. "Rights-Based Approaches: Issues for NGOs." *Development in Practice* 13 (5): 558–64.

Hashemi, Kamran. 2007. "Religious Legal Traditions, Muslim States and the Convention on the Rights of the Child." *Human Rights Quarterly* 29 (1): 194–227.

Hefferan, Tara. 2007. "Finding Faith in Development: Religious Non-governmental Organizations (NGOs) in Argentina and Zimbabwe." *Anthropological Quarterly* 80 (3): 887–96.

Hellum, Anne, and Henriette Sinding Aasen. 2013. *Women's Human Rights: CEDAW in International, Regional and National Law*. Cambridge: Cambridge University Press.

Hellum, Anne, Ingunn Ikdahl, and Patricia Kameri-Mbote. 2015. "Turning the Tide: Engendering the Human Right to Water and Sanitation." In *Water Is Life: Women's Human Rights in National and Local Water Governance in Southern and Eastern Africa*, edited by Anne Hellum, Patricia Kameri-Mbote, and B. C. P. Van Koppen, 32–80. Harare: Weaver Press.

Hellum, Anne, Patricia Kameri-Mbote, and B. C. P. Van Koppen, eds. 2015. *Water Is Life: Women's Human Rights in National and Local Water Governance in Southern and Eastern Africa*. Harare: Weaver Press.

Henneberg, Susan, ed. 2016. *LGBT Rights*. New York: Greenhaven.

Hershey, Megan. 2016. "Understanding the Effects of Faith: A Comparison of Religious and Secular HIV Prevention NGOS in Kenya." *Journal of International Development* 28 (2): 161–76.

Hertzke, Allen. 2006. *Freeing God's Children: The Unlikely Alliance for Global Human Rights*. Lanham, MD: Rowman & Littlefield.

Hessini, Leila. 2007. "Abortion and Islam: Policies and Practice in the Middle East and North Africa." *Reproductive Health Matters* 15 (29): 75–84.

Hogan, Linda. 2015. *Keeping Faith with Human Rights*. Washington, DC: Georgetown University Press.

Hoole, Rajan. 2009. "Sri Lanka: Ethnic Strife, Fratricide, and the Peace vs. Human Rights Dilemma." *Journal of Human Rights Practice* 1 (1): 120–39.

Hoover, Joe. 2013. "Ambiguous Humanity and Democratizing Rights." *Philosophy & Social Criticism* 39 (9): 935–61.

Howard, Rhoda E. 1998. "Human Rights and the Culture Wars: Globalization and the Universality of Human Rights." *International Journal* 53 (1): 94–112.

Hugen, Beryl, and Rachel Venema. 2009. "The Difference of Faith: The Influence of Faith in Human Service Programs." *Journal of Religion & Spirituality in Social Work: Social Thought* 28 (4): 405–29.

Human Rights Campaign. 2018. "Stances of Faiths on LGBTQ Issues: Buddhism." https://www.hrc.org/resources/stances-of-faiths-on-lgbt-issues-buddhism.

———. n.d.-a. "Stances of Faith on LGBTQ Issues: Hinduism." https://www.hrc.org/resources/stances-of-faiths-on-lgbt-issues-hinduism.

———. n.d.-b. "Stances of Faiths on LGBTQ Issues: The United Methodist Church." https://www.hrc.org/resources/stances-of-faiths-on-lgbt-issues-united-methodist-church.

Human Rights Law Centre. n.d. "Homepage." https://www.hrlc.org.au/.

Human Rights Movement: Bir Duino-Kyrgyzstan. 2016. "Story about Us." http://birduino.kg/en/about/.

Human Rights Now. n.d. "Economic Social Cultural Rights." http://hrn.or.jp/eng/economic-social-cultural-rights/.

Hume, Tim. 2016. "Pope Francis Extends Catholic Priests' Power to Forgive Abortion."

CNN, November 21. https://www.cnn.com/2016/11/21/europe/pope-francis-absolve -abortion/index.html.

Hunt, Mary E. 2010. "Women as Leaders in Catholicism." In *Gender and Women's Leadership: A Reference Handbook*, edited by Karen O'Connor, 490–95. Thousand Oaks, CA: Sage.

InnerCity Mission for Children. 2019. "About." https://theinnercitymission.ngo/about/.

Institute for Studies in Global Prosperity. 2013. "Applying Spiritual Principles to Development Practice: The Case of Seva Mandir." *International Journal of Religion and Society* 4 (1–2): 105–30.

International Bible Society. n.d. *Bible, New International Version.* https://www.biblica .com/bible/.

International Committee of the Red Cross. 1949a. "Geneva Convention (I) for the Amelioration of the Condition of the Wounded and Sick in Armed Forces in the Field." https://ihl-databases.icrc.org/applic/ihl/ihl.nsf/INTRO/365?OpenDocument.

———. 1949b. "Geneva Convention (II) for the Amelioration of the Condition of the Wounded, Sick, and Shipwrecked Members of the Armed Forces at Sea." https:// ihl-databases.icrc.org/applic/ihl/ihl.nsf/INTRO/370?OpenDocument.

———. 1949c. "Geneva Convention (III) Relative to the Treatment of Prisoners of War." https://ihl-databases.icrc.org/applic/ihl/ihl.nsf/INTRO/375?OpenDocument.

———. 1949d. "Geneva Convention (IV) Relative to the Protection of Civilian Persons in Time of War." https://ihl-databases.icrc.org/applic/ihl/ihl.nsf/INTRO/380 ?OpenDocument.

———. n.d. "Mandate and Mission." https://www.icrc.org/en/who-we-are/mandate.

International Criminal Court. 2002. "Rome Statute of the International Criminal Court." https://www.icc-cpi.int/resource-library/documents/rs-eng.pdf.

———. n.d. "About." https://www.icc-cpi.int/about.

International Partnership for Human Rights. 2019. "What We Do." https://www .iphronline.org/about/what-we-do.

International Work Group for Indigenous Affairs (IWGIA). 2011. "The American Indian Population Lacks Clean Water." https://www.iwgia.org/en/usa/1192-the -american-indian-population-lacks-clean-water.

———. 2013. "Voices of Water—Indigenous Peoples on the International Water Day." https://www.iwgia.org/en/focus/land-rights/1818-voices-of-water-indigenous -peoples-on-the-internat.

———. 2016. "Israel: Indigenous Arab Bedouins Face Imminent Eviction." https://www .iwgia.org/en/israel/2466-israel-indigenous-arab-bedouins-face-imminent-evic.

Isakovic, Zlatko. 2001. "Choosing between Peace and Human Rights?" *Peace Research* 33 (1): 37–46.

Islamic Conference of Foreign Ministers. 1990. "Cairo Declaration on Human Rights in Islam." http://hrlibrary.umn.edu/instree/cairodeclaration.html.

Islamic Council. 1981. "Universal Islamic Declaration of Human Rights." http://www .alhewar.com/ISLAMDECL.html.

Islamic Relief Worldwide. 2014. "An Islamic Perspective on Human Development." https://www.islamic-relief.org/publications.

Izienicki, Hubert. 2017. "Catholics and Atheists: A Cross-Cultural Qualitative Analysis of Religious Identities among Gay Men." *Sociology of Religion* 78 (3): 263–88.

Jackson, Peter A. 2011. *Queer Bangkok: Twenty-First-Century Markets, Media, and Rights*. Hong Kong: Hong Kong University Press.

Joffe, Alex. 2019. "Human Rights." *Israel Studies* 24 (2): 103–18.

John Paul II, Pope. 1995. "Letter of Pope John Paul II to Women." https://w2.vatican .va/content/john-paul-ii/en/letters/1995/documents/hf_jp-ii_let_29061995_women .html.

Johnsen, Sarah. 2014. "Where's the 'Faith' in 'Faith-Based' Organizations? The Evolution and Practice of Faith-Based Homelessness Services in the UK." *Journal of Social Policy* 43 (2): 413–30.

Johnson, Paul. 2013. "Homosexuality and the African Charter on Human and Peoples Rights: What Can Be Learned from the History of the European Convention on Human Rights?" *Journal of Law and Society* 40 (2): 249–79.

Johnson, Ronald. 2017. "UN Goal-Setting." In *Sustainable Development: Goals and UN Goal-Setting*, edited by Stephen Browne, 68–106. London: Routledge.

Johnston, David L. 2014. "A Muslim and Christian Orientation to Human Rights: Human Dignity and Solidarity." *Indiana International & Comparative Law Review* 24 (4): 899–920.

———. 2015. "Islam and Human Rights: A Growing Rapprochement?" *American Journal of Economics and Sociology* 74 (1): 113–48.

Juergensmeyer, Mark. 2003. *Terror in the Mind of God: The Rise of Religious Violence*. Berkeley: University of California Press.

Kahl, Sigran. 2009. "Religious Doctrines and Poor Relief: A Different Causal Pathway." In *Religion, Class Coalitions, and Welfare State Regimes*, edited by Kees van Kersbergen and Philip Manow, 267–95. Cambridge: Cambridge University Press.

Kahn, Rabbi Yoel H. 1989. "Judaism and Homosexuality." *Journal of Homosexuality* 18 (3–4): 47–82.

Kalmbach, Hilary, and Masooda Bano. 2012. *Women, Leadership and Mosques: Changes in Contemporary Islamic Authority*. Leiden: Brill.

Karam, Azza, and Katherine Marshall. 2016. "Religion, Human Rights and Development: Focusing on Health." *Review of Faith & International Affairs* 14 (3): 106–9.

Kayaoglu, Turan. 2014. "Giving an Inch Only to Lose a Mile: Muslim States, Liberalism, and Human Rights in the United Nations." *Human Rights Quarterly* 36 (1): 61–89.

Kellogg-Briand Pact. 1928. http://avalon.law.yale.edu/20th_century/kbpact.asp.

Kim, Sungmoon. 2015. "Confucianism, Moral Equality, and Human Rights: A Mencian Perspective." *American Journal of Economics and Sociology* 74 (1): 149–85.

Kinderman, Peter. 2009. "The Complexity of Peace and Human Rights." *Peace and Conflict: Journal of Peace Psychology* 15 (3): 305–7.

Kindornay, Shannon, James Ron, and Charli Carpenter. 2012. "Rights-Based Approaches to Development: Implications for NGOs." *Human Rights Quarterly* 34 (2): 472–506.

Klager, Andrew P. 2014. "From Victimization to Empathetic Solidarity: Peace-Building and Human Rights Advocacy in Anabaptist-Mennonite Origins." *Journal of Mennonite Studies* 32: 51–64.

Kligerman, Nicole. 2007. "Homosexuality in Islam: A Difficult Paradox." *Macalester Islam Journal* 2 (3): 53–64.

Koschmann, Matthew. 2013. "Human Rights Collaboration and the Communicative Practice of Religious Identity." *Journal of Communication and Religion* 36 (2): 77–217.

Kraybill, Ron. 1994. "Transition from Rhodesia to Zimbabwe: The Role of Religious Actors." In *Religion, the Missing Dimension of Statecraft*, edited by Douglas Johnston and Cynthia Sampson, 208–57. New York: Oxford University Press.

———. 2000. "Reflections on Twenty Years in Peacebuilding." In *From the Ground Up: Mennonite Contributions to International Peacebuilding*, edited by Cynthia Sampson and John Paul Lederach, 30–44. New York: Oxford University Press.

Kugle, Scott Siraj al-Haqq. 2010. *Homosexuality in Islam: Critical Reflection on Gay, Lesbian, and Transgender Muslims*. Oxford: Oneworld.

Kumar, T. K. Vinod. 2010. "United Nations Peace Process as a Peacemaking and Human Rights Exercise: Lessons from Conflict Resolution in Sierra Leone." *Crime, Law and Social Change* 54 (5): 303–23.

Kuosmanen, Jaakko. 2015. "Repackaging Human Rights: On the Justification and the Function of the Right to Development." *Journal of Global Ethics* 11 (3): 303–20.

Lampen, John. 2015. "The Quaker Peace Testimony in Twentieth-Century Education." *Quaker Studies* 19 (2): 295–304.

Langlaude, Sylvie. 2007. *The Right of the Child to Religious Freedom in International Law*. Leiden: Brill.

Langlois, Anthony J. 2003. "Human Rights without Democracy? A Critique of the Separationist Thesis." *Human Rights Quarterly* 25 (4): 990–1019.

League of Nations. 1924a. "Covenant of the League of Nations." http://avalon.law.yale.edu/20th_century/leagcov.asp.

———. 1924b. "Geneva Declaration of the Rights of the Child." http://www.un-documents.net/gdrc1924.htm.

LeBlanc, Lawrence J. 1996. "Reservations to the Convention on the Rights of the Child: A Macroscopic View of State Practice." *International Journal of Children's Rights* 4 (4): 357–81.

Lederach, John Paul. 1997. *Building Peace*. Washington, DC: US Institute of Peace.

———. 2014. *Reconcile: Conflict Transformation for Ordinary Christians*. Harrisonburg, VA: Herald Press.

Lee, Chelsea, and Robert L. Ostergard Jr. 2017. "Measuring Discrimination Against LGBTQ People: A Cross-National Analysis." *Human Rights Quarterly* 39 (1): 37–72.

Lee, Man, and Karen Lee. 2011. "Religion, Human Rights and the Role of Culture." *International Journal of Human Rights* 15 (6): 887–904.

Lehmann, Karsten. 2013. "Shifting Boundaries between the Religious and the Secular: Religious Organizations in Global Public Space." *Journal of Religion in Europe* 6: 201–28.

———. 2016. *Religious NGOs in International Relations: The Construction of "the Religious" and "the Secular."* London: Routledge.

———. 2019. "Religiously Affiliated NGOs." In *Routledge Handbook of NGOs and International Relations*, edited by Thomas Davies, 397–412. New York: Routledge.

Leurs, Robert. 2012. "Are Faith-Based Organisations Distinctive? Comparing Religious and Secular NGOs in Nigeria." *Development in Practice* 22 (5–6): 704–20.

Levine, James P., and Chitra Raghavan. 2012. *Self-Determination and Women's Rights in Muslim Societies*. Waltham, MA: Brandeis University Press.

Library of Congress. 2015. "Children's Rights: Israel." https://www.loc.gov/law/help /child-rights/israel.php.

Linde, Robyn. 2018. "Gatekeeper Persuasion and Issue Adoption: Amnesty International and the Transnational LGBTQ Network." *Journal of Human Rights* 17 (2): 245–64.

Llewellyn, Jennifer J. 2012. "Integrating Peace, Justice and Development in a Relational Approach to Peacebuilding." *Ethics and Social Welfare* 6 (3): 290–302.

Loeffler, James. 2015. "The Particularist Pursuit of American Universalism: The American Jewish Committee's 1944 'Declaration on Human Rights.'" *Journal of Contemporary History* 50 (2): 274–95.

Lopatka, Adam. 1980. "The Right to Live in Peace as a Human Right." *Security Dialogue* 11 (4): 361–67.

Lough, Benjamin J., and Margaret M. C. Thomas. 2014. "Building a Community of Young Leaders: Experiential Learning in Jewish Social Justice." *Journal of Experiential Education* 37 (3): 248–64.

Loy, David R. 2014. "Why Buddhism and the Modern World Need Each Other: A Buddhist Perspective." *Buddhist-Christian Studies* 34 (1): 39–50.

Maldonado-Torres, Nelson. 2017. "On the Coloniality of Human Rights." *Revista Crítica de Ciências Sociais* 114: 117–36.

Mamdani, Mahmood. 2000. *Beyond Rights Talk and Culture Talk: Comparative Essays on the Politics of Rights and Culture*. New York: St. Martin's Press.

Markowitz, Fran. 2004. "Talking about Culture: Globalization, Human Rights and Anthropology." *Anthropological Theory* 4 (3): 329–52.

Marshall, Katherine. 2013. *Global Institutions of Religion: Ancient Movers, Modern Shakers*. New York: Routledge.

Martin, David, and Rebecca Catto. 2012. "The Religious and the Secular." In *Religion and Change in Modern Britain*, edited by Linda Woodhead and Rebecca Catto, 373–90. New York: Routledge.

McAuliffe, Christopher Michael. 2015. "The Future of Homosexuality in Christian Denominations." *Journal of Psychological Issues in Organizational Culture* 6 (3): 70–76.

McGuinness, Margaret E. 2011. "Peace v. Justice: The Universal Declaration of Human Rights and the Modern Origins of the Debate." *Diplomatic History* 35 (5): 749–68.

Medical Care Development International. n.d. "Water, Sanitation, & Hygiene." http:// www.mcdinternational.org/water-sanitation-hygiene.

Mennonite Central Committee (MCC). n.d. "What We Do: Peace." http://mcc.org /learn/what/peace.

Mertus, Julie A., and Jeffery W. Helsing, eds. 2006. *Human Rights and Conflict: Exploring the Links between Rights, Law, and Peacebuilding*. Washington, DC: US Institute of Peace Press.

Miller, Casey James. 2016. "We Can Only Be Healthy if We Love Ourselves: Queer AIDS NGOs, Kinship, and Alternative Families of Care in China." *AIDS Care* 28 (Suppl. 4): 51–60.

Mittermaier, Amira. 2014. "Beyond Compassion: Islamic Voluntarism in Egypt." *American Ethnologist* 41 (3): 518–31.

Moghadam, Valentine M. 2004. "Patriarchy in Transition: Women and the Changing Family in the Middle East." *Journal of Comparative Family Studies* 35 (2): 137–62.

Moghaddam, Fathali M. 2000. "Toward a Cultural Theory of Human Rights." *Theory & Psychology* 10 (3): 291–312.

Mohanty, Kalpana. 2015. "Peacemaking and Nonviolence in the Hindu Tradition." In *Peacemaking and the Challenge of Violence in World Religions*, edited by Irfan A. Omar and Michael K. Duffey, 178–99. West Sussex, UK: John Wiley.

Monshipouri, Mahmood. 2013. "Identity and Human Rights in the Muslim World: Negotiating Norms in the Age of Globalization." *Human Rights* 1 (2): 37–59.

MOPOTAC-Africa. n.d. "Home." http://www.mopotacafrica.org/.

Morgan, Kimberly J. 2009. "The Religious Foundations of Work-Family Policies in Western Europe." In *Religion, Class Coalitions, and Welfare State Regimes*, edited by Kees van Kersbergen and Philip Manow, 56–90. Cambridge: Cambridge University Press.

Moyn, Samuel. 2015. *Christian Human Rights*. Philadelphia: University of Pennsylvania Press.

Mullally, Siobhán. 2005. "Debating Reproductive Rights in Ireland." *Human Rights Quarterly* 27 (1): 78–104.

Murdie, Amanda, and David R. Davis. 2010. "Problematic Potential: The Human Rights Consequences of Peacekeeping Interventions in Civil Wars." *Human Rights Quarterly* 32 (1): 49–72.

Musallam, Basim F. 1981. "Why Islam Permitted Birth Control." *Arab Studies Quarterly* 3 (2): 181–97.

Mutyaba, Rita. 2011. "Early Marriage: A Violation of Girls' Fundamental Human Rights in Africa." *International Journal of Children's Rights* 19 (2): 339–55.

Mwambene, Lea, and Obdiah Mwaodza. 2017. "Children's Rights Standards and Child Marriage in Malawi." *African Studies Quarterly* 17 (3): 21–43.

Nadler, Richard. 2006. "Judaism and Abortion: The Hijacking of a Tradition." *Human Life Review* 32 (1): 43–52.

Nandy, Shailen, and David Gordon. 2009. "Children Living in Squalor: Shelter, Water and Sanitation Deprivations in Developing Countries." *Everyday Environments of Children's Poverty* 19 (2): 202–28.

Negrón-Gonzales, Melinda. 2012. "Cooperation between Secular and Religious Rights Organizations in Turkey." *Turkish Studies* 13 (3): 415–30.

Neil, Sylvia, and Lisa Fishbayn Joffe. 2012. *Gender, Religion, and Family Law: Theorizing Conflicts between Women's Rights and Cultural Traditions*. Waltham, MA: Brandeis University Press.

Nelson, Paul J., and Ellen Dorsey. 2018. "Who Practices Rights-Based Development? A Progress Report on Work at the Nexus of Human Rights and Development." *World Development* 104: 97–107.

Neufeldt, Reina. 2016. "Impact and Outcomes: The Ethical Perils of Distancing in Peacebuilding Grant Solicitations." *Journal of Peacebuilding & Development* 11 (2): 54–69.

Ngang, Carol C. 2018. "Towards a Right-to-Development Governance in Africa." *Journal of Human Rights* 17 (1): 107–22.

Ngwena, Charles G. 2010. "Inscribing Abortion as a Human Right: Significance of the Protocol on the Rights of Women in Africa." *Human Rights Quarterly* 32 (4): 783–864.

Nicolau, Ingrid. 2014. "Women's Rights in Islam." *Contemporary Readings in Law and Social Justice* 6 (1): 711–20.

Nilsen, Alf. 2016. "Power, Resistance and Development in the Global South: Notes towards a Critical Research Agenda." *International Journal of Politics, Culture & Society* 29 (3): 269–87.

Normand, Roger, and Sarah Zaidi. 2008. *Human Rights at the UN: The Political History of Universal Justice*. Bloomington: Indiana University Press.

O'Brien, Melanie. 2011. "Sexual Exploitation and Beyond: Using the Rome Statute of the International Criminal Court to Prosecute UN Peacekeepers for Gender-Based Crimes." *International Criminal Law Review* 11 (4): 803–27.

Offenheiser, Raymond C., and Susan H. Holcombe. 2003. "Challenges and Opportunities in Implementing a Rights-Based Approach to Development: An Oxfam American Perspective." *Nonprofit and Voluntary Sector Quarterly* 32 (2): 268–301.

Office of the High Commissioner for Human Rights (OHCHR). 2014. "Women's Rights Are Human Rights." https://www.ohchr.org/Documents/Events/WHRD/WomenRightsAreHR.pdf.

———. n.d. "The Independent Expert on Human Rights and International Solidarity." https://www.ohchr.org/EN/Issues/Solidarity/Pages/IESolidarityIndex.aspx.

O'Flaherty, Michael. 2004. "Sierra Leone's Peace Process: The Role of the Human Rights Community." *Human Rights Quarterly* 26 (1): 29–62.

Omar, Irfan A. 2015. "Jihad and Nonviolence in the Islamic Tradition." In *Peacemaking and the Challenge of Violence in World Religions*, edited by Irfan A. Omar and Michael K. Duffey, 9–40. West Sussex, UK: John Wiley.

Organisation for Economic Co-operation and Development (OECD). 2014. "Mainstreaming Cross-Cutting Issues: 7 Lessons from DAC Peer Reviews." https://www.oecd.org/dac/peer-reviews/Final%20publication%20version%20of%20the%207%20Lessons%20mainstreaming%20cross%20cutting%20issues.pdf.

Pace, Sharon. 2012. *Judaism: A Brief Guide to Faith and Practice*. Macon, GA: Smyth & Helwys.

Pal, Amitabh. 2011. *"Islam" Means Peace: Understanding the Muslim Principle of Nonviolence Today*. Santa Barbara, CA: Praeger.

Paludi, Michele Antoinette. 2010. *Feminism and Women's Rights Worldwide*. 3 vols. Westport, CT: Praeger.

Pemberton, Josh. 2017. "Socio-economic Rights in Constitution Aotearoa New Zealand." *New Zealand Universities Law Review* 27 (4A): 918–45.

Penna, David R., and Patricia J. Campbell. 1998. "Human Rights and Culture: Beyond Universality and Relativism." *Third World Quarterly* 19 (1): 7–27.

Pérez, Joseph. 2005. *The Spanish Inquisition: A History*. New Haven, CT: Yale University Press.

Petersen, Marie Juul. 2010. "International Religious NGOs at the United Nations: A

Study of a Group of Religious Organizations." *Journal of Humanitarian Assistance.*
https://sites.tufts.edu/jha/archives/847.

———. 2015. "Conflict or Compatibility? Reflections on the Nexus between Human
Rights, Development and Religion in Muslim Aid Organisations." In *Routledge
Handbook of Religions and Global Development*, edited by Emma Tomalin, 359–72.
Oxon, UK: Routledge.

Pew Research Center. 2017. "The Changing Global Religious Landscape." Religion &
Public Life Project. https://www.pewforum.org/2017/04/05/the-changing-global
-religious-landscape/.

Pinter, Bojana, Marwan Hakim, Daniel Seidmand, Ali Kubbaf, Meera Kisheng, and
Costantino Di Carlo. 2016. "Religion and Family Planning." *European Journal of
Contraception and Reproductive Health Care* 21 (6): 486–95.

Plan International. n.d. "Sexual Health and Rights." https://plan-international.org
/sexual-health#.

Pogge, Thomas, and Mitu Sengupta. 2016. "Assessing the Sustainable Development
Goals from a Human Rights Perspective." *Journal of International and Comparative
Social Policy* 32 (2): 83–97.

Polonko, Karen A., and Lucien X. Lombardo. 2015. "Non-governmental Organizations
and the UN Convention on the Rights of the Child." *Journal of Children's Rights* 23
(1): 133–53.

Public Service International. 2017. "The United Nations General Assembly Approves
Declaration on the Right to Peace." https://www.world-psi.org/en/united-nations
-general-assembly-approves-declaration-right-peace.

Quadango, Jill, and Deana Rohlinger. 2009. "The Religious Factor in U.S. Welfare State
Politics." In *Religion, Class Coalitions, and Welfare State Regimes*, edited by Kees
van Kersbergen and Philip Manow, 236–66. Cambridge: Cambridge University
Press.

Quaker Council for European Affairs. n.d. "QCEA Vision Statement." https://www.qcea
.org/home/about/qcea/.

Radford, Mary F. 2000. "Inheritance Rights of Women under Jewish and Islamic Law."
Boston College International and Comparative Law Review 23 (2): 135–84.

Rashiduzzaman, M. 1997. "The Dichotomy of Islam and Development: NGOs, Women's
Development and Fatawa in Bangladesh." *Contemporary South Asia* 6 (3): 239–46.

Razak, Arisika. 2017. "The Divine Feminist: A Diversity of Perspectives That Honor
Our Mothers' Gardens by Integrating Spirituality and Social Justice." *Integral Review*
13 (1): 72–86.

Regilme, Salvador Santino Jr. 2018. "The Global Politics of Human Rights: From Human Rights to Human Dignity?" *International Political Science Review* 40 (2): 279–
90.

Reidel, Laura. 2010. "What Are Cultural Rights? Protecting Groups with Individual
Rights." *Journal of Human Rights* 9 (1): 65–80.

Renard, John. 2015. *The Handy Islam Answer Book.* Detroit: Visible Ink Press.

Reuter, Tina Kempin. 2012. "Including Minority Rights in Peace Agreements: A Benefit
or Obstacle to Peace Processes after Ethnic Conflicts?" *International Journal on Minority and Group Rights* 19 (4): 359–97.

Rich, Timothy S. 2017. "Religion and Public Perceptions of Gays and Lesbians in South Korea." *Journal of Homosexuality* 64 (5): 606–21.

Rivkin-Fish, Michele, and Cassandra Hartblay. 2014. "When Global LGBTQ Advocacy Became Entangled with New Cold War Sentiment: A Call for Examining Russian Queer Experience." *Brown Journal of World Affairs* 21 (1): 95–111.

Rosch, Eleanor. 2015. "'Peace Is the Strongest Force in the World': Buddhist Paths to Peacemaking and Nonviolence." In *Peacemaking and the Challenge of Violence in World Religions*, edited by Irfan A. Omar and Michael K. Duffey, 142–72. West Sussex, UK: John Wiley.

Rosenberg-Friedman, Lilach. 2018. "Religious-Zionism and Gender: 70 Years of Redefining the Identity of Women in the Military, Religious, and Public Spheres." *Israel Studies* 23 (3): 152–63.

Ross, Susan Deller. 2008. *Women's Human Rights: The International and Comparative Law Casebook*. Philadelphia: University of Pennsylvania Press.

Rouzi, Abdulrahim A. 2013. "Facts and Controversies on Female Genital Mutilation and Islam." *European Journal of Contraception & Reproductive Health Care* 18 (1): 10–14.

Rump, Linda Hartz. 2008. "Is Christianity Oppressive to Women?" *Christianity Today*. http://www.christianitytoday.com/history/2008/august/is-christianity-oppressive -to-women.html.

Russell, Jonathan. 2012. "Human Rights: The Universal Declaration vs. the Cairo Declaration." https://blogs.lse.ac.uk/mec/2012/12/10/1569/.

Saeed, Abdullah. 2018. *Human Rights and Islam an Introduction to Key Debates between Islamic Law and International Human Rights Law*. Cheltenham, UK: Edward Elgar.

Saghaye-Biria, Hakimeh. 2018. "Decolonizing the 'Universal' Human Rights Regime: Questioning American Exceptionalism and Orientalism." *ReOrient* 4 (1): 59–77.

Saleh, Saneya. 1972. "Women in Islam: Their Status in Religious and Traditional Culture." *International Journal of Sociology of the Family* 2 (1): 35–42.

Salek, Lucy V. 2016. "Faith Inspiration in a Secular World: An Islamic Perspective on Humanitarian Principles." *International Review of the Red Cross* 97 (897–98): 345–70.

Salih, Mohamed Abdel Rahim Mohamed. 2002. *Islamic NGOs in Africa: The Promise and Peril of Islamic Voluntarism*. Copenhagen: University of Copenhagen Centre of African Studies.

Saliternik, Michal. 2015. "Reducing the Price of Peace: The Human Rights Responsibilities of Third-Party Facilitators." *Vanderbilt Journal of Transnational Law* 48 (1): 179–243.

Sampson, Cynthia, and John Paul Lederach, eds. 2000. *From the Ground Up: Mennonite Contributions to International Peacebuilding*. Oxford: Oxford University Press.

Sawad, Ahmd Ali. 2017. "Islamic Reservations to Human Rights Treaties and Universality of Human Rights within the Cultural Relativists Paradigm." *Journal of Human Rights* 12 (2): 101–54.

Schabas, William. 1996. "Reservations to the Convention on the Rights of the Child." *Human Rights Quarterly* 18 (2): 472–91.

Schiff, Daniel. 2002. *Abortion in Judaism*. Cambridge: Cambridge University Press.

Schirch, Lisa. 2005. *The Little Book of Strategic Peacebuilding*. Intercourse, PA: Good Books.

———. 2006. "Linking Human Rights and Conflict Transformation: A Peacebuilding Framework." In *Human Rights and Conflict: Exploring the Links between Rights, Law, and Peacebuilding*, edited by Julie A. Mertus and Jeffrey W. Helsing, 63–96. Washington, DC: US Institute of Peace Press.

Schwartz, Dov, and Judith Tydor Baumel. 2005. "Reflections on the Study of Women's Status and Identity in the Religious Zionist Movement." *Review of Rabbinic Judaism* 8 (1): 189–209.

Seljak, David. 2016. "Post-secularism, Multiculturalism, Human Rights, and Religion in Ontario." *Studies in Religion—Sciences Religieuses* 45 (4): 542–65. doi:10.1177/0008429815596547.

Sengupta, Arjun. 2000. "Realising the Right to Development." *Development and Change* 31 (3): 553–78.

———. 2004. "The Human Right to Development." *Oxford Development Studies* 32 (2): 179–203.

Serour, G. I. 2013. "Ethical Issues in Human Reproduction: Islamic Perspectives." *Gynecological Endocrinology* 29 (11): 949–52. doi:10.3109/09513590.2013.825714.

Seung-Soo, Han. 2018. "Addressing Water, Sanitation and Disasters in the Context of the Sustainable Development Goals." *UN Chronicle* 55 (1): 33–36.

Sharma, Arvind. 2010. *Hindu Narratives on Human Rights*. Westport, CT: Praeger.

Sharp, Dustin N. 2013. "Beyond the Post-conflict Checklist: Linking Peacebuilding and Transitional Justice through the Lens of Critique." *Chicago Journal of International Law* 14: 165–96.

Siani, Alberto L. 2014. "The Contemporary Dialectic of United Nations Human Rights." *Clio* 44 (1): 19–50.

Silliman, Jael Miriam, Marlene Gerber Fried, Loretta Ross, and Elena R. Gutiérrez. 2016. *Undivided Rights: Women of Color Organizing for Reproductive Justice*. Chicago: Haymarket Books.

Sirimanne, Chand R. 2016. "Buddhism and Women—The Dhamma Has No Gender." *Journal of International Women's Studies* 1 (2016): 273–92.

Sjoberg, Laura. 2011. "Women and the Genocidal Rape of Women: The Gender Dynamics of Gendered War Crimes." In *Confronting Global Gender Justice: Women's Lives, Human Rights*, edited by Debra Bergoffen, Paula Ruth Gilbert, Tamara Harvey, and Connie L. McNeely, 21–34. London: Routledge.

Sloss, David. 2017. "Human Rights and Constitutional Democracy." *Human Rights Quarterly* 39 (4): 971–86.

Snyder, Sarah B. 2011. *Human Rights Activism and the End of the Cold War : A Transnational History of the Helsinki Network*. Cambridge: Cambridge University Press.

Song, Jiyoung. 2016. "Human Rights in Asia and the West." Carnegie Council for Ethics in International Affairs. https://www.carnegiecouncil.org/publications/articles _papers_reports/763.

Soroptimist International. 2012. "What Do Reproductive Rights Have to Do with Sustainable Development?" https://www.soroptimistinternational.org/what-do -reproductive-rights-have-to-do-with-sustainable-development/.

Staples, Kelly. 2011. "Statelessness, Sentimentality and Human Rights: A Critique of Rorty's Liberal Human Rights Culture." *Philosophy & Social Criticism* 37 (9): 1011–24.

Stevenson, Nick. 2013. "Human(e) Rights and the Cosmopolitan Imagination: Questions of Human Dignity and Cultural Identity." *Cultural Sociology* 8 (2): 180–96.

Subhi, Nasrudin, and David Geelan. 2012. "When Christianity and Homosexuality Collide: Understanding the Potential Intrapersonal Conflict." *Journal of Homosexuality* 59 (10): 1382–1402.

Sumner, Sarah. 2003. *Men and Women in the Church: Building Consensus on Christian Leadership*. Downers Grove, IL: InterVarsity Press.

Tablan, Ferdinand. 2015. "Catholic Social Teachings: Toward a Meaningful Work." *Journal of Business Ethics* 128 (2): 291–303.

Tanyag, Maria. 2017. "Invisible Labor, Invisible Bodies: How the Global Political Economy Affects Reproductive Freedom in the Philippines." *International Feminist Journal of Politics* 19 (1): 39–54.

Tesón, Fernando R. 1985. "International Human Rights and Cultural Relativism." *Virginia Journal of International Law* 25: 869–98.

Tew, Yvonne. 2012. "Beyond 'Asian Values': Rethinking Rights." Working paper, Center for Governance and Human Rights, University of Cambridge. https://www.cghr .polis.cam.ac.uk/publications/cghr_working_papers/wp5.

Third Global Conference on World's Religions. 2016. "Universal Declaration of Human Rights by World Religions." http://worldsreligions2016.org/declaration/.

Thomas, Mark. 2017. *Buddhism*. Broomall, PA: Mason Crest.

Toft, Monica Duffy, Daniel Philpott, and Timothy Samuel Shah. 2011. *God's Century*. New York: Norton.

Tomalin, Emma. 2013. "Religion and Rights-Based Approach to Development." *International Journal of Religion and Society* 4 (1–2): 53–68.

T'ruah. 2019. "About T'ruah." https://www.truah.org/about/.

Tsetsura, Katerina. 2013. "Challenges in Framing Women's Rights as Human Rights at the Domestic Level: A Case Study of NGOs in the Post-Soviet Countries." *Public Relations Review* 39 (4): 406–16.

Türkelli, Gamze Erdem, Wouter Vandenhole, and Arne Vandenbogaerde. 2013. "NGO Impact on Law-Making: The Case of a Complaints Procedure under the International Covenant on Economic, Social and Cultural Rights and the Convention on the Rights of the Child." *Journal of Human Rights Practice* 5 (1): 1–45.

Twombly, Eric C. 2002. "Religious versus Secular Human Service Organizations: Implications for Public Policy." *Social Science Quarterly* 83 (4): 947–61.

Tzouvala, Ntina. 2015. "The Holy See and Children's Rights: International Human Rights Law and Its Ghosts." *Nordic Journal of International Law* 84 (1): 59–88.

UN Committee on the Elimination of Discrimination against Women (CEDAW). 2006. "Declarations, Reservations, Objections and Notifications of Withdrawal of Reservations Relating to the Convention on the Elimination of All Forms of Discrimination against Women." https://www.refworld.org/docid/4ef848ba2.html.

UNICEF. 2018. "Annual Report." https://www.unicef.org/reports/annual-report-2018.

———. n.d. "Child Marriage." https://www.unicef.org/protection/child-marriage.

United Nations. 1945. "Charter of the United Nations." https://www.un.org/en/charter -united-nations/.

———. 1948. "Universal Declaration of Human Rights." http://www.un.org/en /universal-declaration-human-rights/.

———. 1959. "Declaration of the Rights of the Child." https://www.humanium.org/en /convention/text/.

———. 1966a. "International Covenant on Civil and Political Rights." https://www .ohchr.org/en/professionalinterest/pages/ccpr.aspx.

———. 1966b. "International Covenant on Economic, Social and Cultural Rights." https://www.ohchr.org/en/professionalinterest/pages/cescr.aspx.

———. 1972. "Declaration of the United Nations Conference on the Human Environment." http://webarchive.loc.gov/all/20150314024203/http%3A//www.unep.org /Documents.Multilingual/Default.asp?documentid%3D97%26articleid%3D1503.

———. 1979. "Convention on the Elimination of All Forms of Discrimination against Women." http://www.ohchr.org/EN/ProfessionalInterest/Pages/CEDAW.aspx.

———. 1984. "Declaration on the Right of Peoples to Peace." https://www.ohchr.org /EN/ProfessionalInterest/Pages/RightOfPeoplesToPeace.aspx.

———. 1986. "Declaration on the Right to Development." https://www.un.org /documents/ga/res/41/a41r128.htm.

———. 1989. "Convention on the Rights of the Child." https://www.ohchr.org/en /professionalinterest/pages/crc.aspx.

———. 1992. "The Rio Declaration on Environment and Development." www.unesco .org/education/pdf/RIO_E.PDF.

———. 1995. "The United Nations Fourth World Conference on Women." http://www .un.org/womenwatch/daw/beijing/platform/plat1.htm#statement.

———. 2000a. "Optional Protocol to the Convention on the Rights of the Child on the Involvement of Children in Armed Conflict." https://www.ohchr.org/en /professionalinterest/pages/opaccrc.aspx.

———. 2000b. "Optional Protocol to the Convention on the Rights of the Child on the Sale of Children, Child Prostitution and Child Pornography." https://www.ohchr .org/EN/ProfessionalInterest/Pages/OPSCCRC.aspx.

———. 2001. "The Global Agenda for Dialogue among Civilizations." https://www. un.org/documents/ares566e.pdf.

———. 2011. "Human Rights Council Resolution 17/19." https://documents-dds-ny .un.org/doc/UNDOC/GEN/G11/148/76/PDF/G1114876.pdf.

———. 2014. "Women's Rights Are Human Rights." https://www.ohchr.org/Documents /Events/WHRD/WomenRightsAreHR.pdf.

———. 2016. "Resolution Adopted by the Human Rights Council on 1 July 2016." http:// aedidh.org/wp-content/uploads/2016/10/resolution-32-28.pdf.

———. 2017. "Resolution Adopted by the General Assembly on 19 December 2016." https://www.refworld.org/docid/589c72134.html.

———. n.d. "About the Sustainable Development Goals." https://www.un.org /sustainabledevelopment/sustainable-development-goals/.

United Nations Development Programme. n.d. "Human Development Reports. Human Development Index (HDI)." http://hdr.undp.org/en/content/human -development-index-hdi.

United Nations Educational, Scientific and Cultural Organization (UNESCO). 2001. "UNESCO Universal Declaration of Cultural Diversity." http://portal.unesco.org/en /ev.php-URL_ID=13179&URL_DO=DO_TOPIC&URL_SECTION=201.html.

United Nations High Commissioner for Human Rights. 2014. "Prejudice Fuels the Denial of Rights for LGBT People." https://www.ohchr.org/en/NewsEvents/Pages /DisplayNews.aspx?NewsID=14620&LangID=E.

United Nations Women. 2003. "CEDAW 29th Session 30 June to 25 July 2003." https:// www.un.org/womenwatch/daw/cedaw/text/econvention.htm#intro.

——. N.d.-a. "About Us." http://www.unwomen.org/en/about-us/about-un-women.

United Nations Women. N.d.-b. "Intergovernmental Mandates on Gender Mainstreaming." https://www.un.org/womenwatch/osagi/intergovernmentalmandates .htm

UN Watch. 2014. "The Proliferation of 'Human Rights'—A Dictator's Best Friend." http://blog.unwatch.org/index.php/2014/07/04/the-proliferation-of-human-rights -a-dictators-best-friend/.

Uvin, Peter. 2007. "From the Right to Development to the Rights-Based Approach: How 'Human Rights' Entered Development." *Development in Practice* 17 (4–5): 597–606.

Vandenbogaerde, Arne. 2013. "The Right to Development in International Human Rights Law: A Call for Its Dissolution." *Netherlands Quarterly of Human Rights* 31 (2): 187–209.

van Kersbergen, Kees, and Philip Manow. 2009. *Religion, Class Coalitions, and Welfare States*. Cambridge: Cambridge University Press.

Veerman, Philip, and Caroline Sand. 1999. "Religion and Children's Rights." *International Journal of Children's Rights* 7 (4): 385–93.

Verner, Elizabeth. 2015. "Child Marriage in Yemen: A Violation of International Law." *Georgia Journal of International and Comparative Law* 43 (3). https://digital commons.law.uga.edu/gjicl/vol43/iss3/.

Villaroman, Noel G. 2011. "Rescuing a Troubled Concept: An Alternative View of the Right to Development." *Netherlands Quarterly of Human Rights* 29 (1): 13–53.

Villaseñor Alonso, Isabel. 2015. "La Democracia y Los Derechos Humanos: Una Relación Compleja / La Démocratie et Les Droits Humains: Un Rapport Complexe / Democracy and Human Rights: A Complex Relationship." *Foro Internacional* 55 (4): 1115–38.

VIVAT International. 2019. "Vision & Mission." http://vivatinternational.org/about /vision-mission/.

Volf, Miroslav. 2008. "Christianity and Violence." In *War in the Bible and Terrorism in the Twenty-First Century*, edited by E. A. Martens and Richard S. Hess, 1–17. Winona Lake, IN: Eisenbrauns.

Waldorf, Lars. 2013. "Getting the Gunpowder Out of Their Heads: The Limits of Rights-Based DDR." *Human Rights Quarterly* 35 (3): 701–19.

Walters, Julie. 2011. "The Institutionalization of Domestic Violence against Women in the United States." In *Confronting Global Gender Justice: Women's Lives, Human Rights*, edited by Debra Bergoffen, Paula Ruth Gilbert, Tamara Harvey, and Connie L. McNeely, 277–94. London: Routledge.

Weatherby, Georgie Ann. 2010. "Overview: Women as Leaders in Religion and Religious Organizations." In *Gender and Women's Leadership: A Reference Handbook*, edited by Karen O'Connor, 475–81. Thousand Oaks, CA: Sage.

Weber, Max. [1905] 2002. *The Protestant Ethic and the Spirit of Capitalism*. Edited and translated by Peter Baehr and Gordon C. Wells. New York: Penguin.

Wenger, Beth S., and Firoozeh Kashani-Sabet. 2015. *Gender in Judaism and Islam: Common Lives, Uncommon Heritage*. New York: New York University Press.

Williams, Kenneth. 2014. "Justice or Peace? A Proposal for Resolving the Dilemma." *Pace International Law Review* 26: 131–81.

Windborne, Janice. 2006. "New Laws, Old Values: Indigenous Resistance to Children's Rights in Ghana." *Atlantic Journal of Communication* 14 (3): 156–72.

Witte, John, Jr., and Don S. Browning. 2012. "Christianity's Mixed Contributions to Children's Rights: Traditional Teachings, Modern Doubts." *Emory Law Journal* 61: 991–1014.

Witte, John, Jr., and M. Christian Green, eds. 2012. *Religion and Human Rights: An Introduction*. Oxford: Oxford University Press.

Woolley, Sarah. 2005. "Children of Jehovah's Witnesses and Adolescent Jehovah's Witnesses: What Are Their Rights?" *Archives of Disease in Childhood* 90 (7): 715–19.

Xie, Lijia, Stephen L. Eyre, and Judith Barker. 2018. "Domestic Violence Counseling in Rural Northern China: Gender, Social Harmony, and Human Rights." *Violence Against Women* 24 (3): 307–21.

Yunus, Mohd Noor Ahmad. 2017. "Methods of Preventives to Keep Birth Control in the Quran." *Global Journal Al Thaqafah* 7 (2): 204–12.

Zauzmer, Julie. 2016. "Pope Francis Says the Catholic Church Will Probably Never Have Female Priests." *Washington Post*, November 1. https://www.washingtonpost.com/news/acts-of-faith/wp/2016/11/01/pope-francis-says-the-catholic-church-will-likely-never-have-female-priests/?noredirect=on&utm_term=.d33253d8e409.

INDEX

human dignity, *19*, 20, *20*
humanitarian law, 137–38
humanitarian work, 26–28, *27*, 29–30, 72, 74, 78, 156–57, 163, 166
human rights: agreements, 11–12, 172–76 (*see also specific agreements*); attacks on, 49; culture and, 34–41; development, right to, 12, 166; duties vs., 43–44; humanitarian aid distinct from, 74; humanitarian work compared to, 29–30; laws, 137 (*see also* international laws, history of); religion and, 4–6, 15; types of, 18–21, *19*, *20*; as universal, 21; women's rights differentiated from, 109. *See also* children's rights; gender and human rights; peace and conflict; socioeconomic development
Human Rights Commission of Pakistan, 26, 59, 71, 74, 127, 129, 157, 162
Human Rights Council, 50, 75, 83, 139, 142, 162
Human Rights Education Associates (HREA), 124
Human Rights Law Centre, 105–6
Human Rights Now, 68
Human Rights Observatory in Rwanda, 23, 127, 130, 150
human rights organizations: content analysis of websites, 6–7; distribution of, 171; limitations of websites, 168; mission/vision statements, 15, 18; partnering opportunities, 170; religious approaches, 4–6, 15; secular approaches, 169. *See also* Christian organizations; faith-based organizations (FBOs); Jewish organizations; Muslim organizations; non-Abrahamic religions; nongovernmental organizations, funding of; religious vs. secular approaches; secular approaches

ICCPR (International Covenant on Civil and Political Rights), 11, 55, 81, 88, 112–13, 137
ICESCR (International Covenant on Economic, Social, and Cultural Rights), 11, 32–33, 55, 56, 57, 72, 113, 137, 177
IMADR (International Movement against All Forms of Discrimination and Racism), 48
Imam Al-Khoei Foundation, 45
imperialism, culture of, 41
imprisonment and torture, 21
indigenous organizations, 8, 49–50
individualism vs. collectivism culture, 35, 41, 44–50; Christianity and, 38–39; Islam and, 39

Informal Sector Service Center (INSEC), 26, 48, 67, 99, 100, 127
Initiatives of Change International, 140
InnerCity Mission for Children, 125, 127–28
INSEC (Informal Sector Service Center), 26, 48, 67, 99, 100, 127
Institute for Family Policy, 107
Institute for Planetary Synthesis, 42–43, 140
Institutional Review Board (IRB), 8
International Association of Democratic Lawyers, 140
International Bridges to Justice, 22
International Catholic Child Bureau, 69, 127–28
International Committee of the Red Cross, 138
International Conference on Population and Development, 82
International Congress on the Human Right to Peace, 139
International Covenant on Civil and Political Rights (ICCPR), 11, 55, 81, 88, 112–13, 137
International Covenant on Economic, Social, and Cultural Rights (ICESCR), 11, 32–33, 55, 56, 57, 72, 113, 137, 177
International Criminal Court, 138, 141
International Federation for Human Rights (FIDH), 23, 26, 106, 154
International Fellowship of Reconciliation, 106
International Human Rights Funders Group, 110
international laws, history of, 11–12; children's rights, 112–15; culture, 31–34; gender issues, 80–83; humanitarian vs. human rights law, 73; peace/conflict issues, 135–40; socioeconomic development, 56–57. *See also specific laws and agreements*
International Movement against All Forms of Discrimination and Racism (IMADR), 48
International Movement ATD Fourth World, 73, 140
International Organization for the Right to Education and Freedom of Education (OIDEL), 48
International Partnership for Human Rights, 49
International Peace Bureau (IPB), 26, 67, 151–52, 155, 158
International Service for Human Rights, 26, 108, 150

www.ingramcontent.com/pod-product-compliance
Lightning Source LLC
Chambersburg PA
CBHW030322270326
41926CB00010B/1466